Socialism
in Western Europe

Westview Replica Editions

The concept of Westview Replica Editions is a response to the continuing crisis in academic and informational publishing. Library budgets for books have been severely curtailed. Ever larger portions of general library budgets are being diverted from the purchase of books and used for data banks, computers, micromedia, and other methods of information retrieval. Interlibrary loan structures further reduce the edition sizes required to satisfy the needs of the scholarly community. Economic pressures on the university presses and the few private scholarly publishing companies have severely limited the capacity of the industry to properly serve the academic and research communities. As a result, many manuscripts dealing with important subjects, often representing the highest level of scholarship, are no longer economically viable publishing projects--or, if accepted for publication, are typically subject to lead times ranging from one to three years.

Westview Replica Editions are our practical solution to the problem. We accept a manuscript in camera-ready form, typed according to our specifications, and move it immediately into the production process. As always, the selection criteria include the importance of the subject, the work's contribution to scholarship, and its insight, originality of thought, and excellence of exposition. The responsibility for editing and proofreading lies with the author or sponsoring institution. We prepare chapter headings and display pages, file for copyright, and obtain Library of Congress Cataloging in Publication Data. A detailed manual contains simple instructions for preparing the final typescript, and our editorial staff is always available to answer questions.

The end result is a book printed on acid-free paper and bound in sturdy library-quality soft covers. We manufacture these books ourselves using equipment that does not require a lengthy make-ready process and that allows us to publish first editions of 300 to 600 copies and to reprint even smaller quantities as needed. Thus, we can produce Replica Editions quickly and can keep even very specialized books in print as long as there is a demand for them.

About the Book and Author

Socialism in Western Europe: The Experience of a Generation
Steven Philip Kramer

This book explores what socialism in Western Europe meant for the generation that came to maturity after World War I. Dr. Kramer captures individual aspects of the socialist experience through interviews with socialist leaders who have been a significant part of the movement since the 1930s and who represent the great diversity of European socialism. His subjects include Michael Foot, former leader of Britain's Labour Party; Riccardo Lombardi, a historic figure in the Italian Socialist Party; Bruno Kreisky, long-time chancellor of Austria; and Daniel Mayer, secretary-general of the French Socialist Party from 1944 to 1946. Each interview begins with a brief description of the individual and the party. A general introduction interprets the role of this generation in the history of European socialism.

Steven Kramer is associate professor of history at the University of New Mexico. He recently received the International Affairs Fellowship from the Council on Foreign Relations and is also working for the Department of State as a specialist in international political movements.

Socialism
in Western Europe
The Experience of a Generation

Steven Philip Kramer

Routledge
Taylor & Francis Group

LONDON AND NEW YORK

First published 1984 by Westview Press, Inc.

Published 2019 by Routledge
52 Vanderbilt Avenue, New York, NY 10017
2 Park Square, Milton Park, Abingdon, Oxon OX14 4RN

Routledge is an imprint of the Taylor & Francis Group, an informa business

Copyright © 1984 Taylor & Francis

Library of Congress Cataloging in Publication Data
Kramer, Steven.
    Socialism in Western Europe
    (A Westview replica edition)
    Includes bibliographical references.
    1. Socialism--Europe--History--20th century--Sources. 2. Socialists--
Europe--Interviews. I. Title.
HX238.K73   1984   335'.0094   84-7468

ISBN 13: 978-0-367-28773-3 (hbk)

For Sharon

Contents

Abbreviations

EDC, European Defense Community

FGTB, Belgian General Confederation of Labor

ILO, International Labor Office

LO, Swedish Trade Union Confederation

PCF, French Communist Party

PCI, Italian Communist Party

POB, Belgian Labor Party

PSA, Autonomous Socialist Party (France)

PSB, Belgian Socialist Party

PSI, Italian Socialist Party

PSU, Unified Socialist Party (France)

RPF, French Gaullist Party (1947-1953)

SFIO, French Socialist Party

SPD, German Socialist Party

SPO, Austrian Socialist Party

TUC, English Trade Union Congress

Preface

This is a book about what it meant to be a socialist in Western Europe for the generation which came to maturity after World War I. It attempts to capture the subjective aspect of the socialist experience through interviews conducted with socialist leaders who held a significant place in the movement from the 1930s on.

The leaders interviewed represent the diversity of European socialism; they cannot, however, be "representative" of European socialism as a whole. A comprehensive view of the subject can be obtained in a variety of excellent books and articles. But the abundant scholarship on socialism rarely attempts to recreate the atmosphere in which socialists lived and worked, or to reconstruct the collective framework in which they thought. That is the goal of this book.

In the course of previous work, I had interviewed many important figures of European socialism. The interviews were used primarily to supplement the written record. Finally I realized that I was making no use of what interested me most about these interviews, namely, the light they shed on how individuals made decisions and perceived the historical circumstances surrounding them. The story was worth telling, but it was not being told. As time passed, many of the historical actors of the inter-war period died. Unless someone seized the occasion to interview the survivors, a valuable key to the past would be lost.

This book is also a kind of témoignage to a generation I admire enormously. Faced with difficult historical circumstances, they upheld their values. They have something to say to an age which has lost its ideals and romanticism, or feels ashamed to declare them. Their ideas, deeds, and friendships have certainly meant a great deal to me.

The interviews were conducted between September and December 1981. They were recorded on tape, transcribed, edited and then sent back for correction and approval by their subjects. I did the Mayer and Lombardi interviews in French, then translated them; the others were conducted in English. The only exception is the Kreisky interview which was submitted in 1983 in response to written questions.

A series of interviews does not constitute a book. For the interviews to elucidate the experience of socialism, they must be placed in a broader national and even international context. That is the purpose of the brief introductions preceeding each interview and of the general introduction.

The general introduction summarizes the evolution of European socialism prior to the 1920s. In particular, it examines how World War I and the Russian Revolution disrupted the political unity and intellectual self-confidence of the socialist movement. This section gives the background necessary to comprehend what the world of socialism was like when the generation featured in this book made its entry. The introduction then examines problems faced by socialists in the inter-war period, notably the Great Depression and the threat of fascism and then considers socialism's place in the reconstruction of Europe following the Second World War.

But before going further, we must define the way in which the term "generation" will be employed.

The Definition of Generation

In a brilliant and seminal essay on "The Problem of Generation", Karl Mannheim formulates a sociological concept of generation which will be used in this book. For Mannheim a generation, like a social class, represents a given social location. Just as a class may exist objectively but not subjectively, so may a generation be conscious or not conscious of its own existence. A generation is not just a number of individuals coexisting simultaneously; "mere contemporaneity becomes sociologically significant only when it involves participation in the same historical and sociological circumstances."[1] The experiences received at an early stage of existence remain important for the rest of the generation's life: "Early impressions tend to coalesce into a natural view of the world. All later experiences then tend to receive their meaning from this original set, whether they appear as the set's verification and fulfillment or its negation and antithesis."[2] Generation "as an actuality" only comes into existence as the result of specific historical circumstances "where a concrete bond is created between members of a generation by their being exposed to the social and intellectual symptoms of a process of dynamic de-stabilization."[3] Mannheim then defines a more restricted group, which he calls the generation unit:

> The generation unit represents a much more concrete bond than the actual generation as such. Youth experiencing the same concrete historic problems may be said

to be part of the same actual generation;
while those groups within the same actual
generation which work up the material of
their common experience in different,
specific ways, constitute separate
generation units.

The quicker the tempo of social and
cultural change is, then, the greater are
the chances that particular generation
location groups will react to changed
situations by producing their own
entelechy.[4]

Mannheim's definition has many advantages. It
demonstrates how the concept of generation, which is
biological in origin, only assumes social meaning
under given historical circumstances. It posits
generation as one, but not the only factor of
historical analysis, and constructs the definition in
such a way that it is formally parallel with other
concepts, like class. It indicates why different
generation units can exist at the same time,
experiencing the same historical events but reacting
in different yet related ways. It explains why
generation may play an important role in history at
one time, and very little at another. Above all, it
is a dynamic model, well suited to deal with
historical change.

The socialists we meet here were born between
1900 and 1913. On the basis of birthdates, they
belong to one generation. But as mentioned above,
age is a necessary but not sufficient condition for
forming part of a generation unit. All of them came
to adulthood shortly after World War I, a fundamental
watershed for European youth. As socialists, they
reacted in a particular kind of way to their
experiences, as we shall see.

Steven Philip Kramer

FOOTNOTES

[1]Karl Mannheim, "The Problem of Generations," in Essays on the Sociology of Knowledge, edited by Paul Kecksemeti (Oxford, New York, 1952), p. 298.

[2]Ibid.

[3]Ibid., p. 303.

[4]Ibid., p. 304, p. 310.

Acknowledgments

It would have been impossible to prepare this book without the assistance of many kind people. Above all, I am indebted to the statesmen whose interviews appear in the following pages. Not only did they undergo long hours of interviewing, but they also read through and corrected my transcriptions after I had edited them for length and grammar. The only exception to this process was Chancellor Bruno Kreisky, who was ill when I was in Europe and who therefore submitted written responses to my questions.

Some of the interviews I conducted could not be used for this book. I should like to thank Wolfgang Abendroth, Sven Andersson, Claude Bourdet, Leo Friedmann, Roger Ikor, Georges Lefranc, Leo Magits, Gunnar Strang and Reiulf Steen for their cooperation.

The idea for this book was developed in conversation with the late Val Lorwin, a good friend and scholar who is much missed.

My work in Europe was facilitated by Hans Dahlgren, Leif Gustafson and Sigfrid Leijonhufvud in Sweden, Sturle Kojen in Norway, and Johan von Bohnsdorff in Finland. I especially appreciate the kindness of Charles Senninger in Paris.

Jules-Pierre Mondoloni of the French Cultural Services was instrumental in obtaining a fellowship to support my work in France.

Colleagues who read and commented on the first draft of the manuscript include Robert Kern, Jane Slaughter, Richard Tomasson and F. Roy Willis. Other pertinent advice came from Josef Konvitz, Claude-Marie Senninger, John Johnson and Kevin Sharpe. Beth Gard helped answer questions about format.

The secretaries of the History Department, Marian Honhart, Mariana Ibanez, Yolanda Martinez, Arla Sivinski and Avis Trujillo went out of their way to help type the first draft. The University of New Mexico granted me a sabbatical leave for the fall of 1981 without which the necessary interviewing could not have been accomplished.

Peter Durnan, John Hamilton, Dennis Harrington, Richard Harrington, Michael Skol, and William Wood each proofread sections of the final version of the manuscript. Lee Henderson did a masterful job in typing the final draft.

Grace Darling and David Kellog of the Council on Foreign Relations graciously assisted me in deciding where to publish the manuscript. Barbara Ellington of Westview provided valuable editorial guidance.

I am responsible for the translations from French to English of the Mayer and Lombardi interviews. The other interviews were conducted in English.

Steven Philip Kramer

I think socialism is essentially based on trying to build up a society in which the best things that men carry in them, justice and a thirst for freedom, will prevail.

Jef Rens,
Interview with Author

. . . the limitations of the human will in its struggle against the resistance of material things.

Albert Mathiez,
The French Revolution

Introduction

[My generation] saw its life ruined and
destroyed by war. Those who had already
attained adulthood had their programs
developed, their thoughts formed. But the
war seized us at a time...when we needed a
path to follow. And since the war, the men
and women of my generation search not only
for economic equilibrium...but for moral
equilibrium....[1]

> Isabelle Blume, Belgian
> socialist leader

In the years preceding World War I, socialism had
grown rapidly. It had ceased being a marginal
political phenomenon and had become an important
political force in most of Europe. The multitude of
warring little socialist parties in each European
state had disappeared; by 1905 each Western European
nation had one major socialist party. Conflicts
between the various national parties seemed in the
process of being overcome through the good offices of
the International. A sense of expectation and hope
pervaded European socialism; even many non-socialists
conceded that the future belonged to socialism.

Many of the generation which had come to maturity
in the beginning of the 20th century believed
socialism to be not only just but inevitable as
well. They imagined that the advent of socialism
would come about through the continuation of the same
peaceful progression that it saw before its eyes.
World War I disrupted socialism and weakened belief
in its inevitability. The Russian Revolution
challenged the accepted doctrines of Western European
socialists and soon destroyed its political unity.

The generation which became active in European
socialism after the First World War still thought
that socialism was just, but it could no longer
believe quite so firmly that its triumph was
inevitable, nor that reason rather than force was the
motor of human history. Socialism was put on the
defensive by both the forces of the right and
communism. But in order to understand the way in
which this generation saw the world, we must take a
quick glance at socialism before the First World War,
and then examine the consequences of the War and the
Russian Revolution on the movement.

2

Socialism before the War

> There was an atmosphere of intimacy, family, belonging, and of expectancy...that socialism meant an entirely different society....
>
> Jef Rens,
> Interview with Author.

Socialism had not only become a powerful political and social movement before World War I; it had become a way of life, a society within a society. This way of life was informed by the creation of a distinctive world view. Marxism constituted its core, but many other intellectual currents were also incorporated.

Marxism provided a common language and common perspective for European socialism; it also constituted the base for a common program. The Erfurt program adopted in 1891 by German Social Democracy set the SPD on a firm Marxist basis and served as a model for other parties. In most countries, however, knowledge of Marxism was superficial, even among the leadership. In reality, socialist ideology was syncretistic; in each party, Marxism was mixed with varying doses of the native socialist tradition.

The Marxism of the pre-war period was different from that of today. Many of Marx's writings, especially those of the young Marx, were still undiscovered. Marx, moreover, was not so much known through his own works as through those of his popularizers, especially Engels and Kautsky. But the Marxism they propagated bore their own stamp.

Engels tried to transform Marxism into a universal scientific system, something its founder had not intended. Not only was the dialectic to be made into a general social theory, but it was to be applied to the natural world as well. By giving Marxism the air of a general science, Engels served as a leftist Herbert Spencer, attracting philistines who wanted to have a simple explanation for everything. Moreover, his emphasis on the inevitable, almost mechanical, working out of the historical process which would lead to socialism proved a satisfying notion for militants. Engels' view of socialism seemed to make the coming of socialism depend on history, rather than on men; Marx had underlined the role of human volition and consciousness. Kautsky likewise stressed the inevitable, almost mechanical, nature of the revolutionary process. It is not surprising that both the revolutionary left and the revisionist right attacked this point of view. To the former,

Kautsky's "orthodoxy" seemed to justify waiting passively for the collapse of capitalism; the revolution was merely the establishment of socialism on the ruins of a capitalism which had already fallen. Kautsky's views could thus rationalize a refusal to act vigorously to bring about revolution. The deterministic notion of Marxism survived into the post World War I era.

Socialism, like any other great movement which strove for a new world, had a utopian and even religious aspect. It was a kind of faith, as Jef Rens aptly stated:

> There was an atmosphere of intimacy, family, belonging and of expectancy, felt jointly, of things to come; that socialism meant an entirely different society into which one day we would enter. We didn't have any clear idea how, but different from and opposed to the society in which we were living. And it took me quite a bit of time before realizing that what we wanted to accomplish, what we were striving towards was something which was already in process, actually what you call reformism. But it took quite a long time. Probably under the influence of the first French socialists and anarchists, I had the image of an ideal society entirely different from the one in which we were living...So it was, in a way, a world in itself. It had some features of a religion. (Jef Rens, Interview with Author.)

Herbert Tingsten gives a very similar picture in his monumental work on Swedish Social Democracy:

> Capitalism and socialism were regarded as entirely different social systems. The transition from one to the other must occur in a very decided manner. Capitalism would be replaced, or succeeded, by socialism. However, in this connection there was no necessary link with the Marxist theory of crisis in its real sense, but the idea that once won, the victory of socialism would be total implies a domination of the social organisation. It was not predicted that the party would gain a strong position of power without the majority, and even less that once achieved a majority could again be lost. Victory meant total victory, that a new world opinion had become powerful, that the road was open for socialist action....

How socialisation would come about, and
how the socialist society would be created
was rarely discussed. According to Marx
such a discussion was utopian and
unscientific. Certainly it was possible to
predict that the new society would come into
being, but not the forms that it would
take. Instead of making concrete plans,
therefore, one described in general terms
the society of the future as uniting on the
highest level welfare, freedom, happiness
and culture, and thereby, in the eagerness
to make plans that were on a non-utopian
nature, yielded to an even more marked
utopianism.

As a practical movement, Social
Democracy was concerned with short term
goals. The main tasks were limited
social-political reforms and above all a
general political democratising.... The
Marxist theories were quickly rejected in
their more pronounced form....

Whilst the more precise Marxist
doctrines grew weaker, the emotional and
intellectual atmosphere enmeshing these
doctrines remained. The concept of
historical materialism, historical
determinism and the associated developmental
fatalism, the principle of class struggle
and the belief in a total system change, in
the victory of socialism and the realisation
of the ideal society, all this lent colour
and strength to Social Democratic
declarations. Though the party leaders
energetically and effectively worked for
reforms in current (policies) they were
inspired by, and infused their supporters
with, the feeling that the great, the real,
the true for which they fought was something
more, something eternally more vital.

"Socialism" did not consist of social
policy, nor of democratic reforms, nor of
work towards peace and disarmament. Rather
it consisted of a tremendous innovation that
one day must come to pass. In a way that
made comparisons with religious movements
natural a concern with today was united with
a belief in a future, in which were mingled
all the ambitions, hopes and dreams of the
poor classes.[2]

By the 1930s, however, critics of social
democracy castigated it on account of its
amalgam of quasi-religious utopianism and timid

behavior in practice. In <u>The Coming Struggle for Power</u> John Strachey, a communist at the time, attacked socialism by means of a sophisticated version of the Stalinist "social-fascism" line:

> For a long time, however (and in this fact lies the first secret of social democratic power), for just so long indeed, as the national capitalism in question continues to function without sharp, intolerable crises, such a working class will only look outside of capitalism. It will never go outside of capitalism. Its "fantasy life" alone will become socialistic. Such a working class, living in an old, slowly declining, but still rich capitalism, may for a long time, and to a very complete degree, separate its words and thoughts from its actions. In these conditions the workers may become intolerant of anyone who does not use socialistic phraseology when addressing them. The whole terminology of their politics may become socialist. The affirmation of socialism may become a prerequisite for the politicians who lead them. (Our old friend "the nationalization of the means of production, distribution and exchange" will appear on all party programmes and trade union rule books.) The mildest trade union officials will often be required to breathe ferocities from the platform....
> And all the while the real life of such a working class may go on quite as usual, very tamely and quietly, within the limits set for it by capitalism. As the national capitalism in question declines those limits will grow narrower. If only, however, the process is reasonably gradual, nothing will happen. The oratorical socialism of the labour politicians will become more pronounced in nice proportion as they are driven by the exigencies of capitalist decline to make their actions more reactionary. A kind of verbal socialism -- a socialism of the hereafter -- will be established amongst wide circles of the workers. And such a verbal socialism may actually make them support the more easily the hard, and ever more hard, conditions of capitalism. For verbal socialism, like religion, can in these conditions become the

opium of the people. Nor will those workers who have been effectively drugged with the socialism of the hereafter thank anyone (so long as these conditions last) who attempts to dispel the fantasy. (How could it be otherwise? Do we ever thank the man who seeks to wake us from warm dreams to cold reality?)

It is in these economic and psychological circumstances alone the Social Democratic parties flourish. And such have been the conditions of Great Britain and the other nations of Western Europe since the war.[3]

If socialism was motivated by an almost religious fervor, it nevertheless claimed to be scientific. Socialism adopted much of its ideology from liberalism and radicalism, with their faith in science, progress, rationality, and justice. To this intellectual baggage it added one key qualification, that these ideals could only be realized through the attainment of socialism. Socialism was thus both the negation of liberalism and its realization. For this reason, the nature of socialism was different in Catholic and Protestant countries. In the former, liberalism was necessarily opposed to Catholicism; being a practicing Catholic and a liberal were mutually exclusive. Socialism assumed the anti-clerical stance of liberalism. Since Catholicism had become a Weltanschauung, socialism in Catholic countries became an opposing Weltanschauung. Socialism could penetrate the working class only on the condition that the working class become dechristianized. Thus, in Catholic countries, socialism tended to be apocalyptic, and at least rhetorically, more radical than elsewhere. It became a counter-church. In Protestant countries, however, there was no necessary conflict between socialism and religion. Socialism became fused with religious ideals. In England, for example, there was a strong link between socialism and "nonconformist" denominations; in Scandinavia the temperance movement and socialism were often closely tied. Such alliances encouraged reformism. It is interesting to note that with the exception of Germany (which had a mixed Catholic and Protestant population) and Finland, strong Western European communist parties developed only in Catholic countries, perhaps because communism was more effective than socialism after World War I in creating an apocalyptic atmosphere.

The pretension of socialism to be a movement that existed in, but was not part of existing bourgeois society, corresponded with the realities of societies compartmentalized by class and in many cases by religion as well. This helps to explain why socialism in the pre-World War I era attempted to create its own subculture, based on mass institutions like trade unions, cooperatives, mutual-aid societies, and educational programs. This specifically socialist subculture has declined since World War II, but still survives in many places, including Scandinavia, Austria, and Holland. Franz Borkenau aptly describes the socialist subculture of inter-war Austria:

> The socialists succeeded in organizing the workers, not only politically and industrially, but in every imaginable spare-time activity. There were workers' organizations for gymnastics, for hiking and climbing, as for all other sports, for choral singing, for listening to music, for playing chess, not forgetting, of course, the book clubs. Naturally no compulsion was exerted upon the individual socialist to become a footballer or a choral singer, but serious pressure was exerted upon him in the event of his becoming a footballer, or a choral singer, in order that he should only join the socialist club, and no neutral one. Many of these clubs granted their members substantial financial advantages. In addition the socialists, by means of the democratic vote, controlled an increasing number of sick relief insurance funds and similar institutions, and after the War, won control of no less than 47 per cent of the municipalities. The municipalities in their turn carried out large-scale relief work, whose effects in practice combined with those of the private socialist clubs in keeping the worker linked up to the Socialist Party in every conceivable aspect of his life. It was desireable for the socialist worker to have his children born in a municipality ruled by the socialists because there the poorer families enjoyed some financial help at the time of birth. A socialist town council would launch an extensive scheme of kindergartens run on socialist principles of education. Then the boy or girl would enter a preparatory school, again under the supervision of a socialist town council. At the age of leaving school all efforts would be made to make him or her join the socialist youth organization. Such a youth organization

would reject the religious ceremony of
confirmation and carry out a parallel
initiation rite of its own. The preferred
sports for most young men in Austria are
climbing and skiing. The original neutral
organization for these purposes, the
'Deutsch-Osterreichische-Alpen-Verein', had
turned strongly anti-semitic and
anti-socialist. It would hardly encourage
young socialist workers to join. But they
would find an organization of their own, the
'Naturfreunde' with their own shelters,
their own cheap-rate parties, etc. This
would extend to all spheres and through all
stages of life, until at death the socialist
was buried through the cares of a socialist
burial insurance fund, to which he had
contributed during the course of his life.
The rites at this burial would, of course,
be opposed to those of the Catholic
Church.[4]

Another related characteristic of socialism was
its emphasis on education. Socialism preached a
collective solution to human problems, but in
practice individual socialists often showed strong
commitment to the liberal ideal of self-help through
education. Many of the people interviewed in this
book came from poor families but they obtained an
education. Jef Rens passed a high school equivalency
examination and went to the University. Trygve
Bratteli took advantage of socialist study circles.
Daniel Mayer, who had only two years of formal
schooling, was self-taught. The socialists also
inherited the underlying liberal belief in the
fundamentally rational nature of history and of man.
In the last analysis, progress was linked to the
development of man's reason, unlimited progress was
possible because man's capacity for rational
development was without bounds. World War I severely
shook this Enlightenment conception of human nature;
World War II almost destroyed it.

World War I and the Socialist Movement

The war devastated socialism as it
devastated the world.[5]

The First World War produced an explosion of the
latent tensions which necessarily existed within a
movement which claimed to stand for a new order but
which, at the same time, worked within the existing
world.

The most obvious tension within socialism was between revolutionism and reformism. The idea of revolution, abandoned on the practical level, survived on the rhetorical. In most of Western Europe, where some modicum of political and social freedom existed, socialism became a mass organization devoted to parliamentary politics and trade union activity, although this tendency was not without its critics. In any case, by 1900 it was clear that there was a serious divergence between theory and practice.

A second underlying problem was the relationship between internationalism and loyalty to one's own nation. Marx had been categorical; the worker had no country; his loyalty was to his class. This did not prevent socialists from drawing the opposite conclusion from Marx. It was argued that the growth of democracy meant that the worker really did have a fatherland. National loyalty and internationalism could be reconciled by skillfully phrased resolutions, but World War I made the two incompatible.

A third latent conflict in socialism, closely related to the above, was between pacifism and national defense. Marx and Engels had been of several minds on this subject. They had occasionally justified wars for progressive goals, for example, the destruction of Tsarist autocracy, but had also seen war as a threat to socialist development. Socialist members of Parliament frequently demonstrated their opposition to the idea of national defense by voting against military credits; armies after all were often used to suppress strikes rather than to defend frontiers. But the question remained of what would happen in case a real war broke out. Although the International had proclaimed on many occasions its determination to prevent war, its declarations did not go beyond platonic affirmations. And although socialists opposed war, virtually all socialist parties accepted the idea of national defense in case of aggression. But aggression is not always easy to define. In 1914, most socialists were convinced that chauvinism and patriotism had been suppressed within the working class. In a few days in August, the very leaders who had opposed militarism, to say nothing of the rank-and-file, were either swept away by war fever, or did not resist the tide. The illusion that socialism could stop war was replaced by another illusion, that socialists could help their governments win a quick victory leading to a new and peaceful world order. When that illusion too was frustrated, yet another was born, that the war would lead to a world revolution which would destroy capitalism. This belief on the part of the communists destroyed socialist unity, but not capitalism.

By 1917, the unity of the various socialist parties began to crumble. Some parties formally split. One group of socialists continued to support fighting on till victory, another advocated "peace without victory," a position close to that of Woodrow Wilson, while a small number preached "turning the imperialist war into a civil war." This last position would have remained marginal if there had been no Bolshevik Revolution. But once Lenin took power and created the Communist International, he consolidated the war-time splits in the Western European parties which otherwise might have healed. He was able to do this because many socialists felt profoundly guilty for their conduct during the war. Robert Wohl's comment about the centrist element in the French Socialist Party can be applied to other countries: "In their hearts, they felt guilty for War Socialism, for their reckless honeymoon with nationalism and liberalism, and for their failure in the revolutionary eddies of 1919 and 1920.'[6] That guilt drove many to either bolshevism or pacifism in the post-war epoch.

Lenin wanted to destroy the old socialist movement. His intention was not to create socialism in Russia alone; he was too good a Marxist to believe that could be done in a backward nation. But he hoped that the Russian Revolution would spark revolutions in the more advanced nations of the West. Convinced that the proletariat was truly revolutionary but had been betrayed by its leaders, Lenin wanted to draw the working class into a new International. His International was attractive, not because socialists really understood what Leninism meant but because they projected their own hopes onto the far-away Bolshevik experiment. Bolshevism seemed to be a genuine socialist revolution, that was enough; it was symbol, not reality.

What separated socialism from communism in 1921 was not clear. Many reformists went over to Lenin, many radical socialists remained in the "old house." The main difference usually was the attitude towards democracy. Socialists insisted that socialism was an extension of political democracy, that the "dictatorship of the proletariat" had to be at best very limited in time. Their critique of bolshevism as a violation of democracy rather than true democracy turned out to be accurate, but that was by no means clear in 1921.

The split with communism crippled socialism, not only politically, but morally. Communism seemed a movement of action; socialism at best a loose coalition of those who for one reason or another were not communists. Socialists often assumed a defensive attitude towards communism and suffered from an inferiority complex; the more dynamic communists set the terms of debate.

Socialism and Pacifism in the 1920s

> ....you have to situate my generation with respect to the hope of international peace. You have to remember the slogans we shouted: "Nie wieder krieg," "plus jamais de guerre," "plus jamais ça." Our hope, almost the raison d'être of our socialism was peace through Franco-German reconciliation.
>
> Daniel Mayer,
> Interview with Author.

The young men and women active in socialism after World War I had become socialists primarily because of their commitment to pacifism and international reconciliation. The parties of the right in most European nations stressed nationalism, the communists, violent revolution. As Albert Thibaudet wrote in reference to France: "Today, one would say that socialism is the quest for peace. One is socialist to the extent that he places this problem before all others."[7]

The term "pacifism" is being used loosely here. It represents a state of mind resulting from the combination of traditional socialist fears of militarism, utopian liberal or religious notions that education and progress could eliminate war and finally, a feeling of bad conscience or guilt at not have prevented World War I, or not having ended it sooner. Believing that its main cause was the arms race, most socialists were determined to avert another conflict by working for disarmament.

Almost all socialists opposed the Treaty of Versailles, which seemed a peace of vengeance rather than of reconciliation that would open the way to future war. No matter how socialists had felt about World War I, they could now unite in favor of disarmament and in opposition to the Treaty. The issue of war and national defense, which had contributed to the collapse of socialist unity after 1914, now became a basis for unity. As Ziebura states:

> One of the cements of unity of the French Socialist Party, so divided, moreover, on almost all doctrinal and tactical problems, was its profound pacifism. This pacifism showed itself in

the most diverse forms: horror of war,
traditional antimilitarism or ideological
condemnation of war as an instrument of
capitalist imperialism.[8]

In England, Ramsay MacDonald, who had left the
leadership of the Labour Party in 1914 because of his
opposition to war, resumed it in 1922:

> The Labour movement had forgotten its
> support for the wartime coalition and the
> knock-out blow.... it was now more
> MacDonaldite than MacDonald was himself.

Since the arms race was blamed for World War I, "the
only way to avoid war was to disarm."[9]

Likewise, in Sweden, there was a return to
pacifism. In the period preceding World War I, the
so-called "defense nihilists" had supported absolute
disarmament against the position of the party leaders
who, in the words of Tingsten:

> ....insisted on the necessity of
> defense, but attacked militarism as such;
> they combined demands for political and
> social reforms with the defense question;
> they were skeptical towards or critical of
> proposals for increments in arms but
> nevertheless examined such proposals on
> their factual merit.[10]

But for the authority of the party leader,
Branting, the defense-nihilists would have had a
majority in the Congress of 1911. Then came the war,
which seemed to justify Branting. Swedish
preparedness was credited with preserving
neutrality. The hard core of the defense-nihilists
left the party to form the Left Socialists in 1917,
which later became the nucleus of the Communist Party.
Interestingly enough, the question of national
defense arose once again after the war. Since the
prospects of war seemed negligible, many thought
Sweden should give an example through unilateral
disarmament. This position would have prevailed in
the Congress of 1931 had it not been for the
opposition of party leader Per Albin Hansson. The
rise of Hitler soon produced a rapid shift of
opinion: "....only three years after a party
congress had advocated disarmament, a vast majority
in the party was prepared to vote in favor of a
substantial mobilization."[11]

It was no easy task for a socialism identified with pacifism to rapidly alter its stance, as we shall see.

Socialism and the Depression

> Don't forget that my generation was the generation of those who didn't attach much importance, at least in France, to economic problems. Our socialism was based on feeling.
>
> Daniel Mayer,
> Interview with Author.

For decades, historians have berated the statesmen of the late 1920s early 1930s for having applied the remedies of classical economics to the Great Depression, rather than using counter-cyclical responses. This kind of critique, applied with smug satisfaction, is heard less often today, as economists and politicians struggle haltingly against a major economic crisis themselves.

Perhaps what is most difficult to understand is the strange immobilism of European socialists, their apparent willingness to accept classical "liberal" theory, which meant in practice a "deflationary" budget. These leaders saw the economic crisis as just one more of the periodic slumps which had occurred since the Industrial Revolution. These slumps had never lasted long; it was assumed that this would be the case again. When the crisis continued, political leaders did not know what to do.

The reaction to the depression was also related to the experience of the immediate post-war period. The World War had produced economic disarray in Europe. In Germany, inflation had destroyed the middle classes; elsewhere devaluation had consumed the earnings and savings of the workers. European leaders had worked to restore the Gold Standard, believing that it would create the preconditions of economic stability on which prosperity depended. There was reluctance to embark on any experiment which might undermine free trade and the Gold Standard. Thus, the only means available to avert deficits was to cut expenditures, mostly those used for relief of the unemployed.

To the extent to which socialist leaders shared the liberal economic gospel, they had logically to support cuts in spending. As the political representatives of the workers, they could not subscribe to such cuts. But without an alternative economic doctrine, how could they justify their position? In the opposition, it was easy to attack deflation, but there were dangers in being in the opposition. The cuts would be greater if the socialists were not in the government. Moreover, in central Europe, socialists also had to take into account the growing threat of fascism. But the price for remaining in government became increasingly high. In England, Ramsay MacDonald slashed the budget, but in acting as a "statesman" he split the Labour Party. The German Social Democrats at first participated in the Brüning government, but left when they could no longer condone its economic policies. Nevertheless, they then "tolerated" the same government. As Sturmthal says, "the Social Democrats had no economic policy but only a 'relief' policy."[12]

The question is why the socialists did not have an alternative economic policy. One reason was that most socialists were ignorant of economics. Although Keynes had already published some of his ideas, few socialists had heard of him. Instead, they were caught in a logical trap of their own making. If they actually studied Marxist economics, it was through the popularized versions of Engels or Kautsky, versions which, as already noted, presented a very schematized and mechanical view of Marxism. Socialism would come after capitalism collapsed under the weight of its own contradictions. Capitalist productive forces had to be fully developed as a precondition to socialism. But socialists generally agreed that this last stage of capitalism was still far off. Nor did they see the Great Depression as the final collapse of the system.

In short, many socialists argued that the only solution for the capitalist economy was socialism, but socialism was impossible until the necessary conditions came into being. Moreover, capitalism as a system could not be reformed. Since socialists tended to see socialism and capitalism as totally distinct historical epochs, socialist solutions could have no place in a capitalist economy, which had to function under its own economic laws. Their own logic drove them to the conclusion that only liberal remedies could be used under capitalism. The mechanistic thinking of the socialists thus led to a reductio ad absurdum.

A third reason why the socialists proved incompetent in matters economic was their lack of experience in governing. In the pre-war years they had concentrated on easily comprehensible political and social issues: universal manhood suffrage, recognition of trade union rights and short-term improvements of the condition of the workers. In much of central and eastern Europe, they were in effect substituting for a weak or non-existent bourgeoisie which had proven incapable of accomplishing the democratic revolution. So long as universal male suffrage and political democracy had not been attained, there was no possibility of the socialists' governing; thus, they developed the reflex of pure opposition. Even in countries which possessed democratic liberties, the socialist vote before World War I was usually too small to make governmental entry appear imminent. Suddenly, during or after World War I, socialists either participated in governmental coalitions or governed alone. Generally they were unprepared, equipped as they were with only some vague social meliorist ideas and the experience of representing trade-union interests. As Adolf Sturmthal puts it:

> From the turn of the century until the end of the First World War, the European Socialist movement, under its cloak of a revolutionary party, was thus a mere parliamentary instrument of trade unionism. Its real activity was restricted to trade unionist problems.... The lack of a constructive Socialist program on issues outside the realm of labor's traditional pressure-group activity became painfully clear once labor was in political control....[13]

The Great Depression pointed out the essential inadequacy of a socialist movement whose ultimate goals had become more and more detached from its real actions. A faith in the coming of a future society was all very well, as was concern for short-term working-class interests. What was fatal was the lack of connection between the two, the lack of a middle-range strategy. The behavior of the parties was not really reformist, since immediate actions were not related to any general goals. The word opportunist might be more fitting, but this opportunism was hardly pragmatic. The Great Depression should have provided the opportunity for socialists to present their own solutions. Instead, it turned out that in most major European nations, like Germany, England, and France, they had none. That the unpreparedness of European socialism was revealed precisely at the moment when fascism thrust itself onto the stage of history was nothing short of tragic. For the fascists claimed to have answers, and many desperate people wanted assurance. Soon Germany and Austria fell under the fascist heel. Unless socialists in other countries developed a different approach, what fate awaited them? Thus it is not surprising that younger socialists like Jef

Rens gave active support to new leaders who offered
an alternative.

Socialism versus Fascism: The Threat from Within

The Great Depression and the challenge of fascism
from within provided a severe test for socialism in
Europe. German socialism collapsed. The French
Popular Front, initially a real victory both for the
workers and for democracy, failed to create a
national consensus and unintentionally contributed to
polarization. The British Labour Party split and
suffered a humiliating electoral defeat. The Belgian
socialists contributed to getting their country out
of the depression, but found themselves seriously
divided over questionable initiatives in domestic and
foreign policy by some of their leaders. Only on the
northern periphery of Western Europe did experiments
prove successful.

The first experience of fascism came well before
the Great Depression, in a post-war Italy which had
been deeply perturbed by World War I. The war had
not been thrust on Italy; it was the result of a
calculated decision by Italy's elites that their
interests lay in joining the Allies. The war had
little popular support and was opposed by the
Socialist Party. Only a few socialists, like
Mussolini, broke ranks to support participation. The
war aroused greater enthusiasm among the lower middle
and middle classes, especially some of the former who
obtained social mobility by becoming non-commissioned
officers or shock troops. Enraged by the "betrayal"
of the Versailles treaty, they were also incensed by
the anti-war propaganda of the left.

The war had radicalized workers and peasants, who
returned from the front, seized land and went on
strike with the slightest provocation. The mood
seemed revolutionary, but the Socialist Party was
incapable of channeling the radical impulse. Divided
between a reformist minority which would have
preferred to participate in a government coalition
with the more progressive bourgeois elements and a
revolutionary "a maximalist" wing which preached
revolution along soviet lines but did nothing to
prepare for it, the socialists could bring about
neither reform nor revolution. They did, however,
frighten the bourgeoisie, especially with sit-down
strikes in 1921. Since government was ineffective,
the landowners and industrialists relied on vigilante
forces to defend their interest; these groups,
largely constituted from demobilized officers, formed
the emerging fascist movement. The old political
leadership stood aside, as did the "forces of order;"
it was hoped, at least by some of the former, that

once the socialists had suffered at fascist hands
they would be more amenable to compromise. This was
not to be; fascists, who had benefited from the
tolerance of the State, soon discovered that the road
to political power lay open. The March on Rome of
1922 led to a fascist regime (although Mussolini did
not fully consolidate his authority until 1926); the
fascists gained a monopoly of political power, but
left the old elite's economic power intact.

Surprisingly enough, the lesson of Italian
fascism was not readily drawn by either the left or
the right. Despite accurate accounts of fascism by
such left-wing writers as Gaetano Salvemini and
Angelo Tasca, socialists persisted in thinking of
fascism as the last stage of capitalism; they did not
understand the revolutionary character of fascism.
They saw it merely as a tool of Big Capital and
failed to recognize that it had its own social base,
ideology, and dynamic. Likewise, upper classes
elsewhere in Europe did not realize that Mussolini's
triumph had been partly at the expense of the elites,
who lost their political power. This lack of
understanding contributed to the success of Hitler in
Germany.

The coming to power of Adolf Hitler and the rapid
consolidation of Nazi power in Europe produced shock
and consternation throughout the socialist movement.
The German SPD had been the largest, best organized
socialist party in the world. Yet it had been unable
to stop Hitler's rise to power or even to save its
honor by armed resistance. Instead, a few trade
union leaders tried ingloriously and unsuccessfully
to salvage what they could by making a deal with
Hitler.

The German socialist movement had seemed
irresistible in the late 19th and early 20th
century. World War I, however, had been a confusing
and disillusioning experience, its very outbreak and
continuation with support from the working class a
seeming proof of the failure of socialist
internationalism. It resulted in a split between
socialists, mostly reformists, and communists, who
accepted Lenin's Twenty-one Points. But it was not
only the war which damaged socialists' hopes. The
very economic development of Europe was not to their
advantage. Reformists had believed that one day the
workers would constitute 51 percent of the
population. They could then simply vote capitalism
out. Instead, new middle classes emerged. Perhaps
these new middle classes and portions of the old
middle classes and peasantry would have been willing
to follow the SPD had it decided to make a genuine
revolution in 1918. But the socialists had become so
used to working within a system whose doom they

routinely prophesied that they had no clear idea of an alternative. Once in power, the SPD had done little more than decree universal suffrage, call elections and defend the economic interests of the working class. A broad program of social change might well have attracted the middle classes and the peasants: a program for a drab parliamentary regime and support for worker bread and butter demands would certainly not. The socialists were left a minority party, the victims of their own "modest egotism". Unable to offer the blueprint for a new society, the socialists helped create a republic threatened from within by the old elites (Junkers, General Staff, the bureaucracy, the big capitalists, the Church, etc.) -- elites which the party had not even attempted to eliminate in 1918-1919. These elements were never reconciled to socialism -- no matter how reformist -- because they were never reconciled to democracy. Thus by becoming a mild spokesman for working class special interest, the SPD dimmed the enthusiasm of the working class (already rent by the split between socialists and communists) and denied itself support from the middle classes.

By the 1930s it was fascism which seemed the wave of the future. The membership of the Nazi Party was much younger than that of the SPD. Fascism affirmed that it was the revolt of youth against age, of a New Order against the old plutocrats and labor bosses. Fascism had triumphed in Germany. Could it be stopped elsewhere? How could the left regain the initiative? This question was debated at a meeting of the Socialist and Workers International in July 1933.[14]

The meeting demonstrated the growth of significant opposition to the traditional leadership of the old generation of leaders. The "new left," represented by "bourgeois intellectuals" like the Belgian Pierre-Henri Spaak and the French school teacher Marceau Pivert spoke out for such radical steps as the general strike and insurrectionary seizure of power. Pivert opposed the very concept of national defense. Their point of view was neither intellectually sound nor politically practicable, but reflected the frustration felt by many socialists. On the right, a group of French socialists who had just constituted the "neo-socialist" faction repeated their call for a program based on "order, authority, and nation," "strong democracy," and participation in the government. Socialists, they claimed, had to deprive the fascists of their potential base. Leon Blum, the leader of the French Socialist Party, who had already expressed his dismay at the neos' position, wondered what would happen if in their race with fascism for the soul of the middle classes the left started to absorb fascist ideas. The subsequent careers of the neos indicated that Blum had good reason for suspicion.

The old reformist leadership agreed that it was permissible for socialists to exercise power within the capitalist framework to defend democracy against fascism. But they could have nothing to do with "intermediary forms," "introduced by capitalism itself by means of different dictatorial powers which are being established at this time in several countries." Socialism was the logical extension of democracy. Any form of social organization, whether anticapitalist or bolshevik, which limited democracy was unacceptable. Socialism could have nothing in common with fascism. The problem with this position was that it led to a defense of existing democratic institutions whose inability to come to grips with the depression had led to the rise of a mass fascist movement in the first place.

A year after the meeting of the International, yet another major socialist bastion fell; clerical-fascism came to power in Austria. The Austrian socialists may have made errors; the need to prevent the communists from constituting a force on their left may have made them too intransigent at times. Yet compared with the SPD, they were paragons. The SPO had not appealed to right-wing paramilitary units to "save" the nation from bolshevism; instead it tried to create a republican army. The SPO maintained a real intellectual life; "Red Vienna" under socialist administration became a showplace of how working class life could be improved. Yet socialism ultimately failed because it got a few percent less votes in each election than the Catholic Party, which used its majority position to create a clerical-fascist dictatorship step by step. Finally in 1934, Dollfuss went all the way; his coup d'etat provoked a socialist response, but the workers could not defeat the army and a dictatorship was installed. Under younger leaders the Socialist Party went underground as the Revolutionary Socialists of Austria. But clerical-fascism was in turn threatened by the Austrian wing of Nazism and then by direct German aggression. In 1938 Hitler destroyed both clerical-fascism and the underground socialist movement.

One model for dealing with the problems of the depression and the threat of fascism emerged in France. The French political climate had deteriorated badly. On 6 February 1934 massive riots by the right occurred in Paris. The left thought that they presaged a coup d'état. Many socialists and other democrats wanted to join together to meet the threat. Significantly, the Soviet Union finally recognized that its policy of encouraging communist parties to attack socialism rather than fascism as their primary enemy was disastrous. The Communist International made an abrupt shift and now preached the union of all democrats against fascism and cooperation between the democracies and the USSR.

The French Popular Front, an alliance of the Communist, Socialist, and Radical parties, as well as other organizations like the trade unions and the League of the Rights of Man, won the parliamentary elections of 1936, and socialist leader Léon Blum became Prime Minister. In its domestic policy, the government had mixed success. The victory of the left provoked a great wave of spontaneous sit-down strikes, which turned into a general strike. When Blum took office, he organized a conference of business and labor at the Matignon Palace, the seat of government, which led to the recognition of unions and collective bargaining, wage increases, and for the first time, paid vacations. Daniel Mayer, who was covering the meetings for the socialist newspaper, Le Populaire recalls:

> ....there was by chance a woman in the worker delegation who worked in an enterprise whose boss was in the management delegation. He had no idea of the scale of wages of this worker. When she told him how much she earned in his place, he flushed, he stuttered, he was greatly surprised, he was ignorant of the smallness, the shabby character of the wages he was paying. Collective bargaining, the recognition of the right of unionization are probably what gave the working class the notion of sovereignty and dignity which it had not known until then. In that respect, it was a revolution. (Daniel Mayer, Interview with Author.)

On the other hand, the Popular Front was not an economic success. Blum hoped that the increased buying power of the workers would stimulate production and get France out of the depression. This did not happen, in part because the government had not established currency controls and large amounts of money left the country. The government also hesitated to devalue, and when it did, did so too late. It lacked expertise in economics; the influence of Keynes had not yet made itself felt. In the short-lived second Blum government of 1938, Pierre Mendès-France was prepared with modern solutions, but it was too late for the Popular Front.

The Popular Front constituted a breakthrough for the working class but also polarized French politics. It proved impossible to unite France on a coherent foreign policy of resistance to fascism. Moreover, the alliance between socialists and communists was unsatisfactory. The communists took advantage of the Popular Front to infiltrate non-communist working class institutions.

In Britain, divisions within the Labour Party over the economic crisis led not to a synthesis but to a split. The crusade against the policies of the MacDonald government was briefly led by an aristocratic labour leader, Sir Oswald Mosley. In both the Labour and Liberal parties there had been some discussion of Keynesian remedies to the economic crisis. As unemployment worsened, many labourites demanded action. Mosley compared MacDonald and Chancellor of the Exchequer Snowden to "chickens running in front of a motor car and cackling the economy slogans of their opponents."[15] He prepared a long memorandum circulated in January 1930, advocating state intervention in the economy and placing the goal of economic recovery ahead of a balanced budget. This provoked discussion, but was rejected by a labour leadership intimidated by Snowden. Mosley then resigned and set up the short-lived New Party, which gravitated towards Imperial protectionist schemes. In 1932, he abandoned both socialism and democracy and founded the British Union of Fascists.

Mosley's movement towards fascism was largely the result of his impulsive and arrogant character, as well as his cult of physical force. Nevertheless, his economic proposals of 1930 were far closer to the mark than those of the labour leadership, and his frustration was shared by many of the best minds of the party who were, however, unwilling to leave. Like Mussolini, Mosley had embraced socialism in the belief that it was a movement of virility committed to radical change through forceful means. When he found out otherwise, his interest in labour disappeared.

In 1931, MacDonald's government, confronted with serious deficits, was reconstituted as a National Government including tory and liberal ministers. The vast majority of labour saw MacDonald's behavior as betrayal, and labour split. Only a small number of "National Labour" members of parliament followed MacDonald. The elections of 1931 resulted in a smashing defeat for labour, which lost its say in policy-making for the duration of the 1930s.

In Belgium occurred what seemed a hopeful experiment in the use of economic planning to end the depression. The old leadership of the Socialist

Party was caught in the same dilemma as its counterparts in Germany and England. There seemed no middle ground between the impossible dream of socialism and purely negative criticism of the conservative government's deflationary policies. Belgium, an industrial and exporting nation, was hard hit by the depression. The growing fascist movements posed less of a threat than did nazism in Germany, however. Highly nationalistic, the Walloon and Flemish fascists could not work together, whereas the leaders of the three major democratic parties had been accustomed to cooperate since at least 1914. In 1935, when a by-election occurred in Brussels, they united behind Prime Minister Van Zeeland and ignominiously defeated the leader of the Rexists, Leon Dégrelle. Nonetheless the situation of the Socialist Party and the trade unions was difficult. The party leader, Emile Vandervelde, invited Hendrik De Man to return to Belgium and encouraged his efforts to renovate the party.[16]

De Man was the author of the Psychology of Socialism. In this book he attempted to destroy the historicist elements of Marxist thought to go "beyond Marxism" through the discovery of the role of sentiment and ideal in social change and the affirmation of the need for a socialist party which was not restricted to the industrial proletariat. Named to the chair of Social Psychology of the University of Frankfurt in 1929, De Man observed the death of the Weimar Republic and the SPD. He thought he understood why German socialism had failed, and agreed to Vandervelde's request that he return to Belgium. De Man believed that fascism could be stopped and working with a research team that included some of the brightest young people in the party, including Jef Rens, prepared an economic plan designed to eliminate the causes of fascism.[17]

De Man's analysis of fascism took note of the discontent of the middle classes, aroused by their threatened proletarianization and directed against the proletariat. De Man stressed that socialism had become a special interest group, a seeming defender of existing institutions. Anti-fascism alone was not effective: a merely negative approach was what had destroyed the SPD. The party had to orient the anti-capitalism of the middle classes towards socialism. This was all the more necessary since the middle classes, rather than the working class, were growing. De Man stressed the importance of helping the unemployed, who were becoming a fifth class, hostile to a labor movement which appeared to them to be defending only those with jobs. A common denominator was needed for all these groups. The fight against employers interested only the workers;

a struggle for reforms of distribution was rendered difficult because capitalism was in a regressive stage of development. A labor front emphasizing structural reforms had to be created against finance capitalism. It had to strike against under-consumption and unemployment, the causes of the crisis. A mixed economy would replace the faltering capitalist economy. These changes had to be accompanied by a reform of the state.

The linch-pin of the Plan was the nationalization of credit, "the principal means of a managed economy to develop the buying power of the masses of the population in order to assure to all a useful and profitable job, and to increase the general welfare." Basic industries that were under monopoly control would be nationalized. A Commissariat of Transportation would be created. The rest of the economy would remain in private hands, subject to the general directives of the government. Among the many specific goals of the Plan were the stabilization of profits, reduction of working hours, establishment of collective bargaining procedures, increase in foreign trade and creation of a complete system of social security. In addition, changes in the political system were called for. Parliament would be transformed into a streamlined unicameral body elected by universal male suffrage, assisted by consultative councils, whose members would be chosen from outside Parliament by virtue of their expertise. Organisms set up to direct the economy would be endowed with executive powers to assure "rapidity of action and concentration of responsibilities".[18]

The Plan seemed to have several political advantages as well. First, it would enable the party to take the offensive. Second, it seemed to eliminate the issue of whether or not to participate in government by linking participation to "the Plan, the whole Plan, nothing but the Plan". Third, it attracted a generation of young socialists like Jef Rens, Isabelle Blume, Max Buset, Maurits Naessens, some of whom later became disillusioned. Fourth, the Plan seemed to offer a solution to the acrid debate between the left and right of the party. De Man offered the grand vision of Belgium's becoming the "starting place of a vast counter offensive against capitalism ... that will show the world that it is through liberty, and only through liberty, that the order which it seeks with all its strength can be actualized."[19]

The significance of the Plan was not restricted to Belgium; similar experiments were tried elsewhere, and the notion that socialism could be linked with planning and a mixed economy provided a new model for socialist parties which proved especially important after World War II.

In Belgium, the campaign for the Plan reached its height in 1935. At that time, however, the right-wing government fell and a coalition was formed between the socialists and the christian democratic wing of the Catholic party. De Man and Spaak both were included in the ministry; De Man abandoned the campaign for the Plan just as Spaak abandoned his involvement in the Action Socialiste, the leftist faction of the party. Although the government did little to implement the structural reforms suggested by the Plan, it did act effectively against unemployment. The great strikes of 1936, which spilled over from France, also led to improvements in the condition of the working class.

De Man and Spaak were criticized by more traditional socialists for renouncing certain socialist stands on domestic policy, but their policy of governmental participation received trade union support. Spaak's call for "order, authority, and responsibility" and "authoritarian democracy" were both alarming, as was De Man's advocacy of "socialisme national." Grave disputes also occurred over foreign policy.

Both De Man and Spaak supported Belgium's return to an independent foreign policy in 1936, as did most other socialists, but De Man and Spaak interpreted it as meaning neutrality. When the Spanish Civil War broke out, Belgian socialists were emotionally committed to the Republic. But the coalition government would have collapsed if the party had refused to follow Spaak's advice and accede to the opening of commercial relations with Franco in 1938 (it took three party congresses for Spaak to get his way). By late 1938, De Man seems to have lost his faith in political democracy, perhaps partly because his ambition to become Prime Minister had been frustrated. When war came, he and his friends supported neutrality in word as well as in deed; the other wing of the party advocated active moral support for the allies. When Belgium was invaded, De Man stuck by the King, abolished the Belgian Labor Party of which he had been President since April 1939 and tried to establish a labor movement acceptable to the nazis. Spaak left Belgium and participated in the government-in-exile. De Man's career shows that those who wanted most to make socialism into an "active" movement in the 1930s could fall prey to what one writer called "the psychosis of neighboring examples,"[20] once they became convinced that the "New Order" was the wave of the future, and that socialism, like democracy, was outmoded.

More effective solutions to the Great Depression were effected in Scandinavia. Like most of their European counterparts, the Swedish Social Democrats had struggled for complete parliamentary democracy (not achieved until 1920) and short-term social gains. The Marxist core of the party's program had quickly evaporated, with the exception of the socialization of the means of production. The first socialist minority government of 1920 appointed a Board of Socialization to consider specific plans for socializing industries. At the same time, it pursued a purely quotidian program. By the time the depression struck, the Socialization Board had not made any recommendations. It never did. In 1932, the party entered a coalition with the Agrarian Party on the basis of a program of immediate solutions to the economic crisis. The Socialization Board lingered on before giving up the ghost years later. The program of the new government, which included major state involvement in social affairs and protection for the farmers (but not state control over industry) proved enormously successful. The social democrats created the welfare state. The gap between theory and practice was eliminated. But the abandonment of Marxist doctrine did not imply acceptance of sterile reformism. On the contrary, Swedish Social Democracy never forgot its commitment to equality and through its own special brand of pragmatism created new policies to further this goal.

The other Scandinavian socialists also responded successfully to the crisis. The social democratic government under Stauning in Denmark prevented a major industrial crisis in January 1933. The employers insisted on a 20 per cent wage reduction, which was refused by the workers. To avert a lock-out, the government held a marathon discussion session with leaders of the major parties. The result was agreement on devaluation and a ban on strikes and lock-outs for a year. Later, a system of compulsory arbitration was established. Necessity proved the mother of invention. At the same time, the entire system of social legislation was rationalized. The government dealt with the crisis not through nationalization but through manipulation of wages, prices, and taxes:

> Denmark thus possessed a manipulated, if not a planned economy, with a substantially higher degree of regulation than England, France, or the United States. Unlike Sweden, Denmark conducted its policies almost entirely on an empirical basis, without much effort of using theory for guidance or justification. The success

of the Danish experiment can be found in its
political effects -- the Danish farmer was
not driven by dispair into the ranks of
fascism, and the Danish worker did not turn
Communist, although at times unrest was
fairly strong.[21]

In Norway also, the Labor Party entered into a
coalition with the Agrarian Party. The Nygaardvold
government of 1935 represented a shift to
pragmatism. Labor, which had briefly adhered to the
Comintern because of the influence of its radical
syndicalist wing under Martin Tranmael and which had
suffered several schisms, was now united on a program
of reform. Through the efforts of the government
unemployment was drastically reduced, farm prices
improved, industrial peace maintained, social welfare
legislation created:

> Nearly all these measures had been
> accepted in principle, if criticized in
> detail, by all the parties of the Storting,
> a circumstance which helped destroy the
> notion that a large body of right-wing
> extremists was prepared to fight for its
> privileges....Meanwhile, the Labor movement
> had resumed its former close relations with
> the Social-Democratic parties of Sweden and
> Denmark and attached itself to the Socialist
> Labour International....[22]

Thus, by the end of the 1930s, we can already
speak of a "Scandinavian approach to socialism."
Despite the historical differences between Sweden,
Norway, and Denmark, their paths converged. A
welfare state emerged and developed with widespread
support. The success of the experiment was
demonstrated in the 1970s when the socialist parties
all lost power for at least a time. Their
"bourgeois" rivals made little effort to undermine
the welfare state.
The 1930s was an agonizing period for European
socialism. Some of the strongest socialist parties
failed to meet the fascist challenge, and were
liquidated by the resulting regimes. The British
Labour Party was ineffectual, the French socialists
had some success with the Popular Front, but could
not reestablish a national consensus. The Plan in
Belgium inspired enthusiasm, but socialists were
divided over foreign policy. In Scandinavia,
however, socialism embarked on a new course which
would prove a model to other countries.

Socialism versus Fascism: The Threat from Outside

>   We could not throw our pacifism away as
> quickly as Hitler built up his power.
>   Jef Rens,
>   Interview with Author.

In most countries of Western Europe, fascism
never posed a serious internal threat. Fascism
thrived on economic crisis and fear of revolution,
but it could not overcome a long tradition of
political democracy. In France and England, for
example, the lower middle class, a crisis stratum in
Germany and Italy, remained democratic. The triumph
of Hitler was unwelcome, not threatening. Few
contemplated a preemptive war against Hitler, few
realized how quickly Hitler could rearm.
Only after Germany began to rearm and Hitler and
Mussolini embarked on foreign adventures did it
become apparent that they were threats to world
peace. Yet many socialists, committed to pacifism,
believed until March 1939 that Hitler's only foreign
policy goal was to unite all Germans in one reich.
After 1934, there was no unified socialist response
on an international level; some of the most important
socialist parties in Europe no longer existed and
even within the surviving parties, there was no
consensus on appropriate responses.
As Jef Rens said:

>   The problem of fascism was complicated
> by one thing that you shouldn't forget. In
> the years following the First World War, we
> inculcated inside the labor movement of
> Europe, everywhere in Europe, pacifism, as
> almost the most essential feature of
> socialism. And we still practiced that cult
> when Hitler was already in power and
> organizing the remilitarization of Germany.
> So there was more than one weakness on our
> side. This was a real one. And I would say
> that in England it was overriding. You
> could not be a socialist without being a
> pacifist. And we did not want to see the
> danger of Germany's becoming a military
> power....
>   Also, you know, Hitler's march towards
> power in terms of historical development was
> a very quick movement, and it was not so
> easy for an old movement like the labor
> movement, which had through the evils and
> the sufferings of the First World War
> developed a position of pacifism to do away

with that, even watching what was going on in Germany.

We could not throw away our pacifism as quickly as Hitler built up his power. He went very, very, very, very fast; and, of course, a concentration of power in one hand -- as against democracy, where you know, ideas have to be developed through a whole framework of institutions and meetings and so on. (Interview with Author.)

Daniel Mayer stated that he had little difficulty in changing from pacifism to anti-fascism:

I think all the young socialists, except some pacifists understood it, that what the new Germany, the Germany of Hitler was going to become was not the Germany of yesterday. We had to make a rapid turnabout. Whereas we had been supporters of an understanding with the Weimar Republic, there could be no understanding with the Germany of Hitler. Whereas we had been for disarmament ... from one day to the next not only was it necessary not to disarm in the face of the new Germany, but it was necessary, on the contrary, to rearm. (Interview with Author.)

Nevertheless, many socialists remained pacifists in France.

In England, the Labour Party had espoused disarmament during the 1920s. After 1931, the rump of labour was presided over for several years by George Lansbury, an elderly, idealistic Christian who professed an almost total pacifism and whose lieutenant, Sir Stafford Cripps, shared that predilection. Labour included advocates of collective security through the League of Nations who at the same time opposed an increased military budget and favored disarmament. The situation within the party was muddled; it illustrates Rens' comment about how hard it was for socialists to adapt as fast as their opponents. German rearmament and Mussolini's Ethiopian War prompted the trade union leadership, especially Ernest Bevin, to support both League sanctions against Italy and British rearmament. They forced Lansbury out in 1935 and replaced him with Clement Attlee. But even then, labour was not of one mind. The National Government, which purported to be supporting Ethiopia, had been ready to sell it out with the Hoare-Laval agreement; the same government seemed the very incarnation of the class enemy at home. Under such conditions, how could labour vote the defense budget? And then there was Spain.

The Spanish Civil War first seemed to harden labour's position against fascism. But that position was muddied by the government's espousal of non-intervention, in which it alleged it was following the wish of the French Popular Front. Only the gradual discovery that non-intervention was nothing but an alibi for British aloofness from the Republic which permitted Germany and Italy to pump massive quantities of arms into Franco Spain forced labour to reject it. Whatever its faults, however, labour arrived at a firmer anti-fascist position than its opponents on the right. It is not astonishing that the very day of Hitler's invasion of Poland, when Chamberlain was still tergiversating about what England might do, one of his own backbenchers shouted across to the Labour spokesman, Arthur Greenwood, "Speak for England."

In France, as we have seen, pacifism had provided the cement of the Socialist Party during the 1920s. The perceived threat of domestic fascism and the rise of Hitler propelled the party into the Popular Front, although some socialists were not unduly enthusiastic about collaboration with the communists. It was foreign policy rather than domestic which proved most divisive to the socialists in the second half of the decade. How would they respond to the rapid growth of German power?

The party was profoundly divided. On the one extreme, Marceau Pivert, who preached the value of insurrection to stop fascism in France, advocated revolutionary defeatism in case of war. The working class should refuse to defend the fatherland; if Germany began a war, it would turn into world revolution. However nonsensical they may seem, Pivert's ideas had a considerable audience, particularly among teachers and in the Federation of Paris. On the other hand, Jean Zyromski and the Bataille Socialiste (to which Daniel Mayer belonged) supported a coalition with Russia against fascism.

Since 1921, the SFIO had been based on the alliance of Paul Faure, the party's secretary-general, and Léon Blum, the head of the parliamentary group. After 1934, the alliance began to crack. Both Blum and Faure had supported disarmament; as late as 1936 Blum persevered in proposing it to Germany. But it became increasingly clear to Blum that a Grand Alliance against Hitler was needed. By the time of Munich, the party was virtually split; Blum and the Bataille Socialiste versus the Faure and Pivert factions.

As head of government at the time of the outbreak of the Spanish Civil War, Blum immediately sent arms

to the Republic. This excited opposition. The
Radical Party, which was part of the government
coalition, demurred; many socialists opposed aid.
The English informed Blum that if his actions led to
war with Germany, England would not be bound to take
the part of France. Blum was ready to resign, but
the Spanish Ambassador, del Vayo, begged him to
remain. Blum continued covert supply of arms, but
officially France subscribed to non-intervention. By
the logic of things, Blum was forced to support
non-intervention, thereby incurring the wrath of the
communists and some of his own party. It is by no
means clear whether he would have done better to
resign rather than to serve as a cover for
non-intervention. The conservative government used
French adherence to non-intervention to oppose
labour's demands for helping the Republic.

The tragedy was that no governmental coalition
based on a firm commitment to France's allies and
resistance to fascism was possible. The right was
unwilling (with a few noteworthy exceptions), the
radicals uneasy, the socialists divided. There was
no political base for a stable foreign policy:

> The simple truth is that from Munich onwards
> the French Socialist party had fallen into
> two parts because of the dispute about this
> basic problem in public life. It was this
> dispute which reduced it to silent
> impotence. Anxious to preserve the
> appearance of unity, the party avoided
> taking any clear-cut line of action and even
> avoided making any clear-cut declaration for
> that would have revealed its inner divisions
> and would undoubtedly have led to an actual
> split... Thus the party dragged out its
> existence in mistrust and humiliation for
> nearly two more years until at the end its
> very existence was scarcely noticed any
> longer.[23]

In Sweden, as we have seen, there had been strong
sentiment at the 1932 party congress for unilateral
disarmament. By 1936, the vast majority of the party
supported rearmament. The rise of nazism, the
Ethiopian war, the failure of the League all
contributed to this resolve. At the same time, the
party reaffirmed its commitment to the ideal of
disarmament. As one of the former leaders of the
pro-disarmament wing of the party said:

> We must remember that everywhere in
> Europe where a military vacuum exists it is
> immediately filled by Nazi troops. If not

[by] German Nazi troops, then [by] private troops with a nazi spirit from within the country itself.... If a Social democratic party, under the enormous pressure of world events or even because of domestic political conditions, must momentarily redirect itself along the course of retreat on the military question, it has not thereby forsaken its fundamental standpoint. We are most certainly all agreed that as soon as the external situation permits, the antimilitary fight and the fight for arms reduction will be taken up again with all possible force.[24]

In Denmark, according to Carl Landaver, the social democratic government had actually put into effect a program approximating unilateral disarmament:

Even among the small countries, few were so much inclined to rely for their security on the League of Nations as Denmark was under the second Stauning cabinet. The army and navy were reduced to a size hardly sufficient to safeguard the frontiers against even minor infractions of Danish neutrality in the event of war. These forces were wholly inadequate to repel an invasion. After 1933, the Social Democrats recognized that the peace policy had collapsed and that Denmark's example of voluntary unilateral disarmament had not been followed by others. For any serious defense plans, however, the resources of the country were considered too small. When actual invasion came, the country, unable to defend itself, could only maintain its moral integrity through the incorruptible spirit of its citizens.[25]

The Labor and Socialist International reflected the confusion of the socialist movement. After Munich, the smaller countries within it lost faith in English and French resolve to stand up to Hitler, and wanted to avoid taking a stand:

By September 1938 war seemed inevitable, and the small countries bordering on Hitler's Germany hoped to escape the catastrophe by a policy of neutrality. In all these countries except Holland, the Socialist parties were in a leading position inside the government. By going over to a policy of neutrality they

contradicted a policy of collective security
which the Labor and Socialist International
had always supported.[26]

The International's president and secretary, Louis de
Brouckère and Friedrich Adler, both good
internationalists, resigned on 14 May 1939. When the
war started, the International did not even condemn
the aggressor. Once again, the socialist movement
had failed in the face of war.

War, Occupation, and Resistance

> Parri said to me: "We are discussing
> whether or not to engage in armed struggle.
> Let's begin the armed struggle and the
> question will be resolved!"
>
> Riccardo Lombardi,
> Interview with Author.

The inundation of Western Europe by the nazis
seemed to justify the right's claim that democracy
and socialism were obsolete. The fall of France
convinced many that the Swastika would soon float
over Westminister. Few had the foresight of De
Gaulle, who realized that the Axis would not win; the
others could only resist for moral reasons. The vast
majority of the population of the occupied nations,
whatever their political affiliation, wanted peace at
any price, and was willing to straddle the fence if
not actually to collaborate with the Germans.
Vincent Auriol describes how socialist members of
Parliament behaved to Léon Blum in July 1940, during
the session of Parliament which voted full powers to
Pétain:

> Where are the 175 Socialist members of
> Parliament?... Some, of course could not
> come...but the others? Where are they,
> those deputies who in former times acclaimed
> him in a standing ovation in the party
> caucus, in the Chamber, in our congresses,
> at mass meetings? Where are those who,
> seeking election or re-election, called him
> to their district so that he might give them
> his backing with his eloquence, his
> authority, his prestige? Where are those
> who crowded the antechambers of the Matignon
> Palace to solicit favors, those who owed him
> everything ...?"[27]

The temptation to collaborate was great. Many
socialists yielded; they collaborated with
quasi-autonomous "governments" like Vichy if not

directly with the nazis. As time went on, the behavior of the Germans rendered collaboration unpalatable; the changing fortunes of the war ultimately made it irrational, since by 1943 Allied victory seemed probable. The distressing subject of left-wing collaboration with puppet regimes and with Germany has only recently been given serious study.

The efforts to organize underground socialist parties must be seen against this background. The task required immense courage and dedication. The resistance never attracted more than a minority of the population; socialist resistance was the affair of a minority of socialists. The honor of the socialist parties was redeemed by those who took an active role in the resistance. Without them, the party would not have been reborn after the war.

Resistance movements can be classified in several ways. First there was a distinction between internal and external resistance. Communication was difficult between the two and their perspectives often diverged. Frequently the old party leaders who attempted to assert their control from abroad were the very people blamed by the internal resistance for pre-war failures. In some cases, socialist parties operating underground virtually repudiated their pre-occupation leadership.

Resistance movements can also be divided between those which were specifically party organizations and those which were broader movements grouping people from diverse backgrounds. Generally, socialists participated in the latter for several reasons. They did not see the resistance as a matter of partisan politics. The old socialist parties were not always popular among resistance figures. Especially at the beginning of the war, the collapse of the democracies seemed evidence of the failure of the entire system, a system of which the socialist parties were part. Many resistants dreamed of a political order based on new, or at least greatly transformed parties. There were certainly socialists who shared the opinion of French resistance leader Henri Frenay, who wrote in 1943:

> It would be puerile to pretend that in the great trial of France, men have died for the Radical Party or Democratic Alliance, but there are certainly men who belonged to the Radical Party or the Democratic Alliance who died for France in the Resistance. Thus the present reconstruction of parties as they existed before the war would be a grave error.[28]

Many French Socialists had little desire to see the old SFIO reappear, the more so because most of its militants simply sat out the war, and some major leaders like Paul Faure were tainted with appeasement and implicated in Vichy. In Italy, socialists often belonged to Giustizia e Libertà, which was far more active in the resistance than the Socialist Party.

Nevertheless, the old parties did reappear, more or less changed from the pre-war. One reason for their reappearance was the conduct of the communists. After having stayed out of the resistance during the period of the Nazi-Soviet non-aggression pact, the communists joined with great zeal when Russia was invaded. Much more adept at underground activity than the socialists, they formed their own groups and front organizations and infiltrated other organizations as well. Because they acted as a party, they gained much more notoriety than parties whose members fought in non-party movements. The nature of the communist resistance helped transform resistance _mystique_ into _politique_. The socialists could not run the risk of facing the communists at the liberation with no organization of their own. In France there was another reason: De Gaulle, opposed by the Americans, encouraged the rebirth of parties in order to justify his claim to represent France.

In most of Western Europe the old political parties returned. Socialism was one of those old parties. New parties based on the resistance tended to disintegrate. But socialism had a tough battle for survival against a reinvigorated communist movement in the post-war years.

Socialism Master of the Hour? Atrophy and Success: 1945-1968

> Our intention was very clearly to go on further with the policies of the 1930s: full employment, better education, greater social justice.... The real break was the 1930s.
>
> Trygve Bratteli,
> Interview with Author.

> Really, there was nothing more to do in that party.
>
> Daniel Mayer,
> Interview with Author.

It was, in my opinion, in those few months
after 1966 that our greatest opportunity was
lost.

Michael Foot,
Interview with Author.

Shortly after his return from a German
concentration camp, Léon Blum wrote an optimistic
article entitled "Le Socialisme: maître de
l'heure."[29] It reflected the widespread optimism
of Western European socialists that the world could
be changed, that the ideals of socialism would
constitute the basis of a new society. What
precisely were these hopes, and why were they so
quickly disappointed?

Socialists hoped that the world could be
reconstructed on the basis of international peace and
fraternity and that some form of international
organization could be successfully constructed. They
wanted to solve the problems which had divided Europe
and had caused two world wars. They hoped for a
world without blocs and for the continuation of the
Grand Alliance between the USSR and the West. They
hoped that good relations between the West and Russia
would be paralleled by either fusion or close
cooperation between communist and socialist parties.
They often imagined that socialism could become the
dominant force in Europe through the absorption of
Catholics, resistants and members of the middle
classes whose perspective had been broadened by the
war experience. Lastly, they hoped that socialism
would go through a process of renovation and
revitalization which would justify its claims to
leadership. These high hopes were destroyed above
all by the Cold War.

There were strains in the war-time alliance from
the beginning. The post-war order was based not on
ideals but on realpolitik. England and America put
down the left in Greece and intervened, in fashions
less direct, in Italy. The Russians, convinced that
the only way to have "friendly regimes" in Eastern
Europe was to install puppet governments, used the
Red Army to consolidate unpopular communist rule.
The socialist parties of Eastern Europe were either
fused against their will with the communists in
"unity" parties or liquidated. The coup in Prague of
1948 was as much a statement of Stalin's intentions
as the coup there in 1939 had defined Hitler's.
There was a great deal with which one could reproach
America, but Stalinism was much worse. If a choice
had to be made between them it would be for
Atlanticism.

Socialists tried to avoid making a choice between
America and Russia. Once the prospects for a new

world order collapsed, socialists retreated to a second line of defense; Europe should be socialist and independent, a link between East and West. A reconstructed International could constitute a third force. The persistence of resistance front governments including communists, socialists, and christian democrats in France, Italy, and Belgium was evidence of a desire to preserve the fragile unity of the underground. But events in the outer world moved more quickly than within these countries. These resistance front governments were anachronisms. By 1947, the Cold War was too far advanced for anyone to seriously believe that Europe could stay out. Moreover, Europe discovered it could not recover without massive economic assistance which only America could give. With the exception of the Italians, socialists in the great majority took sides with America against Russia, though hardly with enthusiasm.

With the globalization of the Cold War resulting from the Korean conflict, the United States decided that Europe had to contribute land forces to its own defense. NATO had been formed, but that was not enough. German rearmament was called for, an idea which could hardly be popular five years after the collapse of the Third Reich. The way out of German rearmament was to rearm Germany within the framework of a European army. This idea, embodied in the Pleven Plan for a European Defense Community, evoked enormous opposition throughout Western Europe. After years of discussion it was defeated by the French National Assembly in 1954. Socialists were deeply divided. Despite endorsement by the party, half the French socialist members of parliament voted against it; in Belgium the party gave members a free vote. The German Social Democrats opposed the EDC. The rejection of the EDC by the French National Assembly led to the adoption of the London agreements, which ironically provided fewer safeguards than the EDC. The point is that European socialism was in no position to make decisions for Europe; indeed, Europe could not determine its own destiny.

There were, nevertheless, certain exceptions to the general rule of socialist support for the Atlantic alliance. Since neutral Sweden had kept out of both world wars, it was only logical that Swedish socialists should support neutrality. Italy, however, was the only western nation in which a major socialist party maintained a close alliance with the communists for a decade after the liberation. This Popular Front went as far as joint electoral lists in the elections of 1948, elections which proved disastrous to the PSI (the PCI received 135 seats in the Chamber of Deputies, the PSI 51). Although the subsequent socialist congress ended this phase of the alliance, the PSI maintained unity of action with the communists.

How can this apparent anomaly be explained? Italy had been under fascist rule for over two decades. Many socialists attributed Mussolini's rise to power to the fragmentation of the left. Party leader Pietro Nenni and party secretary Lelio Basso were determined not to let this happen again. The communist seemed the most dynamic force on the left; if the price of unity with the communists was a schism with the right of the PSI, so much the worse. In Germany, which also had a long experience with fascism, the socialists blamed the communists for helping to destroy Weimar. In France, fascism never came close to power; there seemed less urgency to maintain a close communist-socialist alliance. But in Italy, the mystique of unity proved all powerful. Moreover, it was reinforced by antagonisms to American and English intervention in Italian affairs.

The third major socialist party which resisted the general movement towards atlanticism was the SPD. When nazism collapsed, it was inevitable that the leadership of the SPD would devolve on those who had been active before 1933. There was no significant underground during the Hitler years; the SPD could not benefit from the fructifying experience of the resistance. The social democrats naturally planned their post-war strategy on the basis of their failure to stop Hitler. Kurt Schumacher who imposed himself as leader, was determined that the SPD would not appear as an anti-national force as it had been perceived after World War I. Schumacher emphasized the defense of German national interests. Strongly anti-communist, he refused to cooperate with the communists and opposed the fusion of communists and socialists in the Soviet zone. Yet despite his bitter hatred of soviet communism and its eastern zone allies, Schumacher and the SPD refused to support the EDC. Schumacher's opposition was derived mostly from his insistence that Germany be treated as an equal; that of the rest of his party, from pacifism. Moreover, Schumacher feared that the EDC would prevent eventual German reunification. German unity was more important that Atlantic solidarity. But this policy proved neither realistic nor electorally profitable. This period provides interesting parallels with the policies followed by the SPD after the collapse of its coalition with the Liberals in 1983.

Thus socialists took sides in the Cold War. Europe could not serve as an instrument for world harmony; it could not even maintain its autonomy in the struggle between the superpowers. But this also helps explain why Europe could not be socialist. Europe needed America, but America was wary of socialism. For a while, it was possible to argue that "socialism was the worst enemy of communism," but when given a chance, the America of the late 1940s and early 1950s preferred to work with christian democrats or conservatives. The equation in the American mind of communism, socialism, and Marxism made socialists appear dubious allies to the USA. By the late 1940s, the political pendulum in Europe started moving back to the right. Socialists either had to accept more conservative policies if they wanted to remain in coalition governments, or else, return to opposition.

The logical corollary of the Cold War, the ghettoization of Western Europe communism, was a major blow to socialist hopes. After 1947, cooperation with the communists became impossible; indeed, socialist ministers often took action to repress communist-initiated political strikes. In the period 1947-1948 there was considerable fear of communist plans for insurrection; such plans did not exist, but the communist parties certainly were instructed by Moscow to disrupt Western Europe, because Moscow feared that America was planning war. The socialists, by becoming an active part of the anti-communist coalition, were forced to the right; they antagonized some of their constituents who blamed them for contributing to the balkanization of the left. At the same time, the inability of communist and socialist parliamentarians to work together strengthened the right. There was no way out; French socialists, for example, lost support because of their anti-communism, Italian socialists lost support because of their alliance with the communists.

The decline of socialist strength in France and Italy was also a result of their organizational inferiority compared with the communists. The old SFIO had almost disappeared during the war; socialist efforts at reconstruction could not keep up with the PCF, which had used the resistance to develop its infrastructure. Likewise, Italian socialist unity of action with the communists had undermined their own organizational integrity in historically socialist regions. In France and Italy the communists got control of the major trade union federations during and after the war. As masses of minimally politicized workers flooded into the unions, the old socialist or anarcho-syndicalist militants were outmaneuvered by the communists, who took control of the trade union centrals and then used this position to consolidate political control over much of the industrial proletariat. The communist tide was

strong wherever the communists had played a major
resistance role. But in countries which had large
well-organized trade unions run by socialists, their
offensive was turned back and communist strength
eroded rapidly after 1947.

Socialism was also weakened by the inability to
break out of a restricted social base, especially in
Catholic countries. Many militants were
anti-clerical and resisted efforts by leaders like
Daniel Mayer to attract Catholic resistants.
Moreover, by the post-war period, Catholic
trade-unions were no longer the old "company unions"
of the past. These unions, as well as the new
"progressive" christian democratic parties resisted
socialist inroads into the practicing Catholic
working class.

Socialism also suffered from identification with
unpopular war-time controls and rationing systems
which the right attacked as "socialist." The desire
to return to "normalcy" became identified with
lifting these controls, which were popularly
identified as the cause, rather than as the result,
of scarcity.

Yet another reason for socialist weakness was the
failure of doctrinal renovation. Socialism had
always been both a spokesman for the future society
and an instrument of reform within capitalism.
Socialism constantly sought equilibrium between the
two roles. Once the initial enthusiasm of the
liberation abated and the belief that a new world
could really be created came to an end, socialist
parties in the West tended towards increasing
moderation and identification with the status quo.
They became essentially governmental parties; whether
to participate in government ceased to be a
theoretical and became a tactical question.
Socialists acted as if there was no alternative to a
bi-polar world, to the dominance of America over
Europe, and as if the mixed, planned economy with its
social welfare programs created after World War II
was the final answer to the social question. They
assumed that the affluent society of the late 1950s
was quite acceptable; only minor changes might be
needed. As George Lichtheim, reflecting that state
of mind, wrote:

> In a fully industrialized society,
> "conservatism" signifies not defense of
> precapitalist interests (e.g., in
> agriculture), but rather the maintenance of
> middle-class values and standards such as
> home ownership, educational privileges, and
> various amenities associated with possession
> of individual property. "Liberalism" may

come to stand for economic planning -- a far cry from Cobdenite or Gladstonian orthodoxy. "Socialism" signifies concern for the status of lower-paid wage earners, while the historic goal of superseding "private ownership of the means of production" is tacitly abandoned, at any rate so long as the economy maintains full employment. The classical case is Scandinavia under Social-Democratic management, but Britain and the remainder of Western Europe show signs of following suit. Under circumstances of this sort, with growing wealth making for political quiescence, socialism loses its revolutionary edge, so that it is finally left to a minority of syndicalists and other enthusiasts to keep the pure flame of faith burning. It is, however, misleading to attribute this change in the political climate to embourgeoisement on the part of the workers or their leaders. The fact is that a society of this kind though it may still be capitalist can no longer be described as bourgeois.[30]

This attitude fitted well with the belief in "the end of ideology." Looking back on this period, the sociologist Walter Korpi elucidates the problem created for Swedish Social Democracy:

The strong reliance by the Social Democrats on the growth strategy made the leaders of the labour movement sometimes appear as parts of the techno-structure, having economic growth as their main goal. Combining compromise politics with a pronounced future orientation also proved difficult for the labour movement. Its leadership became absorbed with day-to-day political responsibilities. The party faced difficulties in developing programmes for continued societal change in the direction of economic democracy. In the eyes of many voters, the Social Democrats gradually became identified with the compromise and growth policies. They also tended to defend most aspects of these policies, often also those that caused dismay among potential supporters....
The bourgeois parties' gradual acceptance of welfare measures once enacted made the Social Democrats seem but one among several reform parties competing for the

right to administer existing society. By focusing on some of the negative aspects of the compromise policies, especially rapid urbanization, regional imbalance, centralization and problems with the environment and with nuclear energy, since the late 1960s the bourgeois parties were able not only to maintain but also to increase their political support....

It would appear that the interpretation suggested here, derived from the Swedish experience, also can help to explain electoral difficulties of social democratic parties in other European countries in the postwar period.[31]

The identification with the existing social order could not be reconciled with Marxism or indeed with almost any radical vision of socialism. Would socialists be willing to reconcile theory and practice? In Germany, after the death of Schumacher, the SPD's Bad Godesberg program of 1959 abandoned Marxism and reaffirmed commitment to a mixed economy. At about the same time, the party ended its opposition to rearmament and became a loyal supporter of the Atlantic community. This change in doctrine gained it political respectability and ultimately power, but also underlay the deepening conflict between the party establishment and the more radical Young Socialists.

Bad Godesberg at least unified theory and practice. In most countries, however, this never occurred. The gap between the two became gigantic in France, Italy, England, and Belgium; Guy Mollet, for example, could justify a policy of colonial reconquest in Marxist terms. In most socialist parties intellectual life stultified; intellectuals were not welcome. In France, non-communist left-wing intellectuals felt bitter contempt for the SFIO and turned to smaller groups and movements.

Socialism's credibility was undermined by the issue of colonialism. In the past, socialists had often declaimed against colonialism, although many had accepted it as a means of uplifting the indigenous populations. Generally European socialist parties paid scant attention to what was happening in the colonial world. In Belgium, a special party congress did discuss the Congo in 1956 but the word independence was not uttered; socialists acted as if there was no rush to give the Congolese an "apprenticeship in democracy." When riots took place in 1959, the socialists demanded immediate independence for the Congo, which certainly was not prepared. The socialist role in colonization seemed further evidence that socialism had little to offer the modern world.

The moderation of post-war socialism was beneficial in electoral terms in countries where communism was weak. Yet even there it was dangerous to become too well integrated into the system. By the late 1960s there was a feeling that the western world, despite its affluence, its new-found political stability, planned economies and social welfare systems, was still not the Good Society. Young people became upset about Vietnam and asked why their governments, even socialist governments, did not take a stand against American involvement. The end of ideology may have seemed a blessing to those who had lived through the 1930s; it did not provide meaning for the young. Socialism, even communism, seemed to have become part of one great repressive system, as Herbert Marcuse's One Dimensional Man suggested. May 1968 demonstrated the depth of hostility to that system, how greatly the socialist parties had lost touch with the younger generation. Without renewal, they ran the risk of slow extinction. Would that renewal take place?

Eurosocialism

....the greatest issue in the world is what is to happen to the nuclear arms race.
Michael Foot,
Interview with Author.

The very right to property must be challenged.
Riccardo Lombardi,
Interview with Author.

When I was about 20 years old, most people believed that really profound change in economic conditions wasn't possible. The big break was to discover that it was possible by appropriate means to control economic conditions. We're in the midst of that discussion again today. To me, it's rather horrifying to listen to these arguments from the 1920s.
Trygve Bratteli,
Interview with Author.

We have not yet learned to become world citizens.
Jef Rens,
Interview with Author.

The evolution of European socialism since 1968 must be seen in its historical context. On the international level, this period has been marked by the rise and fall of détente. The invasion of Afghanistan, the repression in Poland, the Iranian crisis, the increase in Soviet military capability which ended American supremacy, the perception that the Reagan administration's policy was incoherent, all helped to produce a feeling of malaise in Europe. Russia was perceived as more threatening than before, the U.S. as more erratic.

In Western Europe, the period was marked by the rise and subsequent decline of a partial sense of European identity. Economic integration had proceeded apace; England and several other nations had joined the Common Market. Authoritarian regimes in Spain, Portugal, and Greece collapsed; for the first time, all Western Europe lived under democracy.

A European Parliament was elected; some form of European federalism seemed possible. Nevertheless, Europe was very far from being a political unit. The sense of identity was fragile; England, for example, continued to waver in her adherence to the Common Market. And although it seemed politically advisable to add Spain and Portugal to the European Economic Community to help stabilise democracy there, the economic price for the industrial nations, already in crisis, seemed high. The oil crisis of 1973 demonstrated that in times of stress Europe was apt to react along nationalistic lines; a decade later two successive EEC summit meetings in December 1983 and March 1984 failed to reach consensus. Even after it was elected directly, the European Parliament had little authority. But most importantly, Europe had not chosen to develop its own independent military capacity (although France did have its force de frappe). Thus Europe had to remain militarily dependent on the United States or else move towards neutralism and pacifism, which was politically absurd. Nonetheless some of those who had not experienced the German occupation or the Marshall Plan, who knew the U.S. only since the Vietnam era, equated the two superpowers or even saw the U.S. as the major danger to world peace. The debate over INF demonstrated the fissures within individual parties and within the Socialist International. In short, Europe could not constitute a Third Force because it did not have an independent military potential, but resented its dependence.

As détente was breaking down, so was European affluence. The long period of rapid growth ended. The inherent problems of the Western economies were aggravated by the inflation resulting from the Vietnam War, OPEC's price hikes, and the undercutting of European and American industries by Japan and then by the Third World.

Economic downturn rendered incumbent governments unpopular, whether leftist or rightist; no government seemed capable of producing "prosperity in one country." Socialist ministries were turned out in Norway, Denmark, and Holland, brought to power in France and Sweden, and weakened in Austria despite generally good economic conditions. The Mitterrand government, which came to power largely because of the economic failures of Giscard, was soon blamed for its own. Just as the in the 1930s, socialists seemed to possess no answers to the economic crisis. They had assumed that the post-war system of a mixed economy would function sufficiently well to support the elaborate superstructure of the welfare state. No longer was that obvious. It would be necessary either to cut social services, intervene in economic life in a different fashion, or just tinker around in the hopes that prosperity would return.

The coincidence of the end of both détente and prosperity produced an identity crisis in European socialism; it encouraged polarization and tended to strengthen the radical wing within some socialist parties. In England, for example, labour moved to the left (at least by its own standards). One-time outsider Michael Foot was elected Party Leader, but soon Foot was preoccupied by trying to hold the party together. To be sure, Foot stood for withdrawal from the Common Market (but this had not always been an exclusively left/right issue), nationalizations, and opposition to nuclear weapons on British soil, but these were old issues. Unlike Benn and the "hard left", he was firmly wedded to the old parliamentary tradition. He conceived of labour as a party of government; Benn was willing to marginalize it to make it ideologically homogeneous.

In Germany, too, radicalization occurred. Helmut Schmidt experienced increasing difficulty in controlling the left; when the FDP changed alliances in 1983 Schmidt resigned and was replaced by a party leader more acceptable to the left and the greens. The subsequent election, based on economic issues, was made into something of a referendum on the stationing of nuclear weapons on German soil; it may have pushed the social democrats farther in their opposition to new missiles than their leaders really intended. In Holland and Belgium, the euromissile issue also proved radicalizing. But the left opposition lacked any realistic alternatives; it reflected understandable fear and frustration, but had no policy; in the case of Germany, it smacked somewhat of nationalism à la Schumacher.

If Europe as a whole had attained only a partial sense of European consciousness, the same may be said for European socialism. European socialism became eurosocialism, at least on the cosmetic level. The rose replaced diverse and sundry party symbols. Socialism took on a more human face, or at least a younger face; young leaders like Felipe Gonzalez emerged. Socialism was better packaged. The International seemed more conspicuous. But how much had things changed under the glossy surface?

It is hard to find a common denominator for eurosocialism. Generally, eurosocialism tried to break with anticlericalism, to find support from Catholics and former Catholics who had become politically progressive. Eurosocialism showed concern for environmental and ecological issues, which meant putting into question a certain Marxist tendency to think that economic concentration was progressive, that the rate of production was more important than its ecological consequences. The Swedish socialists may have lost in 1976 partly because they advocated nuclear power. Likewise, socialism returned to its historic interest in women's issues and problems of quality of life. In the case of France, eurosocialism meant relinquishing the jacobin legacy of political centralization in line with the Proudhonian concerns of decentralization and self-determination highlighted by May 1968. Eurosocialism implied more attention to the Third World, attention manifested in things like the Brandt report, but also in greater independence from the United States in dealing with Third World issues. The International was opened up to Third World parties, some of which did not belong and socialist leaders were all too quick to identify with the Sandinistas and El Salvador's guerillas. A Lebanese feudal chieftain became a Vice President of the International. At the same time, there was a need to recruit skilled technocrats and managers into positions of prominence in party and government life. Pre-war socialist leaders had often worked their way up in the party or allied organizations, especially trade unions, or were journalists, autodidacts, sometimes literati from bourgeois background. Now trained economists, upper-level bureaucrats, and technicians became more important, for example, Rocard and Chevènement. Eurosocialism was also a reply to eurocommunism, the attempt of western European communist parties to become independent, or at least appear independent, of Moscow and Marxism-Leninism.

How to deal with communists evoked the most divergent response. For example, Mitterrand preached cooperation with a communist party which had already demonstrated that it was neither eurocommunist nor desirous of a left-wing victory; for the first time the French socialists began to "plumer la volaille communiste." In Spain, the issue of relations with the communists became moot; the communist movement collapsed and split. The new Craxi leadership in Italy followed the opposite policy from Mitterrand. Although Craxi talked about becoming the Italian Mitterrand, he waged an anti-Marxist crusade in his party and avoided cooperation with the PCI. The response of socialist parties to eurocommunism seems dictated primarily by national political considerations.

The economic crisis of the 1980s has challenged socialism's claims to possess answers to today's problems, as well as casting doubt on the reality of eurosocialism's new image. It has always been questioned whether socialism should be merely another party of government; in recent years, it seems unclear whether socialism can succeed merely as a party of government.

The people interviewed in this book have participated, in a more or less active way, in the debate raging on the future of socialism. Their points of view are different. What binds them together is a deep belief in socialism as a realizable goal for mankind.

The Scandinavians interviewed demonstrated the greatest optimism about the future of socialism. For them, socialism really is a movement in all senses of the word; the large-scale organization of workers in pursuit of a common goal, but also a movement of history towards greater equality. For them socialism is immanent in the very development of the labor movement. Although the Swedish and Norwegian socialists who figure in this book were all interviewed when their parties were out of power, they were confident that once they returned to power they could put society and the economy back on track. In a sense, Tryve Bratteli's statement that the priority for the rest of the century is to "just go on continuing in the same direction," is not as static or complacent as it sounds. It means that the process of solving new problems in ways that promote the achievement of equality and opportunity will continue. In that respect, Sigrid Ekendahl epitomizes the movement: after retiring from trade union and political affairs, she now works to organize the retired. The only non-Scandinavian with a similar sense of satisfaction about his party was Bruno Kreisky. Interestingly enough, he had spent over a decade in Sweden.

The other persons interviewed were less sanguine about the situation of socialism. Even before the

Mitterrand government came under heavy fire, Daniel Mayer emphasized that the election of Mitterrand did not mean the end of the "Old Regime." The Mitterrand government was not socialist. Socialism in the final analysis involves the withering away of the State, because once human nature is transformed, there is no need for the State. In the meantime, transitional types of regimes were possible. Mayer remains close to the Jaurès-Blum humanist tradition which emphasizes that the transition to socialism is also a process of human and cultural transformation. Implicit in his statement is the need to return from politique to mystique.

Jef Rens is also not satisfied. He is upset by the failure of Belgian socialism to maintain its elan an even its unity, since the French and Dutch-speaking socialists have separated into two independent parties. On a broader level, Rens felt that socialists have to take interest in the problems of the Third World, and become "world citizens."

The two most controversial personalities in the following pages are Michael Foot and Riccardo Lombardi. Contrary to what might have been anticipated a decade ago, Foot became Leader of the Labour Party; no one accused him of doing so out of personal ambition. A resolute idealist, Foot wanted to make the practice of the Labour Party square with its rhetoric. Unfortunately, his positions on the Common Market, NATO, and unilateral disarmament were divisive and Foot proved a beleaguered leader. He tried to pursue the policies of the left of the party with the support of the right and center. But as labour moved towards predictable electoral disaster, it became clear that Foot was unlikely to survive. In some ways, his fate resembles that of an earlier idealist, George Lansbury.

Another critique of current socialist practice comes from Riccardo Lombardi. Lombardi agrees with Mayer that socialist practice must go beyond mere politics; he reproaches Craxi for seeing everything in terms of politics. But Lombardi wants to present a socialist alternative based on worker involvement in the management of the place of work and transformation of the nature of property. In political terms, Lombardi wants to create a coalition of the left which can eventually come to power in order to implement this socialist alternative.

The socialists interviewed in this book were still trying late in their lives to relate the meaning of their own experience to the future of socialism. Let us now turn to their own accounts.

FOOTNOTES

[1] Parti Ouvrier Belge, Congrès, December 1933, p. 118.

[2] Herbert Tingsten, The Swedish Social Democrats (Bedminster, Totowa, New Jersey, 1973), pp. 336-338.

[3] John Strachey, The Coming Struggle for Power (Covici, Friede, New York, 1933), pp. 296-297.

[4] Franz Borkenau, Austria and After (Faber and Faber, London, 1938), pp. 174-175.

[5] Milorad M. Drachkovitch, Les Socialismes français et allemand et le problème de la guerre 1870-1914 (Geneva, 1953), p. 129. The statement was made by L. - O. Frossard.

[6] Robert Wohl, French Communism in the Making 1914-1924 (Stanford University, Stanford, 1966), p. 205.

[7] Albert Thibaudet, Les Idées politiques de la France (Paris, 1932), p. 203.

[8] Gilbert Ziebura, Léon Blum et le parti socialiste 1872 - 1934 (A. Colin, Paris, 1967), p. 255.

[9] David Marquand, Ramsay MacDonald (J. Cape, London, 1977), pp. 332-333.

[10] Tingsten, op. cit., p. 571.

[11] Ibid., p. 577.

[12] Adolf Sturmthal, The Tragedy of European Labor (Columbia University, New York, 1943), p. 141.

[13] Ibid., pp. 18-20.

[14] Proceedings, International Conference of the Labour and Socialist International, Paris, Maison de la Mutualité, August 21-23, 1933.

[15] Michael Foot, Aneurin Bevan, vol. 1 (Atheneum, New York, 1963), p. 130.

[16] The following material comes from my article, "Neo-socialism, the Belgian Case," Res Publica (Brussels, 1976:1).

[17] Henri de Man, Après Coup (Toison d'Or, Brussels, 1941), p. 123.

[18] For the text of the plan, see Peter Dodge, Beyond Marxism, The Faith and Works of Hendrik de Man (Martinus Nijhoff, The Hague, 1966), pp. 232-236.

[19] "Un Plan économique pour la Belgigue, "Mouvement syndical belge, August 23, 1933, p. 298.

[20] Louis Rosenstock-Franck, Democraties en crise: Roosevelt -- Van Zeeland -- Léon Blum (Paris, 1937), p. 62.

[21] Carl Landauer, European Socialism, Vol. 11 (University of California, Berkeley, 1959), p. 1559

[22] T.K. Derry, A History of Modern Norway 1814-1972 (Clarendon, Oxford, 1973), p. 328.

[23] Léon Blum cited in Julius Braunthal, History of the International, vol. 11, (Nelson, London, 1967), p. 489.

[24] Tingsten, op. cit., p. 562.

[25] Landauer, op. cit., p. 1559.

[26] Braunthal, op. cit., p. 490.

[27] Joel Colton, Léon Blum, Humanist in Politics (M.I.T. Press, Cambridge, 1966), pp. 375-376.

[28] Henri Frenay, cited in Henri Michel and Boris Mirkine-Guétzevitch, Les Idées politiques et sociales de la résistance (Presses Universitaires de la France, Paris, 1954), p. 114

[29] L'Oeuvre de Léon Blum 1945-1947 (Albin Michel, Paris, 1958), pp. 65-78.

[30] George Lichtheim, The New Europe (Praeger, New York, 1964), pp. 185-186.

[31] Walter Korpi, The Working Class in Welfare Capitalism (Routledge and Kegan Paul, London, 1978), pp. 322-323.

1
Daniel Mayer
and French Socialism

Daniel Mayer is one of the six people who have served as secretary-general of the French Socialist Party since 1921. He led the party through the difficult years of the underground during World War II and the liberation period.

Mayer comes out of the tradition of humanistic socialism exemplified by Jean Jaurès and Léon Blum; indeed, Blum considered Mayer his political heir. But Mayer was blamed for the party's post-war difficulties and ousted as secretary-general by Guy Mollet in 1946. Although Mayer remained a significant figure in the party until he left it in 1958, it was Mollet, not Mayer, who shaped its policies. Mayer was not the only person to leave the party. Not only did it lose some of its leaders, but it lost much of its electorate. In 1969, its presidential candidate received only four per cent of the vote. Only after Guy Mollet was forced out that year did the long process of reconstruction begin, a reconstruction which drew on many of Mayer's conceptions from the 1944-1946 period. But to understand what Daniel Mayer represents, we must first briefly consider the history of French socialism.

One characteristic of French socialism has been the strength of both revolutionary and reformist traditions. The French Revolution provided the model for revolutionary change in Western Europe. The term "dictatorship of the proletariat," was invented by Blanqui and Marx's elaboration of the concept was based on the "democratic dictatorship" of the Jacobins in 1793-4. Leninism could be implanted in France without seeming to be an alien imposition.

On the other hand, the ideas of the left have always attracted middle class radicals. As Clemenceau said, "the revolution is a bloc," and one of the axioms of the radicals in the Third Republic was "pas d'ennemi à gauche." It was easy for intellectuals to make the transition from radicalism to socialism. Such converts were likely to hold an ethical and reformist conception of socialism. Indeed, St. Simon, Fourier, Proudhon, Louis Blanc and many others had contributed to the adumbration of a native French "utopian" socialist tradition. Marxism arrived in France in the 1880s through the efforts of Jules Guesde; the communards of 1871 knew next to

51

nothing of Marx. Even socialist leaders like Jaurès who assimilated Marx did so with large doses of the native French socialist traditions. For Jaurès and his followers, socialism was the logical extension of democracy; the justification for socialism was ethical rather than historical.

Socialism thus influenced both proletariat and middle classes; its ideological diversity produced both a longing for unity and a tendency to disintegration. In the 1880s no fewer than five socialist parties developed, yet many workers preferred to eschew politics entirely for revolutionary syndicalism. The first attempt to create a coordinating committee of the different socialist parties lasted only from 1899 to 1900. In 1905, through the mediation of the Second International, unity was attained, but the Congress of Tours of 1921 precipitated the permanent split between communists (PCF) and socialists (SFIO).* In many countries the communist-socialist schism produced parties of unequal strength. In France, however, both parties have been strong.

The split did not represent a neat division between revolutionaries and social democrats. The Socialist Party has always included many who think themselves to the left of the PCF. Indeed, if the Communist Party has given the impression (sometimes misleading) of a monolith, the Socialist Party has often seemed a battleground for a wide range of factions. What has separated communists and socialists has been their view of the validity of the Soviet model, the relationship between the PCF and USSR, the nature of party organization, and differing views towards pluralistic democracy.

Daniel Mayer joined the Socialist Party in 1927; in the 1930s he became a reporter and later an editor at the party's daily newspaper, Le Populaire. Like many other young people at the time, Mayer joined the SFIO because of its commitment to justice and world peace.

During the period, relations between communists and socialists were hostile, often violent. The communists centered their attacks on the "brother party." In 1934, however, after the riots of 6 February which appeared to many as an aborted fascist coup, the communists made a dramatic about-face.

---

*The name of the Socialist Party, found in 1905, was officially Section Française de l'Internationale Ouvrière; the socialists retained this name after the 1921 schism. In 1971, the name was changed to Parti Socialiste.

They called for cooperation among all democratic
forces against fascism and for an alliance among the
Western democracies and the Soviet Union. This
Popular Front, first attempted in France, was then
offered as an example for others. Mayer's testimony
provides us with an understanding of how young
socialists brought up on doctrines of pacifism and
international cooperation faced the reality of an
expansionist Germany and what the Popular Front
signified to them. In addition, Mayer gives us a a
remarkable vignette of the two major party leaders,
Léon Blum and Paul Faure.

The cooperation between Blum and Faure and the
political forces they represented, the Jaures
humanist tradition and the guesdist Marxist tradition
was the basis of the SFIO after the schism with the
PCF. Blum served as parliamentary and intellectual
leader; Faure, as secretary-general, administered the
party organization. Their paths began to diverge in
1934. Faure was hesitant about cooperation with the
communists; after all, his main accomplishment as
secretary-general had been to reconstruct the party
against the communists. Blum, on the other hand,
supported the Popular Front. By 1936, the two began
to disagree on foreign policy. Despite his belief in
disarmament, Blum became convinced of the need for an
alliance against fascism; Faure remained a pacifist.
Daniel Mayer provides us with a striking sketch of
the beginnings of the rift between the two men.
After the defeat of 1940, Paul Faure collaborated
with the Vichy regime. Mayer's comments about Faure
in this interview, juxtaposed with what Jef Rens says
about Hendrik De Man, provide insight into what made
some socialists collaborate during the war.

During the war, Mayer emerged as the leader of
the underground party. After the liberation, Blum
hoped Mayer could renovate the old socialist party
and infuse it with socialist humanism. Mayer dreamed
of a party free from collaborators and <u>attentistes</u>,
emancipated from the old anticlerical sectarianism.

Mayer was elected secretary-general at a time
when socialist expectations were high; had not Léon
Blum himself spoken of socialism as "the master of
the hour?" But these hopes proved unfounded. Party
organization was almost nil, the communists were
taking control of the trade unions; De Gaulle, as
head of the provisional government, prevented the
socialists from enacting their structural reforms.
The socialists hoped that the PCF had changed during
the resistance, that unity of action or even organic
unity might be possible. This also was an illusion.
Fearing to govern alone with the more dynamic
Communist Party, the socialists insisted on
tripartism with the MRP (Christian Democrats) in

1946-7; tripartism, however, was not successful in dealing with the disastrous economic situation. It would take Marshall Plan aid to finally bring France out of economic crisis. Successive elections brought a decline in SFIO strength, for which many leftist militants blamed the Blum-Mayer leadership. The rising frustration of the militants led to the rejection of Mayer's <u>rapport moral</u> at the Congress of late August - early September 1946. Mollet replaced Mayer as secretary-general.

Ironically, the accession of Mollet did not result in either electoral success or a shift to the left. Indeed, less than a year later, when Prime Minister Ramadier fired the communist ministers after they had broken government solidarity, the SFIO decided, by a small majority, to remain in the government without the communists. Subsequently, the SFIO participated in "Third Force" governments with the MRP and other centrist parties, directed against both the PCF and the new Gaullist RPF. The Cold War resulted in bitter conflicts between the communists and the government, including the violent strikes of 1948 and their suppression. The CGT split, and a small socialist contingent created its own confederation, Force Ouvrière. The Cold War pushed the PCF back into a rigid Stalinist mold, while the SFIO increasingly lost stature as a party of the left.

The governing majority shifted to the right. How long could socialists consider participation in the interest of the working class? Interestingly enough, it was the self-declared Marxist Mollet who continued supporting governmental participation. After 1950, Mayer opposed it.

A number of issues brought Mayer into conflict with the party leadership. Mayer strongly opposed the European Defense Community. Although the SFIO, at Mollet's insistence, supported it, half the socialist members of parliament, including Mayer, voted against it. Mayer was nearly expelled for this offense. In addition, by 1956 Mayer began to oppose Mollet's Algerian policy. Mollet, after becoming Premier in early 1956, reversed his earlier position and became a "hawk" on the Algerian War. Mayer resigned his seat in Parliament in April 1958. When Mollet committed the SFIO to supporting De Gaulle's return to power after 13 May 1958, that was the last straw for Mayer and others like Edouard Depreux and Robert Verdier; they left the party and created the Parti Socialiste Autonome (PSA) which later fused with other groups to form the Parti Socialiste Unifié (PSU). Not until Mollet's replacement by Alain Savary in 1970 did Mayer return to the Socialist Party, which had found a new name and new leadership. Although Mayer sits in the <u>comité</u>

directeur of the Socialist Party, he has only limited involvement in partisan politics today.

Daniel Mayer's departure from the SFIO meant the end of his political career in the narrow sense; it did not mean the end of his public life. When he became President of the Ligue des Droits de l'Homme (League of the Rights of Man) in 1958, Mayer continued to fight for the same ideals he had defended as a socialist. By the 1970s, he had become one of the grand old men of the French left, continuing the tradition of his mentor, Léon Blum. In 1982 he was named by President Mitterrand to be a member of the Conseil Supérieur de la Magistrature. Shortly afterwards, he was appointed president of the Conseil Constitutionel. As this interview demonstrates, he has continued to think about the meaning of socialism in modern society.

Interview with Daniel Mayer

DANIEL MAYER:

I was born on 29 April 1909 in the 12th arrondissement of Paris. My father was a small merchant, something like a salesman. He did odd jobs and had a lot of troubles. My mother became an orphan very young; she lost her father when she was four and her mother when she was eight. After being cared for by her brothers and sisters for several years, she was finally put into a Rothschild orphanage where she was trained to be a teacher. She entered the orphanage at the age of 13 and left at 26 to marry. In other words, she had no personal life. She developed tuberculosis during the First World War, when I was five and I lost her when I was 12. My father's family was French from the beginning. My mother's was Alsacian. They had refused to become German at the end of the Franco-Prussian War in 1870, so they came to Paris where my mother was born.

Neither practiced religion, although they were among those Jews who, despite not practicing religion, did a little something. My father, for example, did not smoke on Yom Kippur; he ate, but he did not smoke.

I am self-taught. I stayed with my mother until her death. I went to school a year and a half in my whole life, between my mother's death and the age of 14. At 14 I began to work; life was difficult. My father could not continue to pay for my schooling, even though I was more or less on scholarship.

My entry into the worker movement resulted from the shock I felt at the time of the Sacco-Vanzetti affair, towards its tragic end when there were campaigns all over the world asking that Sacco and Vanzetti not be executed. I began to attend the demonstrations organized by the Ligue des Droits de l'Homme. I remember a meeting at the old Trocadéro Theatre, with Léon Jouhaux, who was secretary-general of the Confédération Générale du Travail, Henri Torrès, and Victor Basch, President of the Ligue des Droits de l'Homme. That led me to join the League in September 1927, at the age of 18.

In preparation for the electoral campaign of 1928, Léon Blum, who was deputy of the 20th arrondissement of Paris where I lived, came to give a speech which was rather technical, but very interesting. It was probably above the understanding of a young boy, because it concerned economic and financial problems. At that moment, I felt the need to become active and with a lot of nerve, I went up to the speaker, Léon Blum himself, to ask what I had to do to join the Socialist Party. He turned to the secretary of the section of the 20th arrondissement, a man named Pagès -- I still remember -- "Pagès, would you see this young man." And that's how in December 1927 I joined both the party and the Young Socialists.

Q: What kind of work did you do at that time?

A: I was a salesman for textile factories in the North which manufactured linen, dust cloths, towels, sheets. I had to travel a bit. I let my moustache grow and wore hard collars to make myself look a little older and more serious. When I became a member of the party and of the Young Socialists, I tried to find a regular, sedentary job in Paris. In Paris, the Young Socialists were not numerous; they had 400 members in the whole region. They obviously lacked staff, and it's not arrogance or pride on my part to say that after just a few months I was already a leader. The opposite would have been astonishing. I became the Delegate for Propaganda of the Young Socialists of the Department of the Seine in April or May 1928. Through the intermediary of the brother of a socialist city councillor of Paris, I got a job as an assistant at the Prefecture of the Seine where I worked in the unemployment department; I filed papers the whole day. I did this until my military service, that is to say, until 1930. From 1933 on, I was an apprentice journalist on Le Populaire: two years later I was put in charge of the trade union and social affairs department. Thus, from 1933 on, I finally had a regular profession, a profession which I liked, which excited me and which enabled me to take part in political activity.

Q: What ideological influences affected you at that time?

A: I read much. During the entire period between joining the Socialist Party and leaving for military service, I always had brochures or books in my pocket; every time that I went to speak at a meeting I read in the metro; I had a thirst for reading. In literature, Victor Hugo and to a lesser extent Emile Zola influenced me most. Above all, the epics of Victor Hugo, in particular Les Miserables, that great fresco of the chivalry of modern times which for me was absolutely thrilling and overflowing with lyricism and humanity. In the domain of socialism, it was in large part Jean Jaurès, then the daily articles of Léon Blum, which elucidated issues. They were written in an extremely simple style, clear and transparent, which made one really understand all the problems which arose, even the most complicated. But strangely enough, as I was very attached to the art of public speaking, I was more influenced by the eloquence of Paul Faure, who at that moment was secretary-general of the party, than by the argumentation of Léon Blum. In other words, on an intellectual level, the influence of Blum was preponderant, but with regard to the handling of crowds, with regard to that sort of music which is eloquence, to which I was extremely attached almost all of my life (even if I discover now with a little bit of distance its vanity), it was Paul Faure, popular orator, engagé orator with all that may entail, even a little demagogy, a little bombast who influenced me.

I myself had a certain influence on crowds, even when I was very young, perhaps because I was very young. I remember once when I was about 20 I tried to force a discussion on a deputy named Ballu, a man of the right who was running in a district of Seine-et-Oise, in the Paris Metropolitan area. I was the 14th who tried and the first 13 hadn't succeeded in making themselves heard.* They listened to me, I suppose because my youth must have interested them, and so I benefited from the relatively protective curiosity of the crowd. "We must let this guy be heard." But if I recount all that now, it's not to boast of the achievement of 50 years ago, but because the recollection is amusing.

Q: Did you have much contact with Paul Faure at that time?

A: He suggested to Léon Blum that he hire me as an editor at Le Populaire.

Q: It surprises me that you were so close to Paul Faure. How do you explain his political evolution, which ultimately led him to accept a place on the Conseil National of Vichy?

A: I understand Paul Faure's evolution from 1934, several years before it became generally recognized that he was going astray, that he was deceiving himself. I understand it because of a particular event which I am going to recount to you, which was a bit fortuitous and rather minor. At the

---

*In France it is a common practice to attend the meetings of a candidate of the opposing party and attempt to force him into debate. This is known as porter la contradiction.

Populaire, my office was at the entrance to the
editorial room, at a place where the room was very
narrow and formed a kind of corridor which went in
the direction of Léon Blum's office. Léon Blum
passed by very often when he was accompanying someone
to or from his office. After the fascist
demonstration of 6 February 1934, there was a whole
series of secret conclaves between the leaders of the
parties of the left, the trade union organizations,
etc. Léon Jouhaux, in the name of the Confédération
Générale du Travail (which at that time was the
non-communist organization) decided on a general
strike for 12 February, to reply to the events of the
6th. Léon Blum wanted to add a demonstration to that
notion of a general strike. He thought that it was
not appropriate for the workers on strike to stay
home. He felt they had to demonstrate in the street,
shoulder to shoulder, to manifest the popular will to
stop fascism.

By chance, Léon Blum and Paul Faure passed
through this room transformed into a corridor by its
slenderness and therefore talked about this
practically in front of me, a miniscule, passive
spectator but naturally, listening and hearing.

Up to that point, I had the feeling that Léon
Blum, by virtue of his profile, the very frail
quality of his voice, by the very nature of the
sentiments to which he appealed, which were spirit,
persuasion, etc., was less strong than Paul Faure.
Paul Faure, on contrary, was the thunderer, the one
who appealed to the masses, who urged them to great
public exploits, even perhaps, rather brutal deeds.
And to my great surprise, I hear Paul Faure saying:
"No, there must be no demonstrations, we must not
have any, no, no, I don't wany any. In any case, the
Socialist Party will not convoke them." And in a
tone which I had never heard, always very courteous,
but with sovereign authority, Léon Blum, director of
the Populaire, said to him: "Well, then, my dear
Paul, the Populaire will convoke them." In other
words, I take the responsibility all by myself, as
director of the Populaire, to call for
demonstrations. It was that day that I changed my
conception of the two men. I understood that in the
last analysis, Paul Faure was not courageous, that he
was a coward, that it was one thing to rouse mass
audiences when one had the public on one's side, that
it was another thing to make grave decisions by
oneself. He had shown much courage against the
communists after the schism of Tours, when he
assisted in the resurrection of the Socialist Party.
It took a lot of courage to speak in the communist
areas on the outskirts of Paris, to denounce
bolshevism, but he didn't have the other form of

courage which consists in fighting against a class enemy. In other words, at this exact moment, around 9 or 10 February 1934, I had -- not the prescience of what he would do later on -- but the feeling that he was not the person I had though him to be.

Q: Were you influenced by Marx or by the utopian socialists?

A: More by the utopian socialists. Don't forget that my generation was the generation of those who didn't attach much importance, at least in France, to economic problems. Our socialism was based on feeling. We understood political problems, but we weren't very interested in economic problems. I can tell you that even now I have to make an effort to understand an economic and financial process. Thus I did not undergo the direct or even indirect influence of Marx and the scientific socialists.

Q: Nevertheless, you learned a little bit of them through Jaurès and Blum?

A: Yes, through Jaurès, and also through Léon Blum, also through the speeches I read, the debates between Jaurès and Guesde. It didn't go beyond that.

Q: How did you understand the Great Depression of the 1930s? What did you think had to be done to resolve it?

A: To understand that better, you have to place my generation in relation to the hope of international peace. You have to remember the slogans we shouted: "Nie wider krieg," "plus jamais de guerre," "plus jamais ça." Our hope, almost the raison d'être of our socialism, was peace through Franco-German reconciliation. The result was that when 1930 forced us to confront the beginning of an economic crisis, it was not so much its world-wide character or its French character which affected us, but the influence that it could have, that the unemployed in Germany and France could have, on the problem of French-German relations. Contrary to the communists, who saw the unemployed of the period as rebels, revolutionaries, people who could transform societies, we immediately saw (and without effort) that, on the contrary, the unemployed would be the mercenaries of fascism. Consequently, we had to admit (and really, I think all young socialists except some pacifists understood it) that what the new Germany, the Germany of Hitler, was going to become was not the Germany of yesterday. We had to make a rapid turnabout. Whereas we had been supporters of political liberalism, we had on the contrary, to take a stand against it. Whereas we had been supporters of an understanding with the Weimar Republic, there could be no understanding with the Germany of Hitler. Whereas we had been for disarmament conceived almost as unilateral at certain times (Denmark had attempted an operation of unilateral disarmament, and we were carried away by that), from one day to the next not only was it necessary not to disarm in the face of the new Germany, but it was necessary, on the contrary, to rearm. Which is to say, there again, that we saw economic problems in terms of their political consequences.

Q: This change was not easy. It took four or five years for some socialists, and there were some who never changed.

A: Obviously.

Q: What was your analysis of 6 February 1934? Was it a fascist coup d'état?

A: Yes, an anti-parliamentary coup d'état, since the demonstrations were essentially directed against Parliament, reflecting a desire to align France on a political orientation, if not on men, identical to that of Mussolini and Hitler. February 1934 was only a year after January 1933, Hitler had been the head of Germany for only 13 months; one had the feeling that there was some sort of complicity between the French fascists and the Hitlerites and Italian fascists. Moreover, thanks a little bit to that we could -- because we knew our French adversary well -- carry out our change of attitude towards to Germany more rapidly. Simplistic but sure reasoning: the moment that our French adversaries defended the new Germany, it was the confirmation that the new Germany was bad.

So we came to the origins of the Popular Front. Curiously, it was in this building, Rue Jean-Dolent, that the meetings of the Rassemblement Populaire were held under the chairmanship of the President of the League, Victor Basch, with Emile Kahn as secretary-general (he was also secretary-general of the League) in the very room where we are talking now. I think that its essential, its most important characteristic was not to confine itself to a political program hostile to the right but to add an essentially economic program: public works, the 40 hour week, paid vacations, the Office du Blé, the nationalization of the Bank of France, etc., to make possible a struggle against the economic crisis.

That was the first time the link between politics and economics had been officially recognized and published, that politics was seen as the expression of economics....

Q: To what extent was the Popular Front successful in its internal policies?

A: There is no doubt. The Popular Front, in the strictly political domain, dissolved the fascist leagues and put a stop to what these leagues were planning. In a matter of days it completly transformed the social and economic conditions of the people as in a real revolution. The revolutionary character of the advent of paid vacations cannot be grasped now. The 40 hour week, that is to say, the spreading out on a greater number of men the possible hours of work in an enterprise or in an industry, is what Léon Blum called a sort of partial payment of the dividends owed to the working class for the product of its labor. Officially, 1936 in France was reform, but in reality it was a sort of revolution, to the extent to which one means by revolution a quick mutation in the living conditions of the working class. In a very few days, life was completely transformed. What was perhaps most important.... was the recognition of the rights of the trade unions, that is to say, the fact that the worker was no longer alone against management, as he had previously been. Through collective bargaining, the support of his union, discussions between worker unions and organizations of management, he was defended, he was no longer isolated, he was no longer someone who could be fired from one day to the next. I followed the worker movement since 1933. In certain factories of the Paris region, for example, in the Citroën factories, a worker was dismissed instantly if they saw that his lunch was wrapped in a left-wing newspaper. Not the <u>Humanité</u> or the <u>Populaire</u>! Simply in <u>L'Oeuvre</u>, a newspaper of the liberal left, nothing more.

When the so-called Matignon agreements were concluded (between management and the trade-unions) under the chairmanship of Léon Blum (so-called because they were negotiated at the Matignon Palace, where the Prime Minister's offices are located), there happened to be a woman in the worker delegation who was employed in an enterprise whose boss was in the management delegation. He had no idea of the wages of this worker. When she told him how much she earned in his place, he flushed, he stuttered, he was greatly surprised, he was ignorant of the smallness, the shabby character of the wages he was paying. Collective bargaining, the recognition of the right of unionization are probably what gave the working class the notion of sovereignty and dignity which it had not known until then. In that respect, it was a revolution.

Q: What was your position in the party at that time with respect to foreign policy?

A: I was in the "Batille Socialiste," led by Zyromski, that is to say the current of resistance to Hitlerism, the refusal of any complicity, even of any weakness. But at that time, there were many points of convergence in matters of foreign policy between Zyromski and Blum, just as there were, despite appearances, between Paul Faure and Marceau Pivert, in the form of a pacifism whose limits could not be imagined.

Q: During the period 1934-1939, you took part in national congresses of the party, you spoke for your federation and for your faction against neo-socialism, against Munich, but you were far from being a party leader. You were very young. It was during the resistance that you became a real leader. Would you speak about the experience of the Resistance?

A: I was not taken prisoner, unlike the majority of the French Army. I was lucky. After having located my wife at the end of July 1940, we decided to go ask the members of the party we could find and in whom we had confidence what we should do. We felt we should go to England, without knowing what we could do there that would be useful. It was simply to demonstrate our opposition to the new institutions. So we went to see Marx Dormoy at Montluçon, exactly one year to the day before his assassination. He told us that he didn't see what we could do, adding: "And in addition, you are Jews and you will have extra difficulties." We went down to the Midi, because our intention was eventually to cross the Pyrenees to reach London. We learned from Suzanne Buisson, a party militant, that Léon Blum was in the area of Toulouse. We went there, and asked him how we could get to England and if he knew how to do it. Then he told us that as far as he was concerned, he had indeed been asked to go, but he didn't want to leave France because he had to -- I am trying to remember his exact words -- ultimately defend his actions, defend the Popular Front in a public meeting or before a tribunal if that was necessary. It was real prescience, because he foresaw something of what the Riom Trial would be. But as for us, "I don't know about your military abilities. I have somewhat the impression that you will be two extra mouths to feed whereas here there may be an important task to accomplish, a whole section of public opinion to recapture, an underground party to create, etc."

Then we went to rest several days in the Pyrenees. We had nevertheless gone to see Léon Jouhaux -- he was near Sète -- but that added nothing new. While resting in the Pyrenees we heard successively of the arrest of Vincent Auriol, Léon Blum, etc. Then we went to Marseille, where we made contact with Felix Gouin, who was deputy for Istres in the Bouches-du-Rhône. Our criterion for meetings was obviously to seek out those socialist members of Parliament who had voted against Pétain on 10 July 1940.... That's how we began to lead a little underground action, in particular, Henri Ribière, who subsequently would lead a liberation movement known as Libération-Nord. We went throughout France, going from one place to another to see comrades, to give them the alarm, etc. I personally established the liaison with Bourassol 14 times. The daughter-in-law and the future wife of Léon Blum were at the Hotel des Voyageurs at Riom, very near Bourassol where Léon Blum was imprisoned during the whole course of the Riom trial. He answered us through the intermediary of his daughter-in-law, a very zealous woman, with a very precise mind, who fulfilled her mission like a soldier. At that time, we were also publishing the underground Populaire.

When we had to designate a delegate of the Socialist Party for the National Council of the Resistance we first chose André Le Troquer, who had been one of Léon Blum's lawyers at the Riom trial. When he left for London, I was chosen. I went in particular to London, between two moons, as we used to say, between April and May 1943, where I fulfilled a triple mission. First I reaffirmed to Camille Huysmans, the President of the Socialist International, the fidelity of the SFIO to the International. I confirmed to De Gaulle that we were with him in the battle against the occupier, in which he was the symbol, the leader and discussed with him a certain number of possibilities, in particular an idea originated Léon Blum which was the prototype of the National Council of the Resistance (what Léon Blum called the Executive Committee of the French Resistance). The third mission, simultaneously the least noble and most delicate, consisted in appeasing the internal divisions of the socialist group at London, which was split between pro- and anti-gaullists. Naturally, they were all resistants, but some said De Gaulle was a future dictator and others said that, on the contrary, he was going to enable us to save and reestablish the Republic.

Q: What was your opinion on that subject?

A: I had a very nuanced opinion. I thought that De Gaulle represented a period in the history of France that had to be utilized, that he was strictly the only one absolutely the only one, capable of unifying the Resistance, who was able to speak in the name of France, that it was absolutely necessary that we uphold him, and that, in addition, we would see him at work once we were back in Paris. We even sent letters to Roosevelt, obviously clandestinely, at a time when he began to support Giraud a little too much for our taste. During this seven week stay at London, I thought it appropriate to have a text adopted which would be a manifesto of the Socialist Party to the people of France, a clandestine manifesto, but evidently with maximum publicity. I asked some comrades in London to write sections of it and isolated myself in the outskirts of London, at Twickenham, to write up the document. I had it approved successively by the socialists at London, by the socialists of the southern zone, by the underground executive committee, and it became a manifesto which we published in the underground Populaire. Mission accomplished.

Q: The communists infiltrated the movements of the resistance, at the same time that they created their own movements. Do you regret that the socialists didn't create their own purely socialist movement?

A: No, I don't regret it at all, given that we wouldn't have had the material means to have a military organization and that it was much more loyal to belong to units grouping the whole gamut of resistants, rather than having a personal army. No, no, I don't regret that at all. I was going to say that if it was to be redone...let's hope not, but in the end, it's exactly what had to be done, it was a symbol of the unity of the Resistance.

Q: The communists nevertheless benefited from having their own organization.

A: They would have done it some other way. When one is dealing with people who are not loyal, their disloyalty can be exercised in all sorts of ways.

Q: Finally, we arrive at the Liberation. Certain people have criticized you for having conducted too rigorous a purge of the party.

A: We had one sole criterion...we put out of the party all the elected officials who had voted for Pétain in July, 1940. That seemed the least we could do. Do you think that was too harsh?

With the exception of several special cases, we declared that all those who had voted for Pétain were out of the party, except for two who had voted for Pétain but took part in the Resistance soon afterwards. We studied the cases of those who had not been present. We kept most of those who did not have the opportunity to vote for Pétain because they were not at Vichy. After the Liberation, the party was no longer the same as the resistance party because a large number of its members who had done nothing during the war returned. And they felt themselves very close to the deputies who had been excluded, since they themselves had done nothing and, had they been deputies, they would perhaps have voted for Pétain. Despite that, really, if it had to be redone, I would start all over again....

Q: What was the state of the party at the Liberation?

A: There was nothing left. The underground party had no organizational structures. It had people in charge, but they, for reasons of security, during the underground period, intentionally didn't know each other. In those places here and there where it had maintained its organization, it was because the militants had done nothing during the war. Now, independent of political considerations, I didn't have an administrative temperament: I am not a good administrative secretary; it doesn't interest me.

Q: There was a difficult cohabitation inside the party between the resistants and many old militants.

A: Obviously. And then, there was another thing they reproached us for. We had a congress decide -- we never took unilateral, dictatorial measures -- that the time spent in the Resistance counted in measuring seniority for new members. To be a candidate in the elections, according to the old statutes, three years of membership in the party was required, to be a member of the CAP (Commission Administrative Permanente) five years. Naturally, all those who had been candidates before the war and who had done nothing during the war, but who wanted to become involved in politics once again found that their place had been taken by others.

Q: There was also opposition to your efforts to bring in Christian resistants. This effort was renewed more successfully in the 1970s.

A: Indeed, it did not work. There is a very French phenomenon: the anticlerical laic who, as soon as something isn't going well, brings up laicity as an Indian digs up his tomahawk. You know the speech of Léon Blum to the congress of 1946. Well, that's where you will find the explanation, when Léon Blum says: "You are afraid, you are afraid of women, you are afraid of young people, you are afraid of renovation, you are afraid, you are afraid ..." There was a kind of petit-bourgeois possessiveness on the part of certain members of the party and they were afraid of all that smacked of renovation.

Q: The SFIO also had difficult political problems. From February 1945 on, it was evident that De Gaulle was hostile to much of the economic and social program of the socialists. The communists very quickly seemed what they had been before the war, frères ennemis. Organic unity with the communists, or even unity of action became impossible. In retrospect, do you think that there was an alternative to the policies followed by the Socialist Party, policies which proved electorally unsuccessful?

A: Honestly, I don't think so. What would have been necessary and wasn't in our power, was that the MRP be willing to lose part of its electorate. The founders of the MRP were socially on the left. If the MRP had agreed to cut itself off from its right-wing electorate, tripartism would have assumed a different aspect. Then afterwards, of course, there was the EDC.

Q: If the socialists had pushed De Gaulle to follow the economic and social program of Mendès-France, perhaps that could have changed things. But did the socialist recognize the importance of the question?

A: No, I don't think so. Only Augustin Laurent realized it. We accepted much too much of the policy of facility. Could we have influenced De Gaulle? I always considered Pleven a nefarious man in all respects. If the socialists had resolutely backed Mendès-France, would De Gaulle have yielded, or would he have stood by Pleven? I don't know. But it's certainly a historian's hypothesis.

Q: You were the target for all those in the party who were dissatisfied.

A: They used about every argument, including remarks that weren't arguments. For example, a whispering camapign -- naturally it was never said at the rostrum of a congress -- but ... "Léon Blum, leader of the party, Daniel Mayer, secretary-general of the party, that makes two Jews," a little anti-semitism.

Q: The attack against you was also an attack against Léon Blum. Since when had you been close to him?

A: During the war, and thereafter. After 1945, we went to see him regularly every week and we spoke on the phone almost every day.

Q: You wanted to resign as secretary-general in 1945.

A: I should have listened to my wife -- she was the one who was right -- she told me: "You have been secretary for a certain period. That period is over. You shouldn't continue." My wife was the greatest influence on my life. Her influence was based exclusively on example, in the realm of morality and wisdom. When you write your book, I hope that you won't forget her. But Vincent Auriol and Léon Blum strongly insisted that I continue, and so I continued. I still think my wife was right. Imagine that someone else was appointed in 1945 -- it would probably have been Augustin Laurent, deputy of the Nord. One would never have heard of Guy Mollet.

Q: Perhaps.

A: The party wouldn't have undergone a period of decadence, there wouldn't have been a socialist Prime Minister waging the Algerian War.

Q: But wouldn't the forces represented by Guy Mollet have pushed another secretary-general to follow in the same direction?

A: That would nevertheless have been more difficult with Augustin Laurent, who controlled the Federation of the Nord. The discontent would have continued to be directed against me as former secretary-general. There would have been fewer

complaints against the new one. You are right. The
hostile forces would have always existed within the
party; that's true. But they couldn't have
manifested themselves in the same way, and perhaps
they wouldn't have manifested themselves under the
name of Guy Mollet. One cannot rewrite history, we
don't know.

Q: As secretary-general, you could have used the
means at your disposal to manipulate the votes at the
Congress of 1946?

A: Ah, no, I wouldn't do that. Even today I
don't know how to do that. There is an essential
loyalty in me, which some consider naiveté, if you
will, but I am absolutely incapable of doing that.
When I give a lecture, I begin by saying to the
public: you have to know in what perspective I see
things so that you can judge and so that eventually
you can think differently from the way I think. For
me, freedom of thought, freedom of action, are
absolutely sacred, beginning with the opponent's.
Imagine that I did the same thing as they, and won.
They will be the winners, because they will have
polluted me to the point that I used their methods.

Q: But if you could have avoided the Algerian
War under a socialist Prime Minister?

A: But one didn't know in 1946 that he would
later dishonor himself by waging the Algerian War.

Q: Despite your defeat as secretary-general of
the SFIO you remained quite active in politics.

A: I was deputy from Paris and minister in the
all-socialist government of Léon Blum. Previously I
had refused to be minister under De Gaulle because I
felt, and still feel, that the secretary-general of a
party cannot be minister. He would involve the party
too much in government policies whereas, on the
contrary, the party must retain a certain autonomy.
When I had to reply to the communists in public
meetings, I found an argument which made my defeat
glorious. In my district, when I gave the voters an
account of my work, the communists said that it was
all the more necessary to vote against me since I had
been rejected even inside my party. I answered that
the day when the rapport moral of their
secretary-general was rejected, that proof of
internal democracy would mark a big step towards
working-class unity, and that I prided myself on the
fact that I had led the party to the point that it
was sufficiently mature to be able to reject the

rapport moral of its secretary-general....Which did
not rule out other feelings of a personal nature.

Q: Then you became Minister of Labor and Social
Security in the purely socialist government of Léon
Blum from December 1946 to January 1947.

A: To some extent, I chose that ministry,
because, before the war, as I told you, I had been
responsible for the economic and labor section of the
Populaire, and labor affairs were always very
important to me. I maintained friendly relations
with most trade union leaders, communist as well as
socialist. Generally speaking, we spoke in the
familiar form to each other. I relinquished the
ministry to a communist during the Ramadier
government, which included communists and the MRP. I
returned to the Ministry of Labor in the beginning of
May 1947, after the departure of the communists, and
I remained there until October 1949.

Q: The aftermath of the revocation of the
communists in the Ramadier government must have made
your life in the ministry difficult.

A: Even today, there are communist historians
who say that Ramadier threw out the communist
ministers, as if he committed an aggression. They
completely neglect to say that the communist deputies
in the National Assembly had not voted in favor of
the government to which they belonged.
On May Day, 1947, there was a big demonstration
at the Place de la Concorde with tens of thousands of
participants to celebrate the Festival of Labor. The
Socialist Party chose me as its representative. As
that was not a particularly agreeable task -- we knew
that there would be incidents, perhaps even violence
-- I was full of gratitude towards the secretariat of
the party for having given me such a mission, which
naturally, I fulfilled. There was a lot of noise, a
lot of tumult. At a given moment Marcel Cachin
wanted to calm down the public which was abusing me
and I declared spontaneously that I didn't have to
speak under the protection of Marcel Cachin (a
communist leader of the period) but that I placed
myself exclusively under the protection of the
working-class. From that time on, the people quieted
down and listened to me perfectly. Three days later,
Paul Ramadier asked me to return to the position of
Minister of Labor.
The main battle I led was the defense of Social
Security. There was an outcry against me, howlings
from the right when I included dental surgery as
something which could be reimbursed by Social

Security, which had not been the case before. There was outcry against me from the insurance companies when I took preventive measures in order to diminish the number of accidents on the job. I succeeded in organizing elections for the administrative councils of the central Social Security treasuries, which had been a worker demand. At this moment, <u>Nicole Questiaux</u> is reinstituting the process of choosing these councils by election. Clearly that proves what is involved is a general political and social question: Whether the working class can democratically run the institutions which specifically concern it, or whether management should do so.

There was also a much less positive side to my work as Minister of Labor during the big strikes which assaulted the county in 1947-8, and even a little in 1949. But my work was essentially one of conciliation, arbitration, and maintaining wages. My relations with the trade-union organizations prove that in certain cases it was possible to make use of personal friendships to try to resolve problems. It's a matter of trust, when you know someone, you have a little more confidence in him, even if he appears to you, as the socialists appeared, alas, at that time to the communists, almost as a class enemy. Let me give an example. There were troubles in the electrical industry and the Federation of Electrical Workers, which was mostly led by communists, called a strike. The Prime Minister declared that so long as there was the threat of a strike, there was no possibility of discussion. That's what the bosses often say and there is nothing more stupid, because it's precisely during periods of conflict that one should meet....I went to the Hotel Matignon. A large number of journalists were there. Most of them were members of the same journalist's union to which I belonged before the war, to which I still pay dues. They said to me: "Do you have a lot of work?" -- "Yes, I have a lot. For example, this evening I'll stay at my desk alone until very very late." Some of them understand what I was driving at.

In any case, that evening around 9:00 o'clock the concierge came to tell me: "Monsieur le Ministre, there is a man from the Federation of Electrical Workers who would like to see you." -- "Show him in." He enters and says to me: "So you agree to see us." -- "Naturally, why not? I should especially like to see Marcel Paul" (the leader of the union, member of the PCF, former Minister of Industrial Production under De Gaulle, and deputy at another time). He couldn't have been very far from the ministry, because two minutes later he arrived at my office. The conversation began naturally this way:

"So, you're the one who wants to meet us. I want it clear that I'm not taking the initiative." -- "Listen. We are going to discuss the heart of the matter. Perhaps at 4:00 a.m. you'll be delighted to say that you took the initiative, or perhaps you'll want me to say I did. If you wish, we'll solve that problem when we have finished discussing the real issue." We talked till about 3:00 p.m. At three o'clock, I suggested to him that an arbitrator be chosen. It was understood that as soon as the arbitrator was announced, the strike would be called off and that the government would end its threats. Then he said to me: "Maybe we can reach an agreement, but it depends on who would be the arbitrator." I suggest Grunebaum Balin, knowing that he was well-liked by the worker organizations. Grunebaum Balin had been a member of the Conseil d'Etat and was a friend of Léon Blum.... Naturally, I saw a big smile on his face because he knew that an arbitration by Grunebaum Balin would not be hostile to the working class. I telephoned my Prime Minister because before any final decision I had to let him know what was happening. Three in the morning. Since he knew that Grunebaum Balin would be favorable to the electricians, he said: "that will be expensive, but OK." And from my office, Marcel Paul, President of the Federation of Electrical Workers gave the order to his federation, which was on alert, to postpone the strike. That is an event which has not been discussed, or has been discussed very little, whereas one hears of those other strikes which did indeed take place and which were often brutal.

Those who wish me well, those who like me, those who have painted a favorable picture of me according to their lights, do not admit what I am going to say to you now about the intervention of the police in the miners' villages, in the mines. There were very violent strikes in the mines. The communists wanted to force everyone to go on strike; the socialists felt that there was no reason for going on strike. Often, while the miners were in the mines, the wives of socialist miners were mistreated in the villages. The windows of their houses were smashed, there were fights and the communists were extremely brutal, to such a degree that the socialist fraction of the miners unions in the Nord and Pas de Calais asked for the intervention of the police. Jules Moch, Minister of the Interior, directed the police to intervene in the corons (miners villages) simply to safeguard the right to work. Before giving the order, he telephoned me, as Minister of Labor, to tell me, "In half an hour, we will enter the villages." And I answered: "je suis solidaire" (I share the responsibility with you). Well, when I tell this to those to whom I was referring just before, those who like me, they are absolutely convinced that it's not so, that I did not say to Jules Moch "je suis solidaire". In all the books, in all the accounts, all the responsibility falls on Jules Moch. It's true that he was Minister of the Interior, it's true that he was responsible, it's true that at the demand of the socialist miners he had the police go into the miners' villages. But it is also true that in my opinion there was nothing else to do and that it would be dishonest and disloyal to deny it or keep it quiet. Otherwise, there would have been a massacre of socialist miners by communist miners in the course of more violent incidents.

A certain number of historians have such predefined points of view that when I say that to a historian who wants to consider Jules Moch to be the only person responsible, it's for naught! A communist historian who is no longer living questioned me when he was writing a book on this period. I told him word for word what I have just told you and when I read his book there wasn't one line of what I had said. Jules Moch was still the one and only person responsible!

Q: Well, I promise you that I will not cut this part of the interview! The socialists had no choice?

A: No, not only couldn't they do otherwise in the government, but they couldn't do otherwise in the mines. That much said, much has been extrapolated from it, and probably Jules Moch's judgment and my judgment are totally different. I am absolutely convinced that, contrary to what has been said, the communists had no desire to create an insurrection, to seize control of the State. A certain number of errors and injustices had been permitted to accumulate, and naturally the Communist Party, to justify its opposition to the government, took advantage of them. And then don't forget that 1947 was the beginning of the Cold War. I don't believe in the least in a plot, I don't believe at all that there were precise orders coming from Moscow, I don't believe that Maurice Thorez telephoned every morning to Stalin to ask him what to do. But it happens that there was a coincidence between the role played by the Soviets and the Communist International on the international level and the interests of the French Communist Party. In other terms, they had no problem of conscience. Thus, I have never believed the story of a plot. Subsequently, Jules Moch made himself a bit ridiculous in talking about plots when one day

Jacques Duclos was found in a taxi with some pigeons....

Q: Were you aware of the development of the Force Ouvrière schism?

A: Yes, naturally, and I can bear witness very firmly to the fact that Léon Jouhaux, secretary-general of the CGT, was never in favor of it. I can tell you that I myself, Minister of Labor at that time, was never in favor of it. Contrary to all the rumors which have circulated, I never gave financial support -- moreover, I didn't have any, where would I have found it? -- to the trade unions to create a schism.

Q: Do you agree with Roger Quilliot in his history of the SFIO that your departure as minister signified the end of the period in which socialist participation benefited the working class?

A: I prefer that Roger Quilliot say it rather than I, but is absolutely uncontestable that after, if not 1949, at least 1951, socialist participation was probably not justifed. In a coalition in which the socialists participate, class divisions in society are reflected in the government. It was necessary, therefore that the worker parties be sufficiently strong and their representatives sufficiently firm to counterbalance the will of the bourgeoisie... Until 1949, we gave proof of firmness. Afterwards, I think that the bourgeoisie, having used the Socialist Party during the reconstruction, wanted to return to pre-war norms, and that the relationship of forces was insufficient to justify socialist particiption.... In the absence of communists in the coalition government, the socialists had to represent the totality of working-class demands. In other words, we would have had to refuse to accept what took place, immobilism, and the virtual numerical rejection of the communist votes. The socialist participation from 1950 to 1958 implied accepting the fact that the strength of the communists was severed from that of the working class, whereas we should have represented both socialists and communists. That's why the socialist influence played so small a role....

Q: During the 1950s you became a rebel in the party?

A: What were the major issues which separated me from the majority of the Socialist Party between 1949 and 1958? There was the problem of the EDC in 1952,

1953, 1954; after 1956, the Algerian War and in 1958 the acceptance of the coup d'état of 13 May.

On several occasions, we stated our determination to oppose German rearmament and all the decisions of our congresses were opposed to it. When the idea of what was called the EDC arose in the minds of several European statesmen, the creation of an integrated army in which there would be German units, the issue was what we called "Vatican Europe." This European army presupposed in the first instance the rearmament of Germany, yet there was a large movement of German young people "Ohne Uns" (Without Us) and German Social Democracy which were opposed to rearmament. It turns out that the SFIO was closer to the MRP than to the German socialists.

And suddenly, one day we learn that the affair had advanced considerably and that there was an understanding between the MRP and the SFIO on establishing that European Defense Community. Some of us took a position against the EDC, and I must say that in the party, just as everywhere in France at the time, it was something which affected our consciences, which immediately produced very strong feelings, very great agitation...It seems to have been about as passionate an issue as the Dreyfus Affair had been. In any case, the atmosphere within the Socialist Party was very close to frenzy. I say it all the more since I too was very impassioned and maybe I still am. For I consider that the position of the Socialist Party in favor of the EDC was something approaching treason, in any case, the violation of all its past positions. I remember having given a speech in the National Assembly in the name of the socialist group against German rearmament, a speech which had been judged sufficiently good and orthodox by the leadership of the party for it to have been published as a brochure with a preface by Guy Mollet's assistant, Pierre Commin. Then, in a few weeks, the party changed position and decided to vote for the rearmament of Germany, which was to be included in the European Defense Community.

Q: You were excluded from the party because of your position on the EDC?

A: I learned of my exclusion from the party while listening to the radio at 7 o'clock in the morning. The Comité directeur, or rather, the Commission on Conflicts, had decided to exclude Jules Moch, Max Lejeune, and myself, because in the debate in the National Assembly, we had in an official capacity opposed the EDC. I was Chairman of the Committee on Foreign Affairs, Jules Moch and Max

Lejeune were rapporteurs for the committee. What followed showed that our motives were not the same. 52 members of Parliament broke party discipline. We appealed immediately the appeal was suspensive, and consequently, we continued to exercise our parliamentary prerogatives. But let me give you an idea of the atmosphere. Legally, we remained members of the parliamentary group and naturally the very day that our exclusion was announced, we showed up. There were members of the group who didn't want us to enter the caucus room, saying that we were excluded. It was necessary to explain to them the juridical aspect because morally they were satisfied that we were no longer members of the socialist group. Well, later on, we were amnistied, I'm really not sure what happened; there was a whole series of bizarre proceedings.

To give you an idea of the complicity between the MRP and certain members of the SFIO, at that time, I was President of the Foreign Affairs Committee and Pierre Mendès-France was President of the Finance Committee. Custom, though not the rules, had it that the same party could not control both. Mendès-France was ill for some time. So the strategists of the MRP and the SFIO cooked up the following scheme: since Mendès-France was ill, it would be declared that he could no longer chair the Finance Committee. Christian Pineau, SFIO (who subsequently became Minister of Foreign Affairs) would be asked to chair it. But since both committees could not under a socialist, Daniel Mayer would be asked to step down in favor of Maurice Schumann. As a result both chairmen would be favorable to the EDC. Fortunately for himself, and for his friends, Mendès-France was not seriously ill. Two weeks later, he returned, and this delightful scheme did not see the light. But a similar scheme did succeed later, as you will see.

Q: Did the solution arrived at after the failure of the EDC seem preferable to you to the EDC?

A: Certainly not. Listen, I can tell you something and I don't mind if you publish it, something which moreover is going to seem contradictory. I was a member of Parliament 14 years. That is to say, I participated in numerous votes. The only vote which I regret is that by which I accepted the substitute solution for the EDC. Because that solution also included the rearmament of Germany; it had all the defects of the EDC without perhaps having its advantages. And, what will seem contradictory to you: if it were to happen again, even knowing everything that we know that was going to happen, I would vote the same way. I would do so because it was a Mendès-France government. Because Mendes-France had raised the question of confidence, because of future economic and social policy, because of the problem of Tunisia and what might be foreseen at the time concerning Algeria (the hostilities were not yet official, but they could be intuited -- not how violent they would become, but what hidden dangers might be involved), I would vote the same way, while regretting my vote. It is one of those contradictions which is somewhat tragic, somewhat dramatic for someone who has a conscience, and a political conscience to boot.

Q: Was there another solution?

A: To stand up to the Americans, because in the long run, the Americans saw the EDC as a European shield against Moscow. This was part of that atmosphere familiar to Americans, which they sometimes create themselves. A danger may exist potentially, but they magnify it, exaggerate it, multiply it. Well, the threat of the EDC and of German rearmament should have been bartered for significant Soviet disarmament. But it was not possible to build Europe on an integrated army. There was no European political framework and an army must be in the service of a political stance.

Second conflict: the Algerian War. I tell you from the outset, I did not initially foresee the independence of Algeria. You know there are numerous people who tell you: "From the beginning, I knew that Algeria was going to be independent, etc." It took me two or three years to envision the idea of Algerian independence, that is to say, I began to become conscious of it around 1956 or 1957. The whole program of the Socialist Party was based on peace in Algeria, the formulas of Guy Mollet "against this stupid war," "against the most foolish right in the world," were very strident.

Q: Afterwards, he changed his position after his trip to Algeria.

A: But, more and more, we learned that the French army was subjected to all sorts of tasks, and in particular, that there were torture centers...And that we didn't accept. There were a very few of us within the party who denounced torture, and the atmosphere in the sections was extremely turbulent. It went as far as physical combat. We had conducted an electoral campaign which ended in the victory of the Republican Front. I had been designated almost unanimously by the militants by secret ballot to head the list. The electoral campaign had been filled with camaraderie and friendship. Well, not more than a month and a half after, when after 6 February I denounced the new political line to the militants of my section without employing the word which was a little hard -- treason -- the same comrades who had voted for me to head the list, who liked me, shook their fists at me, wanted to jump on me and beat me up. Because they could not believe that people like Max Lejeune, Robert Lacoste, Guy Mollet, good comrades, could accept such policies. So we had to be lying.

Moreover, you have to recall the atmosphere of the press. The day we denounced the execution of three or four members of the FLN, the first page of France-Soir showed the body of a little European girl torn apart by a bomb planted by the FLN. So -- people aren't subtle -- the moment you say that it is wrong to execute the FLN, you must approve those who blew to pieces the body of that child.

It was no longer a political choice. It was no longer a political debate. It was a debate of a moral and human character. There are those who accept torture; there are those who don't accept it; and those who accept torture don't say so, they deny it exists. They say that it isn't true and that, out of ambition, for personal reasons, or to get even, we were slanderers.

So I come back to the fact that finally Maurice Schumann, with socialist complicity, became Chairman of the Committee on Foreign Affairs. A proposal came before the National Assembly to create what I called a "racist curfew." The Algerians inhabiting France were supposed to be back home before nine p.m. In other words, all those who had a swarthy face were arrested in the street after nine o'clock. I refused to vote for this racist curfew. Unfortunately, the bill didn't come back unamended from the Senate. It was sent back once, twice, three times and the leadership of the party didn't accept my argument that, when I broke discipline, it was over the same vote, thus, only once. They decided that I had broken party discipline three or four times. Now, there was a whole scale of penalties. You start by being censured by letter, then publicly, then afterwards there is a withdrawal of your mandate. The last penalty they inflicted on me was to force me to resign as Chairman of the Committee on Foreign Affairs of the National Assembly. I had just been reelected unanimously, because -- better you say it in your book than that it come from my mouth -- I was a very good president! (Laughs). And the candidate supported by the socialists to replace me was -- Maurice Schumann! I resigned from Parliament in 1958, before the 13th of May. I gave myself a birthday present by resigning on 29 April 1958, because I was going to have to break discipline again, obliged by conscience, because of the fate accorded to the Madagascan separatists who had been put in prison by the government. The Socialist Party, against all expectation and against all previous decisions, had decided to approve the sanctions taken against the Madagascan separatists. Since I knew I couldn't vote for that, that I was going to break party discipline and that I had arrived on the scale of penalties where all that remained was exclusion from the party, and that in any case I could not be excluded from the party and still maintain my seat, I resigned from the National Assembly.

Q: Finally, the SFIO upheld the investiture of De Gaulle after the 13th of May, and Guy Mollet served as Minister of State in the De Gaulle government.

A: Really, there was nothing more to do in that party. That's when the Autonomous Socialist Party (PSA) was created. The person who took the initiative, Edouard Depreux was better suited than any one else to give the signal to depart from the SFIO, because although opposed to the EDC, he had not broken party discipline. Although fiercely against the policies of Robert Lacoste and Guy Mollet, he had never broken party discipline. He was much more respected than we were; he could not be accused of being a systematic opponent, because he remained faithful to the notion that the party is never wrong.

I must tell you that after 54 years as a militant the PSA arouses in me the fondest memories. We were all faithful to the doctrine, loyal, incapable of the slightest calculated gesture, incapable of having personal designs, of pronouncing, as they say now, les petites phrases [insinuating or loaded sentences] incapable of the least machiavelianism. And we were liberated from the authority of the SFIO which had become more and more degrading, humiliating, finally dishonoring (but we didn't know that yet, dishonor only came in the following years, which led to the pursuit of the Algerian War after our own departure in 1958). So, we were happy to see each other in the sections, happy to meet each other. Whereas before, there was a kind of obsession at the idea of seeing the other militants at a section meeting: what was going to occur? When would it end? Would there be a brawl? How would we vote? There was a kind of moral, intellectual, almost physical relief.

Afterwards, probably it couldn't be otherwise, the PSA was transformed into the PSU [Parti

Socialiste Unifie]. There certainly were some positive additions; I think of the <u>Tribune of Communism</u> with a chap like <u>Jean Poperen</u> and some of his friends, not very numerous.

But there were also new elements who were tumultuous, noisy, and useless...Do you know that Israeli anecdote: a fellow who is looking for work goes to find a friend in a high place in the State. He says to him: "Can you help me find work?" The other answers: "Moischele, Moischele, you're intelligent, you're disinterested, you're loyal, you're honest. If only there were 50 people like you in the country, it would be wonderful. But there aren't 50, there are 10,000!" When in a PSU section you met, not thousands, but several dozen such fellows, it was absolutely impossible. I remember section meetings -- my wife and I belonged to the 18th arrondissement section -- I remember meetings where people would arrive, and the secretary would propose three items for the agenda, A, B, and C. "Ah, that's good," says one of the militants, "I'm in complete agreement, only question B should come before question A." There is a discussion which lasts until 11 p.m. to determine whether question B will be before question A or after. At 11 p.m. there is a vote, and by then, when the issues themselves begin to be discussed, the most earnest members leave, because they have to go to work in the morning.

In 1967 the PSU took a very ambiguous stand on the Six Day War. The positions taken by some members would have led practically to the liquidation of the State of Israel...Life became intolerable. My wife and I left the PSU without a great deal of regret.

I'll give you an example to explain this lack of regret. There were problems in Syria. Leaders of the PSU came to ask my wife and me if we would be members of a delegation which would go to Syria because the Syrian Baath party had invited the French socialists of the PSU. We immediately said yes. It was important, and we considered that the request was a gesture of fraternal friendship and political understanding. "But," they said later "you cannot go to Syria, because you won't obtain a visa. Your names are Daniel and Cletta Mayer." So we said, "You must demand it," and we expected from them some kind of gesture of solidarity. You know what they proposed? "Well, maybe we can get false papers for you." They accepted that Jews could be refused visas because they were Jews. They didn't show solidarity with those who were victims of that refusal of a visa. That's how they have to be judged.

Q: The PSU was transformed from a party of the left to a party of the extreme left (gauchiste), whereas the PSA had represented a purified socialism?

A: Exactly. For about two years we were members of no party. I must say that for people who had been politically active since their childhood, we felt a little like deserters. We were uneasy: "Well, we are no longer in the struggle." And then Alain Savary replaced Guy Mollet, and a very gratifying scene took place. Savary asked my wife and me if he could visit. He had just been chosen as secretary. Of course we said yes. He came to our house in the afternoon and began to talk. He told us that now that he was secretary, we would certainly not return to the party, but join the new party. Taking out of his pocket two cards in our names he said, "I suspected you would, I brought your two cards." That was very warm and moving.

Q: At a given moment, did your political activities became less important that your other activities, for example, in the Ligue des Droits de l'Homme?

A: Certainly. The exact date can be given, March 1958. The Ligue des Droits de l'Homme had as its president Emile Kahn, who was 81 years old and probaby must have felt himself to be immortal, like all old men. He had not in the least prepared the way for a successor. He died in January 1958, in full activity. I had joined the Ligue des Droits de l'Homme in 1927, but I was not a member of the Central Committee. For two months, the members of the Central Committee looked vainly for a president. Then Georges Gombault, a journalist on France-Soir, met me one day. He had been one of the directors of the newspaper France during the war in London, a newspaper published by French socialists and resistants close to socialism who were hostile to De Gaulle. He said to me: "Wouldn't you possibly like to be President of the Ligue des Droits de l'Homme?" It was an idea which came just like that, but it came at the right time. If De Gaulle hadn't had a microphone on 18 June 1940, history would have been different. If Hitler had had work when he was a painter in Vienna instead of being unemployed... The meeting of an individual and a period or instrument is very important. If Georges Gombault had asked me six months or two years before if I wanted to be President of the Ligue, I would have answered, "Certainly not, because of my political life, etc." But this was the beginning of a decline of my political life, and I vaguely sensed that I was going to resign from Parliament. I was still a deputy, but things were going from bad to worse for the reasons I told you.

I had been a member of Parliament for 14 years, but during that time I was very rarely just an MP. I was minister or Chairman of the Foreign Affairs Committee, and that's what is important and interesting. To be just a deputy, especially from Paris, presents very little interest. To hold office hours where M. Dupont comes to say: "Would you take care of my social security case?" and where M. Durand tells you: "My son is going to do his military service. Can he do it in the Paris region?" That has no interest whatever, not for someone of my temperament. Well, I saw the prospect of a vacuum, perhaps a need for activity. I vaguely sensed that my political activity was going to be less. So I said yes. And then the Central Committee unanimously named me as President of the Ligue. That was in March 1958. I resigned from Parliament the 29th of April. Thus my activity shifted, but did not change its focus...I was President of the Ligue 17 years and then became President of the International Federation.

Q: There was discussion of a possible candidacy on your part in the presidential elections of 1965.

A: The PSU had decided to present my candidacy. François Mitterrand, who was to be candidate for the first time, was then seeking the nomination; he came to see me and asked me if I wanted to be a candidate. He wanted to know because he was negotiating with the communists and socialists to be the sole candidate of the left. So I told him that if there was a single candidate of the left, there was no question of my running.

Q: Did you suffer from anti-semitism in your political career?

A: With several rare exceptions, I don't think that I suffered from anti-semitism. In any case, I was not aware of it.

Q: During your life as a militant, what was the greatest success of the socialist movement, and what was its greatest defeat?

A: The great success was not the electoral success of the Front Populaire but the rapidity and the substantial nature of its reforms, which had an uncontestably revolutionary character in transforming life. We have already talked of that. Naturally, the election of François Mitterrand and the legislative elections which followed which gave us an absolute majority must be considered as a success for the Socialist Party. But I think it's too soon to measure the quality of these successes, which for the moment are only electoral. The real problem is unemployment and that is partly beyond our control because it isn't a specifically national problem. The difficulties which we encounter are perhaps surmountable, but much understanding is necessary from the principal victims of unemployment. That's the tragedy and it isn't only French.

The defeat, not perhaps a defeat of the party, but I think an occasion that was lost, was May 1968. I think that in 1968 the conditions for a revolution were brought together. By that I mean to say that there was a movement of young people and a worker movement in total ferment which wanted for once not only a change in material conditions but also a moral change. The convergence of the students and workers did not take place, in large part because the CGT and the Communist Party in fact betrayed the movement. Also, because the vision of the students and that of the workers wasn't exactly the same, in the sense that the students wanted to go beyond the affluent society and the workers had not yet benefited from it. It was a defeat for the worker movement, but it wasn't totally a defeat, because since May 1968 nothing is exactly the way it was before, the relations between men, between organizations, between parents and children, teachers and students, professors and students, within the Church, the trade unions, and who knows what...But it would have been necessary to push it a bit more. Today the majority of participants in 1968 are convinced that they were beaten.

Q: The same thing happened in the United States with the anti-Vietnam War Movement.

A: It was doubtless the same phenomenon. At the very beginning, I didn't understand the movement. It was my wife who understood immediately and who said to me: "Let's go to the Sorbonne." I have an absolutely poignant memory. There was a young boy who went to demonstrate with other high school students near the Renault plant. The workers refused to admit them. They were pursued by the <u>CRS</u>. One of them, while running, was so afraid of the CRS who were following with their truncheons, their guns, etc. that he fell in the Seine and died instantaneously. He lived in the 17th arrondissement of Paris, near the Porte d'Asnières. We went to his funeral. The rose did not yet exist as the symbol of any party. The young high school students lined the route, each one holding a rose with a long stem. They were absolutely motionless. It was extraordinary, absolutely extraordinary. Not a word. An overwhelming, absolutely poignant rememberance. Afterwards, there were controversies. Had the CRS killed him? I remember a meeting at the Mutualité where I was booed but afterwards, people understood. I said: "What differences does that make? No matter how he died they killed him by scaring him, by making him fall in the water." The boy was what, 15 years old? I don't even remember his name. I wish I remembered it....

Q: To conclude, would you speak of your conception of socialism?

A: There is a semantic dispute. I refuse to employ the word socialism for the Eastern bloc. They are not socialist states. Those who identify the socialist ideal with the reality of the eastern countries are estranged from socialism. It's a swindle.

A second comment, symmetrical to the first. Since the election of François Mitterrand and the legislative elections, some speak of a socialist regime in France. It is not a socialist regime either. When one speaks of Giscard d'Estaing, in current parlance, you hear people say, "Under the old regime." The Old Regime was before 1789.... We are still in a thoroughly capitalist society. We try to modify it, so there will be less injustice, a little more equity. That has absolutely nothing to do with socialism. Socialism, such as I conceive it -- perhaps it's a jeu d'ésprit -- is in the last analysis the total ownership of the riches of all by all, eventually as in the anarchist formula, after the withering away of the State, that is to say, when there will no longer be a need for the State apparatus. No army, no police, no system of justice because socialism will have transformed the human being. I know I am speaking of something that may take thousands of years. All I can say is, that is socialism.

In the meantime, one can imagine transitional regimes where socialism is inspired by the model of reforms and efforts towards justice accomplished by certain countries, like Sweden. On a structural level, but with liberty added, the Yugoslav system is worth studying closely, all the more so because it is not rigid. A long time ago, I did a book on Yugoslavia. As soon as it was written, it was already out of date, because their institutions are constantly in movement. We should be able to orient ourselves on that; it constitutes one model. Then, if it was generalized, the model of the Kibbutz. Without a doubt, of what I have seen, they come closest to socialism such as I dreamt of it in my adolescence. Everyone works for the whole and works in his place, that is to say, the place that he chooses, for which he has a vocation. In the end, one can proceed by rotations, you do the dishes today, but you are an engineer and tomorrow you organize a theatrical performance where Aeschylus is performed. And it is not dishonorable to do the dishes and wipe the nose of your comrade's kid because you're in charge of the day-care today. Socialism is a combination of all that, but with liberty.

You know, when I was 18 years old, I was convinced that I would see socialism. Reassure yourself, I have become wiser. Now I am 72, and I am convinced that I won't see it. And that's more certain than my faith when I was 18. Still, I am profoundly convinced that socialism as I depict it will come one day. But as a friend who belonged to the Bund used to say, "the paths of life are not superhighways."

Glossary of Names, Organizations and Terms
in the Mayer Interview*

--<u>Vicent Auriol</u> (1884-1966). Socialist militant, Minister of Finance (1936-1937), later the first President of the Fourth Republic (1947-1954).

--<u>The Bund</u>. Jewish social democratic organization established in Western Russia in 1897; abolished following the Bolshevik Revolution and reconstituted in independent Poland.

--<u>CRS</u> <u>Compagnies Republicaines de Sécurité</u> (Republican Security Corps). An organization of heavily armed police established after the Liberation. They gained a reputation for "police brutality," especially against students.

--<u>Marx Dormoy</u> (1881-1941). Socialist militant of Jewish origin, Minister of the Interior (1937-1938). Placed under house arrest by Vichy, he was murdered by members of a secret fascist organization known as the Cagoule.

--<u>"economic and social programs of Mendès-France."</u> Following the war, Minister of the National Economy, Mendès-France wanted to exchange banknotes to detect profits made by collaboration and also to prevent a run-away inflation. In addition, he had a broad plan for restructuring the French economy around a core of nationalized industries. When De Gaulle accepted his rival Pleven's plan to limit the money supply through a loan, Mendès-France resigned. It has been said that De Gaulle later regretted his decision.

--<u>February 6</u>. On this date in 1956, Guy Mollet paid a visit to Algiers, and was confronted by an angry mob of <u>colons</u>. On his return, he began to shift his Algerian policy towards a hard-line <u>Algérie Française</u> stance.

--<u>FLN</u> Front de Libération National (National Liberation Front). The organization behind the Algerian war for independence.

--<u>General Henri Giraud</u> (1879-1949). Candidate backed by the U.S. as leader of the Free French against De Gaulle because of his lack of concern with

---

*The names, organizations and terms glossed are underlined in the body of the text.

"political" questions; he was quickly outmaneuvered by De Gaulle in 1943.

--Jules Guesde (1845-1922). One of the founders of French socialism; exponent of a dogmatic and narrow form of Marxism.

--"Jacques Duclos was found in a taxi with some pigeons." Jacques Duclos (1896-1975) led the communist underground during the occupation and was leader of the communist parliamentary group 1946-1958. He was a candidate for President of the Republic in 1969. In 1952, the communists demonstrated against the visit of Admiral Ridgeway. The government arrested Jacques Duclos in flagrant delict, alledgedly with a pistol, carrier pigeons and wireless transmitter in his car. Far from spying, he was returning from hunting. The "wireless" was a car radio. This ludricrous affair was interpreted as part of an effort to outlaw the Communist Party. If so, it backfired.

--Robert Lacoste (1898-   ). Socialist trade-union leader and member of Parliament appointed by Guy Mollet as Resident Minister in Algeria (1956-1958).

--Augustin Laurent (1896-   ). Long-time mayor of Lille and "boss" of the powerful socialist Federation of the Nord.

--Max Lejeune (1909-   ). Socialist deputy and minister in the Fourth Republic, he supported a hard-line on Algeria. He left the Socialist Party in 1973 to found the Mouvement Démocrate Socialiste.

--Ligue des Droits de l'Homme (League of the Rights of Man). An organization dedicated to the protection of human rights and liberties founded in 1898 during the Dreyfus Affair. It has been politically tied to the parties of the non-communist left.

--Office du blé (Wheat Office). A state office similar to the AAA created by the Blum government in 1936 to stabilize the price of wheat for farmers.

--René Pleven (1901-   ). Minister of Finance (1944-1946), frequent minister in the Fourth Republic; Prime Minister (1950-1951). Created the idea of the European Defense Community.

--Jean Poperen (1925-   ). Former communist, founder of Tribune du communisme (1958), member of Executive PSU (1960), member of executive, Socialist

Party (1971), National Secretary for propaganda of Socialist Party since 1975.

--Nicole Questiaux (1930-   ). Minister of Social Security in the Mauroy government.

--Republican Front. An electoral alliance formed of the SFIO, Radicals friendly to Mendès-France, the UDSR, and some gaullists for the election of 1956. The resignation of Mendès-France as Minister of the Finance on 23 May 1956 in opposition to the Mollet government's Algerian policies marked its breakdown.

--Maurice Schumann (1911-   ). Early gaullist supporter, spokesman for Free France, later one of the founders of the MRP, Schumann was minister in both Fourth and Fifth Republics.

--Maurice Thorez (1900-1964). Secretary-General of the French Communist Party from 1930, Minister of State 1944-1947.

--"those socialist members of Parliament who had voted against Pétain on 10 July 1940." On 10 July 1940 a joint session of Parliament was held to amend the Constitution. This session abolished the Republic and replaced it with the Etat Français under Marshal Pétain. Only 35 of the 158 socialist MPs voted against this change. There was a total of 80 negative votes.

--Henri Torrès (1891-1966). Lawyer and left-wing activist, involved in many political trials.

--Riom Trial. A trial of the leaders of the Third Republic, including Blum, Daladier, and Gamelin conducted by Vichy between 10 February and 11 April 1942. The accused, who had been sentenced to prison before being tried, were charged with responsibility for the military defeat. Their defense helped restore some credibility to the Third Republic. The trial was interrupted by the Germans, who were angry that it was being used to determine why France lost, rather than blaming the accused for starting the war.

2
Jef Rens
and Belgian Socialism

The Belgian Socialist Party was founded in 1885.* Its ideology was defined nine years later in the Charter of Quaregnon. Organizationally, the party was closer to the German and Austrian model than the French. By virtue of the principle of collective affiliation, all members of socialist trade unions, mutual-aid societies and cooperatives were automatically party members. The Maison du Peuple was general headquarters of the movement in every town. The party was composed mostly of industrial workers.

Although doctrinally the party held firmly to the principles of Marxism until long after World War II, its activity was always reformist. Because Belgium did not possess universal male suffrage, its attainment was the party's main goal. By giving primacy to the suffrage issue the party was in effect paying homage to the values of parliamentary politics. In 1893, universal male suffrage was obtained, but with plural votes for the upper classes. Not until 1919 was one man one vote promulgated (female suffrage came after World War II).

World War I integrated the party into Belgian society. In other countries, socialist parties could debate the merits of national defense; for little Belgium, taken by surprise, her neutrality violated, the victim of German atrocities, the question was moot. The three great parties: Catholic, Socialist, and Liberal, learned to cooperate. They would do so again in 1936 to deflate Rexism; they would strive to preserve Belgian identity during the Second World War; they would jointly lay the foundations of the welfare state during the occupation itself.

After World War I, the POB continued in the cabinet for several years, having lost its doctrinal allergy to participating in the government of the "bourgeois state." It could afford to be reformist because it faced no significant "revolutionary"

---

*The original name of the party was the Parti Ouvrier Belge (POB); in 1945 the name was changed to Parti Socialiste Belge (PSB).

opposition on the left. Although a communist party split off in 1921, its strength was minimal; socialist control over the trade unions was never really threatened.

The rise of the POB was contained, however, because it had difficulty attracting Catholic workers. Before 1885, Belgium was split between liberals and Catholics. Socialism was an offshoot of the liberal culture. As was the case in many Catholic nations, the terms left and right referred primarily to a party's stand on clericalism. Because it was anti-clerical, the POB attracted dechristianized workers, but not Catholic workers. After World War II, Catholic trade union membership overtook socialist. Even today the party is marked by anti-clericalism.

Socialism has been affected by the ethnic and linguistic divisions of Belgian society. Belgium is divided into two main groups, the Flemish and Walloons, the first originally speaking a variant of Dutch, the second a Romance language resembling French. In the 19th century, the Flemish adopted standard Dutch, the Walloons French. For the first hundred years, Belgium was dominated by French. The industrial areas were located in Wallonia; there Flemish workers became French speakers. Government, administration, education were all conducted in French; even the bourgeoisie of Flemish cities spoke French. Ultimately, a Flemish movement developed. Since 1945, demographic and economic trends have been reversed. The language cleavage cut across class and religion, which were the basis of the old parties. Between the wars, a compromise was found, but after 1961 the linguistic issue erupted again. New parties based on this question cut into the hegemony of the traditional parties: each of the latter ultimately responded by splitting into two linguistically homogeneous parties. In order to avoid the loss of their electorate to linguistic nationalist parties, Catholics, socialists, and liberals absorbed at least some of the nationalist message themselves. Today, there are two Belgian socialist parties, completely independent; cooperation between the two is by no means a matter of course.

Jef Rens, the subject of this interview, is perhaps the most respected elder statesman of the Belgian socialist movement. Of Flemish working class background, he became a docker and an active socialist; attracted by ideas, he returned to school and eventually obtained the doctorate. He applied his education to the problems faced by the trade union movement and the party in the 1930s.

Many of Jef Rens' reflections deal with the person and ideas of Hendrik De Man. Rens studied with De Man in Frankfurt in 1932 and worked with him when De Man returned to Belgium in 1933 to develop the campaign for the Plan du Travail. But their paths diverged. In 1941, Rens denounced his old teacher on the BBC, but he has never stopped pondering the meaning of the career of De Man.

After the war, Rens became deputy director of the International Labor Organization. There he developed an acute consciousness of the problems of the Third World. He returned to Belgium in the 1960s and presided over the advisory councils of the Coopération au Développement, the National Labor Council, (the equivalent, but much more important, of the National Labor Relations Board in the United States) and the National Science Council, the most prestigious positions in the Belgian State. His retirement did not diminish his enormous intellectual curiosity and concern with the world of politics and ideas.

Interview with Jef Rens

JEF RENS:

Both my parents were typical working people. My mother was the eldest of a family of ten, all working in the brickmaking industry in Boon which was at that time, I think, the greatest brickmaking center of Belgium. My mother went to work at the age of nine. So she hadn't gone to school much and she married without knowing how to read and write. She learned to read from my father and became a very active and interested reader who devoted a great part of her time to reading books, generally novels, history. She never learned to write properly; she wrote like a child of seven or eight. During most of her life, she didn't care about religion, but in old age she came back to her old faith, Catholicism, and died piously in the Church. She was a very lovely mother I could not have had a better one, and although she was of a typical working class family, she became really, in her way of behaving, a very delicate lady.

My father was also of a working class family, but instead of making bricks they cut diamonds, which in Antwerp is a very old trade. It has been practiced there for four or five centuries. He came out of a more liberal family, liberal in the old sense of the word, a very great interest in being independent. He was a very great admirer of President Krueger and he took over a number of Krueger's sayings like "Practice good, don't expect anything in return." But he was a very good man, a very good worker; in the end he tried to become a small entrepreneur, but it didn't work and so he died poor, in rather miserable conditions. Fortunately I was there, but that hurt his pride very much. He was almost hermetically closed to religion, although some of his sisters practiced.

Neither of my two brothers practiced religion, nor did I, but like my mother, I am turning back to the faith in which I had been brought up in my childhood years. But actually, faith has always been a problem to me and I think it is in me.

Q: But from what you say there is nothing in your family background that would explain why you became so actively involved in political and trade union life.

A: Oh, yes, my grandfather, the father of my mother, was one of the first socialists in Boon. His youngest son was a trade unionist and they were considered rebels in their village.

Q: Was your father at all politically active?

A: No. My father was anti-party, he was a liberal in the old Antwerp sense of the word. He voted liberal, and he was tolerant, he understood perfectly well why I became a socialist and I think he approved. He was happy to see that I was doing rather well, my name was in the paper... but he had no sense of solidarity. He was, I would say, a rather solitary figure, whereas on my mother's side my grandfather was in the movement.

Q: Well, tell me something about your own development and your education.

A: I started to work in an automobile factory, Minerva Motors, in 1921. We had come back in 1919 from Holland, where we had been refugees during the war. Then I lost my job and went to work in the port. I had a few good years, heavy work, some of it as a dock worker and most of the time a sort of jack of all trades. I was a very sturdy young man...not heavy but muscular and good in sports. As a young fellow I couldn't set my mind on learning a trade, I just couldn't, so I took this rather heavy job. But I had a reasonably good income, now and then there was a little unemployment but not very much. My second brother who was not very good at all in school, had left at the age of fourteen and started, at the advice of my father, to learn the job of cleaving diamonds, which is a very complicated and long-term apprenticeship. After four years he became very good at it; they paid him half the salary of a full-fledged cleaver and that was about twice as much as what I earned. In the meantime I had started to work as a propagandist in the labor movement, distributing tracts, so my brother, who was a very fine chap, said: "Jef, aren't you a fool? Why don't you learn cleaving diamonds like me and in a few years you will make twice or three times as much money as you are making now." I said, "Yes, but I haven't got a lot of time. I'm beginning to get old." He said, "Well, I will teach you." I spent three years and never got good at it. It was a closed-shop trade. There was a very first class trade union of diamond workers in Amsterdam, organized by a man called Henry Polak and Jan van Zutphen. They were two very great chaps, among the best trade unionists I came across in my life, because to them it was not just a question of obtaining better working conditions, better pay, shorter hours, but it was also a question of cultural promotion. So their trade union weekly papers were really of tremendous educational value and they made other people out of the workers of that day.

One day I came across a boy, he was Jewish, and he was wearing the white cap of a student before the war. I think it was the only time in my life that I had a feeling of jealousy. I rather haltingly, mockingly said: "You can allow yourself to study, your father is rich." This was not true and he became offended and said: "What I am doing, you can do too if you want." I remember the conversation; it was decisive for my whole life. He said, "You know you can take the exam which is the equivalent of the final exam of secondary school. It is given by a special official body which meets two times a year and delivers diplomas equivalent to those given by the secondary schools." And he very generously said, "I will help you. I will help you with everything which is related to mathematics, physics and science." So I pondered a few days and then I went to see him and accepted the offer. That must have been September. He went to his room and got a number of books and said, "You start with this." And he organized two sessions a week for two hours each, and made me absorb algebra and geometry. He gave me also a number of books on history. I had one teacher, one, because the exam for the jury included a translation from English into French. French was a language that was only second to me, but I had gone to evening schools quite a bit at the advice of my mother. She always said you have to be clean, polite, and learn French without which you got nowhere in this world.

Q: Did you have any resentment about having to learn French?

A: None. I was very Flemish nationalistic, but had no resentment. I felt resentment when I was in the army, I hated it, but I didn't stay long because I had ear trouble. And then, it must have been February, a very severe winter ... you know the diamond industry is a very strange industry, suddenly a slump breaks out, no one knows where it comes from, what is the reason, and then woe to the diamond workers and the merchants alike. They are very strange people; when they work and earn money, they spend it all ostentatiously and have great fun, and when the slump comes and there's no income, oh! Saving they don't know. I have known times in my family when there was just nothing to eat, so I went to visit a friend in the hope that his mother would offer me a slice of bread, which generally occurred. So in those months I could study almost eighteen hours a day. And then came the first session of the university exams.

So my friend said, "You know what you should do? If you apply to take this examination, you have not got the slightest chance, but since you have never taken it you will at least have the experience of how it works. In September you will fail again, but next year in July, you will make it." So I followed his advice and I sent in my money. I was convoked to this jury central and succeeded the first time, just about; I nearly failed in French. I was very good in history, even in mathematics.

So I started to take university courses, but I couldn't follow them, I had to work. From time to time I went to Brussels at least to see each professor once. I was very much encouraged by my fellow workers. They were all very interested to see that one of their own was going to the university. I did this three years to get my licence en sciences sociales and then I did a fourth year to get a second licence in economics. Then suddenly there was a big slump following the American Wall Street crash of 1929. In Belgium we felt the crash one year later because we had a Universal Exhibition and that maintained a somewhat artificial activity. That exhibition closed on 30 September 1930. The next day when I went to my shop it was closed -- no more work.

One day I came across a friend of mine from the labor movement, Gust De Muynck, the brother-in-law of Hendrik De Man. He is one of the nicest chaps I know. He said, "Won't you come work with me." I had learned from the papers that he had been appointed director of the first radio news in Flemish. He said, "Well I have three vacant jobs, one is for a liberal, one for a Catholic, and one for a socialist. You can be my socialist editor." So I said, "Do you think that I can compose newscasts?" And he replied, "Well, I don't know whether I can do it myself." I started in early 1931.

Once while I was unemployed I had gone to visit Herman Vos who was still the leader of the Flemish Frontpartei, a very fine chap and a great orator who exercised a great influence on people in different parties. He said, "Well, instead of wasting your time and doing nothing why don't you prepare something in order to get a fellowship from the Alexander von Humboldt Foundation. In June came news from the Alexander von Humboldt Foundation that I got one of the two fellowships. I received a leave of absence from my job at the radio.

I went first to Berlin, but then I decided to go to Frankfurt. I had a letter of recommendation from Gust De Muynck's wife, Yvonne, to her brother, Hendrik De Man, who was then teaching at the University of Frankfurt.

Q: Before discussing your experiences in Frankfurt, could you talk about your prior ideological and intellectual development?

A: I think it is very typical of youngsters of my generation. When I worked for Minerva Motors I already had contact with a trade union at the plant. At this time I began a search for the truth. I went quite often to a book shop owned by an old anarchist, Jan Madou, in one of the lower class districts in the heart of Antwerp, a little old book shop, very stuffy. Madou had a long beard, he was a typical, almost symbolic figure of his trend, but I learned a lot of names from him. He spoke to me about Bakunin, about Kropotkin, about Elisée Reclus and so on. And I bought some little books by him about these people, who have made quite a lasting influence on me, in particular their concept of freedom and the idea that power inevitably leads to more power, which leads to abuse of power and oppression. I have come across this idea in an entirely different version set forth by a man who was not originally an anarchist, Carlo Rosselli, who I knew; he was a lovely fellow, you know he was murdered on orders of Mussolini. He wrote a little book: Le Socialisme libéral. I think it contains one of the most complete and even up-to-date definitions of socialism I know.

But I did not go only to Jan Madou. The Socialist Party in Antwerp was then very active, so I went to the socialist center, called "Cooperator," and they had a book shop too. I bought some books there and I met quite a number of people of all sorts who were members of the party and went to their meetings. It has now completely changed; there is no more such party life nowadays in Antwerp, but at that time the party met at least once a month, and everybody could speak. When not yet 20, I started to stand up and to make a point and that is the way Gust de Muynck got to know me and appreciate me. He was the head of the socialist youth movement to which I belonged. I was searching for the truth and approaching without inhibition people belonging to different types. In the end, I think I fell back on what one would call the center-left in the party, a cautious and sometimes tough opposition to the party bosses. But I wanted to remain in the party. Though some of my friends said it was no use, I thought you had to remain in the party to change the party, which

you couldn't do from the outside. There was no use
in just splitting away and becoming a little minority
group.

Q: Were there any people in the Socialist Party
at that time whom you especially admired?

A: Yes, there were several people. A man whom I
admired, but got to know intimately only much later,
was Camille Huysmans. In Antwerp he was the top man,
but I couldn't approach him at that time. A man I
admired much was the second man called Willi
Eckelers, a metallurgist. He was very interested in
the young people and the students, the labor youth
movement created by Gust de Muynck, and he encouraged
it. And then there was the man who I am proud I
brought to the Party, Herman Vos.
   I brought in Herman Vos. I had a conversation
with him in 1932, shortly after Parliament had
adopted the first laws on language, the Compromis des
Belges. He said, "Well, this legislation takes the
ground from under the Frontpartei which no longer has
a raison d'existence. And I consider," he said,
"that in the Frontpartei now everybody has to go to
the party to which philosophically he belongs." And
I asked him, "In your case?" "In my case," he said,
"the Socialist Party." And then I asked him, "May I
present your candidacy to the party?" And he said,
"With pleasure." And this created quite an uproar,
because the man who at first was against him was
Camille Huysmans. I was no child anymore. I knew
perfectly well that the main source of income of
Herman Vos, Senator of the Frontpartei and director
of their newspaper (which had little circulation) was
his Senator's salary. So I said if he got admitted
into our party, we should give him the post of
provincial Coopted Senator. And Camille Huysmans had
a candidate of his own, a chap from Luxemburg who
couldn't even speak Flemish. There were several
cases like that before the First World War when the
main leader of the Socialist Party in Antwerp had
been Dr. Terwagne who could not speak Flemish. That,
of course, has now become unthinkable. But Willi
Eckelers immediately saw the advantage of having
Herman Vos, a very distinguished leader, with us. He
would probably bring in with him quite a number of
his electorate. And that is actually what happened.

Q: Now perhaps we can talk about your experience
at Frankfurt. There you studied with De Man?

A: Not only De Man. I studied with Paul
Tillich, Karl Mannheim, Karl Seidman, Karl Zossman.
But I think what was most interesting was the whole

political atmosphere of Germany on the eve of the breakdown. And it was there that I decided to try to prepare a thesis on the social foundations of National Socialism. I presented the thesis in 1935 in Brussels; De Man was a member of the jury as was Louis de Brouckère. The main theme of the thesis was the politization of the middle classes and the radicalization -- but in the wrong way -- of the working class. I took National Socialism seriously.

Q: De Man had talked about this. Did you share his point of view?

A: On this point, yes. I think De Man was right in analyzing what he called the proletarization of the middle classes, which did not result in their developing a consciousness of being proletarian; on the contrary they revolted against that idea, they wanted to remain distinct from and above the working class. The radicalization of the socialist workers and communist workers followed a line opposed to the leadership of the Socialist and the Communist parties. "They are leading us nowhere," they thought, so they followed Hitler. I saw real workers marching with the Hitler movement in Frankfurt, disgusted or discouraged by the passivity of the leadership of the Communist and Socialist parties. The only way out for them was unity, and both these parties were against it. The SAP was too weak, too small, just a splinter group and could not have any influence. The whole scene on the left side was one of disorder, disunity.

Q: When did you leave Germany?

A: In August 1932.

Q: When you returned to Belgium, was it with a strong fear that the same kind of thing could happen in Belgium?

A: No. You remember the adventure of Degrelle? He tried to create a mass fascist movement. And then came a spontaneous reaction of the old parties, which put their forces together behind the candidacy of Van Zeeland in the election and Van Zeeland gave Degrelle a beating like hell. No, there is a very strange trend in Belgian public opinion, at least in the past, to rise above disunity at moments of crisis or danger.

Q: A kind of strength born of fragility, the recognition of the intrinsic weakness of the country which, in order to survive, has to hold together.

What did you see as the essential task that had to be accomplished when you returned to Belgium?

A: Unemployment.

Q: Unemployment?

A: When I came back to Belgium, following the promise of Gust de Muynck, I got my job back at the radio. Then I found a job in the trade union movement. I became editor of the magazine of the Commission Syndicale, the Le Mouvement Syndical Belge at the end of 1932. And I would say it was the beginning of a period of the seven or eight best years of my life, because I soon became a member of the secretariat of the Commission Syndicale. It was composed of three chaps, Camille Mertens, Joseph Bondas and Edouard De Vlaminck. Each of them was older than my father. I was extremely well treated, not only with great humanity, but with very great and warm sympathy by the three of them. We became very close friends. They were somewhat tired, and gave me as much responsibility as I could bear, and that was quite a lot.

Shortly after, I was also asked to write weekly columns for Le Travail, a daily newspaper in Verviers, and Le Journal de Charleroi, in French. In the beginning it took me a lot of time, but after five years I could write a readable leader in a couple of hours. Between these two papers, I was paid 75 francs; that almost took care of the rent of our house.

I became a well known and a sharp columnist, and I believed in my cause. As a result, I got more and more invitations to give speeches in the evenings in the provinces. If I had accepted them all (I once discussed it with my wife) she would never see me again. So I said, I'm going to impose a rule on myself, never accept more than three evenings a week, and one Sunday out of two, and I stuck to that rule. In the eyes of a number of militants de province I was a bad propagandist because I didn't go everywhere. I told them I needed free time to study and replenish my stock of ideas, and do some reading and find out what was going on abroad....

Q: How did you think the movement should deal with the problem of unemployment? Of course, it was easy enough to oppose the "Government of Bankers," but what positive measures did you recommend?

A: Well, actually, the remedies we proposed in the economic field were new. We fought to improve unemployment allowances and we fought to provide

income for those who had involuntarily lost their
jobs. One thing happened as a result of De Man's
return. He had a number of very good ideas; he
wanted socialism to penetrate into other social
categories of the population. He organized
discussion meetings with high and middle level civil
servants and some people from industry, not in the
Maison du Peuple, but in the Fondation Universitaire.

Q: The period after 1933 would be one of
dramatic change and great conflict for the Belgian
labor movement. Would you say something about <u>Emile
Vandervelde</u>, who was ending his career as party
leader at this time?
    Looking back at the history of socialism, it
seems that Vandervelde belongs to a particular
generation, the same generation of men like Léon
Blum, Otto Bauer, people who were formed before 1914,
who believed in a progressive evolution of the human
race through education, who considered themselves to
be Marxists, but were profoundly reformist rather
than revolutionary, who chose not to go along with
Lenin. They belonged to a generation that was very
positivistic and frequently came from a cultivated
bourgeois background. But, faced with the Great
Depression, a problem which Vandervelde was
confronting in his sixties, they were not quite sure
what to do. Would that be a fair assessment?

A: I think so. I think it is quite an accurate
picture, except when you say Vandervelde belongs to
the generation of Blum. I would say rather, the
generation of Jaurès, closer to Jaurès than to Blum,
although a very good friend of Blum.

Q: What did Vandervelde represent for the
Belgian labor movement at this time?

A: He was THE leader. He was the <u>PATRON</u>. He
was the only man to whom they gave the name of their
employer to in a sentimental way, as belonging to
them. He was a rather ugly looking chap, rather
small. He was a leader. HE WAS A LEADER; he held
the party together, he built it up and forced respect
everywhere. In his conception of reformist
evolution, he put the party above the trade unions,
above the cooperatives and above the <u>mutualités</u>. He
considered all three of them as <u>creations of</u> the
party to promote the furtherance of socialism. And I
remember, it was almost tragic, the day that, with my
initiative, we held a special congress to change the
statute of the trade unions. And one of the changes
was to substitute for "Commission Syndicale"
"Confédération Générale du Travail de Belgique

(CGTB)." Vandervelde, very old then and not in good health came to that meeting, and in the corridor he begged me "Rens, don't do it. Don't make this change. Let La Commission Syndicale remain the child of the party." I said, "But patron, you must understand." And he went away a very sad man; that was shocking for him.

Q: In Belgium, before World War II, what exactly did the Socialist Party and labor movement mean for the average party or trade union member? What role did it play in their lives?

A: I think a tremendous role. I couldn't think of it in words other than as the role of the large family. There was an atmosphere of intimacy, family, belonging, and of expectancy, felt jointly, of things to come; that socialism meant an entirely different society into which one day we would enter. We didn't have any clear idea how, but different from and opposed to the society in which we were living. And it took me quite a bit of time before realizing that what we wanted to accomplish, what we were striving towards was something which was already in process, actually what you call reformism. But it took me quite a long time. Probably under the influence of the first French socialists and anarchists, I had the image of an ideal society entirely different from the one in which we were living. The labor movement centered around La Maison du Peuple, which in Charleroi was called Le Palais du Peuple, and the tragedy is that the Palais du Peuple now has been sold, as the labor movement no longer could carry the expenses involved. And in La Maison du Peuple, you generally found the offices of the socialist mutualité, of one or more trade unions, of the cooperatives; if you were a member of the party, you were supposed to buy every year -- and you had to prove it -- a certain amount of commodities or goods or items from the cooperatives. It was quite a high figure, a good part of your income. So it was, in a way, a world in itself. I don't say a state in a state, but a world in itself, animated by the great orators, the high priests, like De Brouckère, Jules Destrée, Camille Huysmans, Anseele. Of course that was a time when the Word was pronounced on things to come, and that could be in general terms and in a very lofty and personal way. It had some features of a religion.

Q: The Great Depression provoked an increasing amount of criticism of the old leadership, especially from the radical left, whose leading spokesman at the time was a young firebrand by the name of Paul-Henri

Spaak. Did you have much contact with this Action
Socialiste group at the time?

A: As I told you, I was somewhere towards the
left of center. I played the role of moderator in
the Commission Syndicale, somewhat like Vandervelde
in the party. While working at the radio, I met one
of the other leaders of the Action Socialiste, Walter
Dauge, who was a speaker on the French language
radio. Although I didn't share his views, we became
good friends.

To give you an idea of the Action Socialiste, I
can tell you one story. Dauge asked me to do a
meeting with him at Flénu; he was the son of a miner
from there. I've never seen such posters! "Walter
Dauge, le mineur de Borinage" -- he had never been a
miner! "Jef Rens, Le Docker d'Anvers, parleront à la
Maison du Peuple à huit heures!" ("Walter Dauge, the
miner of the Borinage and Jef Rens, the docker from
Antwerp will speak at the Peoples' House at eight
o'clock!") When Dauge came to work in Brussels he
was dressed like I am, a tie, grey trousers, a decent
jacket, but there he had no jacket, no tie, and his
hair was in disorder. So we spoke, and after the
meeting (this is interesting from the point of view
of Walter's psychology), we went to the counter of
the Maison du Peuple to have a glass of beer. And
the manager, who was appointed by the cooperative,
said: "Walter, what you are doing is not decent."
And he said, "What? What do you mean?" "To appear
this way, in front of our workers. Take an example
from Mr. Rens. He at least shows by the way he is
dressed that he respects our workers. And you, you
downgrade them by presenting yourself in a way you
are not usually dressed." I was very struck by the
remark. I made a mental note for myself. Now Dauge
ended up very badly; he became a trotskyist and ended
his life as a fascist.

There's one very interesting thing about which I
think very little if anything is written. He
organized a meeting in Paris between Spaak and
Trotsky. I think nothing transpired there; I know
that Trotsky didn't think anything of Spaak. That I
found out from Victor Serge; but I have never seen a
text written by Trotsky about that meeting. I asked
Spaak several times; but he always evaded me.

Q: You may recall the comment made in 1949 by
Spaak when he was addressing the Socialist Party
Congress. He held up a copy of The Communist
Manifesto and said that he had just read it for the
first time, and that after this reading, he decided
that it needed some revision. (Laughs) So

considering that, I doubt whether Trotsky found too much of interest in him.

A: No, it didn't work.

Q: In 1933, Emile Vandervelde asked Hendrik De Man to return to Belgium to work actively for the Party. De Man organized a great movement for "Le Plan," in which you were actively involved. The Plan constituted a kind of governmental contract, a series of reforms the POB would implement to deal with the crisis if it were given an electoral mandate. Then the conservative "Government of the Bankers" of Theunis, Gutt, and De Broqueville collapsed.

A: In place of it, over a weekend, there appeared a government under the leadership of Paul Van Zeeland in which we found De Man and Spaak. De Man greatly disappointed a number of his closest collaborators, including myself, Max Buset, and Isabelle Blume. Not so much because he had entered the government, but the way he entered it, without giving us any warning, without having come to explain; we never saw him again at our meetings, he just ceased coming. De Man and his close followers and friends had the habit of attending meetings which took place once a week, generally on Friday, in La Taverne Britannique behind Parliament, where we prepared the next issue of the weekly paper, Plan. Having become a minister, De Man ceased to come and did not give any explanation, not in writing, not by word.

Spaak entered the government during the weekend, and in the course of the week following the constitution of the government, there was a sort of study day in one of the homes the trade unions and the party possessed along the coast. I went there by train, and found myself in the same compartment with Isabelle Blume. And who passes there and joins us? Spaak. And very strange, the first thing that struck me was that he wore fine leather gloves. I had never seen Spaak wearing gloves before. I found it very funny. I didn't say very much but Isabelle Blume took the offensive. She was a very loud woman, and she said: "How could you enter this government, you the leader of the Action Socialiste?" "Je crois," dit-il "Que chacun rencontre dans sa vie un certain nombre, un nombre limité de chances. J'ai vu ma chance passer et je l'ai pris." ("I believe that everyone encounters a certain number of opportunities in his life, a limited number. I saw my chance and took it.") That was the whole justification he gave for his entry into the government, in which, I must say, he became a hard-working and decisive minister.

In the period previous to the constitution of the
government, in the trade union movement, there were a
number of elements, especially Mertens, who insisted
that he should be expelled from the party. And I
always tried to moderate them, saying that I didn't
think that fundamentally Spaak was an extremist. Let
us be patient. I was very young, but that was, I
think, rather wise in judgment. Vandervelde took the
same position in the party executive. So he was not
expelled; he became a minister, Minister of
Transport, and in less than no time he had the Union
of Transport Workers on his side, because he took
decisions to find them jobs. He decided to renew
work on the railroad junction between the North and
the South stations. There was a big, idle field; for
40 years work had ceased, and that, of course,
provided hundreds, if not thousands of jobs in
Brussels alone.

Q: In short, the explanation of Spaak and De
Man's behavior was on one level, personal ambition;
on another, that given a position of power in the
government, they would be able to serve the interest
of the working class, provide employment, improve the
standard of living. That was certainly done by the
Van Zeeland goverment.

A: You must not forget Spaak belongs to a family
at whose table he had come across, even as a young
boy, a statesman, like Paul-Emile Janson, his uncle,
or Hymans and Jaspar, all leading figures. For him
to enter from le salon de famille into Parliament,
was to go from one place to another. He came across
the same people. It was his world. His mother was a
socialist senator. Politics was just in terms of
power. To be just a member of Parliament was to
them, nothing, one had to be minister. You must have
this background in your mind, in order to be able to
understand his motivations.

Q: And yet a man like Spaak was accepted by the
socialists? Why?

A: His extraordinary oratory. And then,
Vandervelde, who in my opinion, was always looking
for young elements to attract to the labor movement.
To a man like Vandervelde, obtaining the affiliation
of Spaak was a point in favor of the labor movement.
So he recommended him to Joseph Wauters in the first
government in which socialists participated, and he
became the chef de cabinet of Joseph Wauters. Spaak
had a vague but real social conception, that is
without doubt.

Q: Van Zeeland brought about some reforms, though far less than those contained in "Le Plan du Travail." He did significantly reduce unemployment. Then following the Popular Front victory in France, the outbreak of a General Strike ...

A: In 1936, after the outbreak of the strike in France, the workers in our country left the shops, quite spontaneously, and without a really planned program. The members of the bureau of the Commission Syndicale came together and said: "This is going to be a general strike and we must formulate the claims to put up as a program for the strikers." And that was a very interesting discussion. The first claim was something the boys themselves had felt already, a considerable increase of wages. As a result of the devaluation, prices had gone up and wages had not followed to that extent. Then the second was the reduction of the hours of work to 40 hours a week. Then they said we must put into that program "la liberté syndicale," (freedom to organize) because, especially in the Walloon part, freedom of association was not accepted by the employers. So for a yes and a no, you were put on the street. You couldn't defend yourself. And then one of our comrades, in a very moving intervention said: "Il faut que nous demandions six jours de congé payé. Nous sommes tout de même la classe la plus nombreuse qui passe toute sa vie d'un bout à l'autre peinant sans obtenir un jour de congé. Il faut faire de cela une de nos revendications fortes." ("We must ask for six days of paid vacation. After all, we are the most numerous class, which spends it entire life laboring without getting a day of vacation. We must make that one of our major demands.") So we did. And he was right, of all the points of the program, the one which moved public opinion most was that related to paid holidays. The non-worker citizens of the country, for the first time, realized that the majority of their fellow citizens had spent their lifetime without one day of vacation. The strike had broken out in the beginning of June, and Mertens had already left for the meeting of the Governing Body of the International Labor Office in Geneva and had been followed a few days later by Bondas. I plunged heart and soul into the action, and for one month, I don't think that I ever slept at home. I sometimes went in the day for an hour, half an hour, to change shirts, give a kiss to my wife and the kids. Every evening, 3 or 4 meetings. The first phase, to get the workers out of the shops was immediately followed by meeting with the government, with Van Zeeland, a whole bunch of ministers, Delattre, sometimes Spaak, sometimes De Man. And then meetings in our own National

Committee, and then finally meetings with the employers, under the auspices and in the presence of the government. It was a life like that, but it was big fun. I gave the full measure of what I could do. The most heavy task was at the end, to put an end to the strike, and persuade the workers that even if they hadn't won from every point -- notably reduction of hours -- that they had gained a very big victory. They got between a 10 and 15 per cent increase of wages, the minimum wage of 32 francs, freedom of association, they got six holidays with pay, and thus another 2 per cent wage increase. But you know, it is at a moment like that, that the communists come out of their dark corners and make the workers believe that they have been defeated. I spent a couple of weeks attending very tough meetings and was even assaulted by the communists. They drag on the meetings and then the majority of the people become tired and leave one after the other. In the end you are confronted with a hard core of extremists and to win against them is tough. But I think we came out all right. And then a few weeks after the end of the strike we had a special congress to draw up the balance of what had been achieved and not achieved. The president of the mine workers, Nicolas Dethier took the floor and said, at the end of the meeting: "I have an announcement that I want to make, a proposal which is unique because appointments are not made by congress, but by the National Committee. I want us to appoint here and now Jef Rens as full-fledged secretary of the Commission Syndicale." I got a standing ovation from the congress and became secretary.

Q: You became the fourth.

A: Mertens was very nice. He got visibly, conspiciously, more pleasure out of my success as speaker at congress meetings than he got out of his own successes. So he called me in one day; he said: "Well, you are going to stay here after we have left, so we should now start thinking of our successors. And you look around to see who you want to bring in and we can discuss afterwards about the new appointments." So we brought in Paul Finet, Louis Major, and Léon Watillon. The man I would really have liked to bring in was a mine worker, Alfred Musset and then his boss came to see me and said: "Don't take him away. He's the only man who keeps our shop going. If he leaves, the miners' union in Charleroi won't resist." So I didn't insist; I couldn't insist. Then the war came; the Germans took him and killed him.

Q: Well, after the war, I've been told, that if you had wanted to be the secretary-general of the FGTB, you could have easily ...

A: Well, you see, it is one of the saddest points of my life on which you are touching now. In the bottom of my heart I feel that I have not done my duty in not going back to Belgium, and the main reason -- and this is something which I have never expressed to anybody -- I didn't go back to Belgium was for the sake of my wife, who started to -- well, I can't find any other words, to become allergic, or almost started to hate Belgium. When the war broke out, I sent her to her parents in North Africa. One day or another, the Germans would march in, so in November 1939, I said: "You'd better go to Oran and wait for the events which are bound to come." So she went and then she saw the months pass. In April, without warning, without asking me, she came back to me in Belgium. And then when the Germans entered Belgium, for some moments she lost her mind. You see, with the two little children, with all the stories which were going around in our country about the First World War cruelties committed by the Germans, she lost her mind, although nothing happened. We fled south and she was out of her mind for weeks. We were separated during the war. She joined me at the end of the war in London. We had two children, two lovely boys. And when I saw the sadness coming over her to have to go back to Belgium, I did the wrong thing. Dore Smets, with whom I wrote a book, once said: "If Jef Rens had come back to Belgium in 1945, the whole socialist history of the Low Countries would have been different." At the conference of the ILO in Paris, in the summer of 1945, I was asked to meet jointly with Louis Major and André Renard. Louis spoke, he was the more talkative, and said: "Bondas est sur le point de prendre la retraite." ("Bondas is about to finish up.) And actually before the war, retirement age in the Commission Syndicale was 60, and Bondas would have reached the retirement age in 1941 and in 1945 it had already been arranged that he should go. Mertens had left at 60, just before the Germans entered, so Bondas took the place of Mertens, and I took the place of the deputy secretary-general, Bondas. It was arranged that if Bondas left, I would succeed him. So in 1945 Louis said in the presence of André Renard: "Bondas est sur le point de finir. Au congrès qui vient en quelques mois, il démissionne. Finet aimerait prendre sa place. Mais nous deux, nous sommes d'accord pour que ce ne soit pas Finet, parce qu'il n'a pas assez de caractère. André voudrait être secrétaire-général, mais moi je

ne suis pas d'accord. Moi, je voudrais aussi l'être,
mais Renard n'est pas d'accord. Mais nous sommes
tous les deux d'accord que tu acceptes le
secrétariat-général." ("Bondas is about to finish
up. At the congress a few months from now, he is
resigning. Finet would like to take his place. But
we two agree that we don't want Finet, because he
doesn't have enough character. Andre wants to be
secretary-general, but I don't agree. I'd like to be
secretary-general, but Renard doesn't agree. But we
both agree that you should accept the position.")

Q: You were the only person who probably could
have dealt with the two of them.

A: I could. There's a Flemish expression:
things past cannot be redone.

Q: Socialist participation in a coalition
government involved acceptance of a foreign policy
which angered many militants because it did not seem
to be sufficiently anti-fascist. Vandervelde, was
losing control of the Party by 1937-1938...

A: That was a tragic year for him, a tragic
end. Spaak always maintained towards Vandervelde, as
far as I could observe, not intimacy, but good
manners. But De Man became cool, as you can read in
what he wrote about Vandervelde which I think is
abominable, abominable.

Q: They more or less forced Vandervelde's
resignation from the government.

A: And then as you say, I'm glad that you know
it because it's not known generally, Vandervelde not
only called De Man back to Belgium when he saw Hitler
coming to power, but did everything to provide him
with an income. Vandervelde went to see an
industrialist who lent a big sum of money to finance
the Institut d'Etudes Sociales. And he had de Man
appointed as director of this institute and gave him
three other posts. He intervened at the Université
Libre de Bruxelles to have De Man appointed
professor. So I must say Vandervelde behaved towards
De Man as a real gentleman, and he was paid back in
very, very, bad money. You know, I have become very
critical, perhaps less of some of his ideas, but
about the person. De Man, as a thinker put forward
some things of value, but as a person he was
abominable.

Q: You know, we've spoken about De Man for a
long time, and since I first met you, seven or eight

years ago, it seems as if your attitude towards De Man has become increasingly negative.

A: No, in the early '30s, I think he made contributions towards a better analysis of the National Socialist and fascist movements, the role of the middle class, the fact that their material, physical proletarization was not accompanied on the level of consciousness. He realized that you just could not do away with National Socialism, as was done by some Marxists, by saying that it was the last crisis of capitalism; there was something more than that to it. The last capitalist crisis could not bring into movement such large masses of people. But I have seen sides of his character which were disturbing, and that, of course, accumulated throughout the years.

Q: What is frightening, is the direction de Man took on foreign affairs. We've already seen, from what you've said, that fascism did not really pose a threat to Belgium from within if the socialists and other parties followed a reasonable policy against it, but the threat from the outside was a very real one. Vandervelde seems to see it much more clearly than de Man and Spaak.

A: There is no doubt that the danger of fascism was seen more clearly by Vandervelde and De Brouckère and Camille Huysmans, than by Spaak and De Man. There's no doubt in my mind about that.

Q: But why?

A: Probably the labor movement, the Socialist Party should not have been in the government because there was an insoluble question, that was Burgos. On the one hand, as a socialist, there was no accommodation possible with Franco, and on the other hand, the international rules between governments oblige you always to recognize a de facto government.

Q: So, once again, it was the sacrifice of the ideal in pursuit of material success. What do you think of Henri Rolin's accusation against Spaak in 1938, at the time of the Burgos affair? He said that Spaak was "un agent de défaitisme international." (An agent of international defeatism.)

A: I think he came close to the truth, I don't go further because the alternative would have been for the party not to be in the government. Once in the government, it was difficult to escape the kind of position Spaak had to take.

Q: But Isabelle Blume also put it very well. She said it was not simply that Spaak took the wrong positions, but he took them with so much enthusiasm.

A: Yes, though he took the wrong positions, through his oratory he always carried with him the majority of the party.

Q: To go back to you, your position personally. I recall very clearly reading your article of March 1939 after the German entry into Prague, which represents a radical change in position on foreign policy. Up until that time, you had more or less followed the position of the government in terms of foreign policy. How did you see the international events of the 1930s and why did March 1939 represent the change for you?

A: That is a good question, and it is an awkward question to answer. I was the chef de cabinet of Spaak. And as we saw the effects of the policy of that government, more and more we became convinced that it was wrong. But it's not so easy to come to that conclusion and draw from that conclusion the step to leave the government and take a position. So when the government fell, I felt free to express myself as I felt.

Q: If one could live the 1930s over, would there be anything you would do differently?

A: Yes, I would not have entered into Spaak's cabinet, surely not, and would have maintained my full freedom of fighting and expressing my opinion in the trade union movement, which I did, as I said, the day after I left the government and in very vigorous terms.

Q: Would you say that it was a mistake possibly for the Socialist Party to have entered a government in which it had to sacrifice ideological needs for certain socio-economic advantages?

A: This question you put now is different from the question you put before. In the question you put before, you said knowing what you know now; and the question you put now is about entering a government without knowing what was in store. And I think we entered the government in the main to make a supreme effort to do away with unemployment. One must have lived with the fear of that period that was haunting every worker's family, even those in which the man was working, the fear of losing their job. I think the Van Zeeland government altered the situation.

The devaluation had, as a result, the immediate renewal of economic activity and in less than a year, you have 100,000 fewer unemployed.

The problem of fascism was complicated by one thing that you shouldn't forget. In the years following the First World War, we inculcated pacifism inside the labor movement in Europe, everywhere in Europe, as almost the most essential feature of socialism. And we still practiced that cult when Hitler was already in power and organizing the remilitarization of Germany. So there was more than one weakness on our side. This was a real one. And I would say that in England it was overriding. You could not be a socialist without being a pacifist. And we did not want to see the danger of Germany's becoming a military power. But I saw it in preparing my thesis. For the first time, and that is the contribution Hitler has to my mind, I had to learn to think in terms of power, which was his only term of thought, but was not the main feature of the labor movement in Europe.

Q: At what time do you think that you became certain that Hitler was planning an offensive war to take over Europe?

A: In 1935 and it was a professor during discussions of the public lesson for my thesis defense at the University who drew our attention to Hitler's threat to peace. I think on the whole, I made a rather good summary, but I missed the main point. I said that a socio-economic regime of that kind could not in the long run stand the pressure of its own public opinion, and that, sooner or later, that regime would break down internally. And this professor said: "Don't you think rather that it would break down as a result of outside intervention, in a war provoked by that regime?" And that made me think.

Q: But wouldn't it be fair to say that although you saw the possibility of a war provoked by Germany, that at that same time you counted on England and France to be strong enough to resist, as in 1914?

A: We thought so and there, of course, we were entirely wrong. For instance, I sincerely believed that the French army was invincible, and even believed that after the fall of Poland. And then there was the propaganda. You should have seen those huge posters as big as this whole wall all over France: "Nous sommes les plus forts," ("We are the strongest.") in three colors. And we saw the

silhouette of the French army on one side and that of
the English fleet on the other side.

Also, you know, Hitler's march towards power in
terms of historical development was a very quick
movement, and it was not so easy for an old movement
like the labor movement, which had through the evils
and the sufferings of the First World War developed a
position of pacifism to do away with that, even
watching what was going on in Germany. We could not
throw away our pacifism as quickly as Hitler built up
his power. He went very, very, very, very fast; and,
of course, a concentration of power in one hand, as
against democracy, where you know, ideas have to be
developed through a whole framework of institutions
and meetings and so on.

Q: De Man became aware very quickly, as you once
pointed out to me, of the weaknesses of the
democracies. But ironically, precisely because he
saw how strong Germany was, he decided to try to
remove Belgium from involvement in war, and so
prepared the groundwork for collaboration, already in
the late 1930s.

A: To what extent a man as intelligent as he
was, and that he was, really believed that by taking
that position he could keep our country outside the
war, remains to me still a very great puzzle.

Q: Do you have any idea what he expected or
hoped for from the position he took?

A: Having observed the way he acted afterwards,
I wouldn't be surprised if in a hidden corner of his
mind, he hadn't seen all that was forthcoming, and
made up his mind to try to accommodate himself inside
that regime, and try to do the best for the labor
movement within the new framework, within the New
Order. I wouldn't be surprised if that already had
been in his mind before Hitler actually overran
Belgium. But, of course, I have no evidence of
that. This is the first time a question of that kind
has been put to me. But I wouldn't be surprised,
seeing how quickly he crossed the line and tried to
compose with the new authorities and dissolved the
old trade union movement and set up a new movement
under his leadership.

Q: You once said that De Man's evolution in an
anti-democratic way was based on two things: his
perception of the increasing weakness of the
democracies' response to fascism; and his own failure
in his great ambition of becoming Prime Minister.

A: Yes, I think that, I still think that. Now for the first, there was quite a widespread criticism among the intellectuals of the labor movement in Europe (I saw them in Holland, in France, in my own country, in Austria), with the weaknesses of democracy, the incapacity of democracy to deal properly with the real problems of our time. Of course, if you take that critical position, you are more apt once democracy is lost to compose with the new power. But fundamentally, I think that de Man, in doing what he did in '40, after the Germans occupied the country, denied his own ideas spelled out in many of his books, The Psychology of Socialism and The Socialist Idea. He acted contrary to his own ideas. And there I can find no other explanation than that De Man the person was well below the thinker. As a person he could be abominable.

Well, did I ever tell you about my association with the German International Socialistische Kampfbund? You know the name of the man who played a very big role in the postwar orientation of the German Socialist Party, Willi Eichler. He belonged to this branch of the German Socialist Party, very small, but very interesting very interesting, because they motivated their socialist faith not by Marxism, but by neo-Kantism, and they had a philosophe, a man called Professor Nelson. If I remember rightly he was teaching at the Marburg University and he wrote a book basing socialism on ethics, which became the banner of this group who called themselves the International Socialist Kampfbund. Nelson died rather young, I think he was fifty, or not yet fifty, and Willi Eichler took over the leadership of this group. They were not large, but extraordinarily devoted. Most of them did not marry, although some did. They lived together in small groups, between five and ten; a house was set up, and they put all of their earnings in the same pocket, used very little for their personal necessities, and devoted most of it to their socialist propaganda purposes. After von Papen had come into power, there was a great disorder in the labor movement. A large part of the younger generation of Germans felt that they were without choice. Suddenly there appeared a new daily paper, Der Funke, which for several weeks was distributed in the streets. It was printed on four pages and sold at a very low price. No publicity whatsoever, and one cry, unity, unity, unity over and over, between socialist, communists, and even Christian trade unions, against the danger of fascism. Extraordinarily well written in a German which was no longer used in newspapers, sounding like a cry, a cry of truth, and it made quite a sensation. However, it had no effect on the leadership, they were just morally dead, and then after a few months it ceased to appear. I then heard for the first time about the existence of the International Socialist Kampfbund. I was intrigued by it.

One day, in September or October 1939, just after the war broke out, I got a visit from a man who called himself Pierre Robert. His real name was René Bertholet from an old socialist family in Geneva. I knew his brother, I belonged to the same Socialist Party section later when I lived in Geneva. Pierre was a fascinating chap, he was oriented toward Germany, and he had remained in Germany after Hitler came into power. He published this same paper, Der Funke against Hitler. He was caught, was tried, got three years and was freed in '36. So in '39 he came to see me and said, after having conversed awhile, "Yes, well, I wonder whether you have not become too important for what I have in mind to ask you." So I reacted, "Well, now you have said too much and too little, what is it?" So he said, "Well I belong to the ISK" and then I became interested. "A number of our people have immigrated and we have set up our center in Paris. We have established contact with the Cinquième Bureau, because now that France and England are at war with Germany we feel that we are allied to France and England and we are offering them our services." So I asked him what those services were. "We offered to sabotage, in all neutral countries around Germany, any train or boat transporting to Germany commodities which can be used for war purposes. For which we want the Ve Bureau to give us false passports and ammunition, both." So I said, "Have you already set up such groups?" "Yes," he said, "and you would be surprised to hear who was leading them. In Denmark we have a cell which is helped by nobody less than a prominent leader of the Danish Trade Union Confederation, Jensen. In Holland we have a cell which is headed very actively by Edo Fimmen, who was the secretary-general of the International Transport Workers, a very powerful figure although politically somewhat marginal. In Luxemburg we have two people," (one of whom later became Minister of Labor after the war). "In Switzerland, the President of the Party, Dr. Hans Oprecht, and he's doing the job personally." And they had somebody whose name I forgot in Yugoslavia. "But we have nobody in Belgium, and I was thinking about you, but with your responsibilities for all these important problems of adjusting wages to prices or blocking prices, I am thinking that you have already become too important to be involved in this." I said, "the job consists of what?" "The job consists of placing bombs in trains which you would know are loaded with materiel

which can and will be used for war purposes. Or with
a magnet, sticking them under the waterline of the
boat. All these bombs have clockwork, so you can
adjust when the explosion takes place up to 72
hours." I was a little scared. I said, "I can't
reply right away, give me 24 hours to reflect." And
I had decided that I would put the question to
Bondas, ask him his opinion, and if he said go ahead,
I would go ahead. I didn't sleep that night. I had
just received as a present from the Metalworkers
Federation a very big steel desk with four sets of
drawers. I thought I could use those to put the
bombs in. I first spoke to Bondas and Bondas
listened to my story and said: "All depends on how
you feel. If you have the courage to do it, go
ahead." When Pierre Robert came back to get my
answer I said, "What do I do?" And he explained:
"In a few days or a few weeks a man will present
himself under the name of Otto," -- it was his real
name, Otto Pfister, a Bavarian woodworker, a huge
fellow. For days and weeks I didn't hear anything,
until one day while I was very busy writing a paper a
secretary came in and said, "Citoyen Rens, il y a un
citoyen Otto qui veut vous voir." ("Citizen Rens,
there is a citizen Otto who wants to see you." In
the Belgian socialist movement, the term "citizen" is
the official form of address.) And in came Otto,
tall, a head taller than I, with two apparently heavy
valises. He said, "I'm Otto, I want to explain,"
(without any introduction) "how it works." These
bombs looked very nice, you would be very pleased to
have them on your chimney. They were in three
pieces, one was the load, the middle piece was the
clockwork, and the third piece was the detonator. As
long as the three pieces were separate from each
other, nothing could happen, but if you put the three
pieces together, and wound up the clock and put the
detonator on a certain hour it becomes dangerous. I
asked him what was the explosion capacity. He said
they could "blow up this whole district into the
air." So I put these things in my drawers. After
this visit I set up a cell in Liège and to it
belonged among others two Germans, a father and son,
who lived in Verviers. I went every ten days with
two valises full of bombs and travelled first class.
And once sitting opposite me was the president of
Cockerill, the biggest factory producing arms. And I
had these two little valises sitting there and talked
with him about serious social matters concerning
Belgium.

After a while I decided to take Louis Major into
it so we had somebody who knew the port of Antwerp.
The last time we were together on this job, we left
Saint-Vith on the German border (it was one of the

former German territories that was incorporated after the First World War) between 7 and 8 o'clock in the evening, and there was a whole trainload filled with tires, big tires for aircraft made by Englebert, a Belgian tire manufacturer. We had put the timer on for a long time, 58 hours. Before we left at 8 o'clock we asked one of our companions, a railroad worker, what was the situation on the other side. He laughed and said, "The last days, listening to the rumor which came across the border we thought that this was the big day. But today everything has been quiet." Major and I arrived at Antwerp at 11 o'clock in the evening on the direct train from Liege to Antwerp and at 6 o'clock the next morning Louis Major was again at my home, because at 5 o'clock the invasion had started. So you ask me what I did. In a certain way this was the resistance before the occupation and against the rule of neutrality. We did it with conviction. I came to America in September 1941 to attend the first wartime International Labor Conference in New York. You know, traveling in that time by clipper was something; on the arrival of the clipper, the names of passengers were in the paper and Spaak and I stayed in the St. Regis. I had hardly opened my baggage when there was a ring. "Yes?" "Mr. Rens" Otto, here," "Otto who?" "Otto Pfister." I nearly collapsed! "Where are you?" "Right here in New York." So he and his wife came and joined me, and he told his whole story of his arrest and escape. He was a very great man. He volunteered in the American army and in 1945 was fighting in Germany where he jumped as a parachutist behind the lines. And I saw him the last time just after the war was over and he was about to take an army boat in Antwerp back to the States. I heard from people in the Socialist Kampfbund that he had gotten a job at Douglas Aircraft in Santa Monica.

Amazing chap. They were good people. Pierre Robert organized a very big technical assistance program, Pindorama, in northern Brazil that was financed by the German trade unions and he died there. They were good socialists. After the war Willi Eichler became one of the authors of the Bad Godesberg Program.

Q: What did you do when the Germans invaded? Was the trade union movement prepared?

A: Well, yes, we had prepared. We had forseen that the war would affect us, and then of course, one always sees a war more or less in terms of the last war, so we thought that there would always be at least a small part of Belgium which would remain unoccupied and that probably the government would go there. And the trade union movement, in full agreement with the Socialist Party, decided that as soon as the government would transfer its seat, we would transfer ours to the same place. We thought the government would go to Ostende. And we went to Ostende, but the government had already booked all the hotels and all pensions. We could not find a single house. So we decided to go to Koksijde which is not far from Ostende and close to the French border and rented a big villa there. Here we come back to De Man. Spontaneously on the morning of the 10th of May, the main leaders of the trade union federations, all of them, went to the CGT. De Man came for a short while, and we discussed quite openly that we could go to Koksijde and stay there. De Man was there and he didn't open his mouth. After the Germans had occupied the whole of Belgium and after the capitulation of the Belgian army, De Man made a violent attack on the trade union leaders who he accused of having deserted their posts with the money of their members. It was one of the features which showed his character in a negative way. If he had to criticize that decision then he should have done it when we were discussing it there.

So we went to Koksijde. I met two ministers by accident on the street, Balthazar and Soudan. They said, "Well, the Germans are advancing so rapidly that in a few days they will take Brussels." And then I was terrorized by the idea that the Germans would enter into our office and find all those bombs. So, I said to my wife -- she was out of her mind -- I said, "I have to go to Brussels, you just wait here," and she nearly went mad, fearing that I might be caught. I told my brother what was at stake. He had a car, and so we drove to Brussels against the stream of refugees. So in I came, unexpectedly, on a Tuesday; it was a day set aside for a meeting of the bureau, and all the staff, but not one member of the bureau was there. I said, "This is what we have to do. My drawers are filled with bombs, we have to get them away from here because if the Germans find them it will be held against the labor movement." One of the staff was the concierge of the union of employés (white-collar workers) and he said, "In the courtyard of our union there is a little hole," (he called it in Flemish a sterput) "and you can throw these bombs in there, and they will fall into the waters of the Senne," (a little river that was vaulted over). We made two trips, and we brought the whole load into the hole in the courtyard of the white collar workers union. You can imagine what the Germans would have thought if they had found the stuff. After that, my brother and I returned to Koksijde.

From Koksijde we went to Nantes, to the Bourse du Travail, where Bondas knew the secretary. This was the single darkest period of my life, those weeks following the invasion. The capitulation of France was unbelievable to us. We convoked a meeting of the bureau of the CGTB in Toulouse on the 12th of August. We decided three things. First, we would suspend the CGTB for the duration of the hostilities. Second, each of the secretaries of the confederation or the big federations would get one year's salary, and then be on his own. Third, everyone was free to do what he felt he had to do, remain in France, return to Belgium or go to England. I went to England where I found all the leaders of the Transport Workers Union and was joined afterwards by quite a number of trade unionists. In England I was asked to give a series of talks on Belgium on the BBC, one a week in French, one in Flemish.

One of those talks was addressed straight to De Man. I started by telling him how disappointed I was by his behavior. I told De Man: "I actually think you are a fourfold traitor. A traitor to your country, our country, by trying to work together with those who invaded and occupied our territory; a traitor to our party which stands for everything which is the opposite of what Hitler stands for; a traitor to your own ideas because I think you acted contrary to what you have advocated in the credo of your book on the Psychology of Socialism; and a traitor to all those, including me, who had such a great confidence in you." And I was told that he had heard of it, and took it very much to heart.

Q: To what extent do you think that Marxism still has any value for the Socialist movement?

A: I would say that indirectly and in a general way, the influence is still very great. What do I mean by indirectly? Or in a general way? There are people in the labor movement and outside the labor movement who are convinced that economic factors are determinant for social life in general. But indirectly, because of those who advance those views, very few of them have read Marx. So the direct influence of Marx, I would say, is rather small, even among the most prominent leaders of the labor movement. I think their reading goes very little beyond the Communist Manifesto.

Q: Were you strongly influenced by Marx at any time in your intellectual development?

A: Oh, yes, but strangely enough, or not strangely enough, I think it was much more by what he wrote in his youth. Three years ago I published an article on what Hendrik De Man had written in 1932 on a manuscript of Marx which had been discovered only in 1930-31 called "Philosophy and Economy."

Q: What are the intellectual influences which have been important for you other than Marx?

A: Jaurès in the first instance and the French Socialist Proudhon; Elisée Reclus; Bakunin; Kropotkin. In later years, the English socialists, Cripps, before he became a member of Parliament, the Fabian Society, Lansbury.

Q: For the Belgian socialist movement in general?

A: Marx to some extent, but mostly Marx through Vandervelde. I think the intellectual influence of Vandervelde on the leadership of the party was tremendous, second to none.

Q: Would you say that after World War II there is a major difference in the intellectual orientation of the socialist movement? Is there a decline in the influence of Marxism? Is there a decline in the influence of philosophy in general, and more of a pragmatic attitude?

A: I think more like that. For example, one fresh or new note was brought into the movement by André Renard invoking Sorel, but that was very superficial and I think passing.

Q: During the period of the war, you were working directly for the Belgian government in exile. And what were your specific functions, what was the title of your post?

A: Well, my title was Counselor of the Government and, for quite a while, I was the only one. I had a specific duty: to prepare solutions for the post-war problems. So I set up a committee which became very large.

For instance, we prepared in great detail (and it was applied in almost the same form) the statute for the Conseil d'Etat, which didn't exist before the war. And then we devoted a very large part of our attention in trying to find out the needs of the Belgian population in cereals, oils, meat and so on. We used the revenue of mineral sales from the Congo to purchase wheat.

In 1943, <u>Pierlot</u> asked me to become a member of the government. I didn't accept. I didn't think that I could make -- and I was probably wrong -- a contribution. I said that I had no mandate and my entry into government would not reinforce it. That could only be brought about by having a resistance figure from the left come from occupied Belgium. Among a number of political figures I had recommended, Pierlot picked Bondas and I wrote to Bondas who became a member of government.

Q: One thing which distinguished Belgium from other countries like France is that in the course of the war, a general consensus was reached on a whole set of problems. And it helped to bring about the transformation of Belgium from a liberal society to a welfare society.

A: That's true and it was due to a handful of people who met during the whole of the war coming from different parties and developing this spirit in a small circle. They spread it out over the rest of the country.

Q: Would it be correct to say that the moments when socialism has perhaps played the most important role in Belgium were both during the First and Second World Wars, when socialist ideas penetrated into other groups, into other parties, and in each case you have a consensus which moves closer to a social democratic ideal?

A: I would not say socialist ideas, because that would be resented, but social concepts which had been advanced before by socialist parties, penetrating later other parties as well. In that respect you are right.

Q: How would you measure the accomplishments of the socialist movement in Belgium and in Europe?

A: The first major accomplishment is the right to vote shortly before the First World War. Then the forty hour week just after the First World War. And then the <u>commissions paritaires</u> in which the employers were forced to sit down and negotiate with their workers was a tremendous step forward. I had known the time when an employer came down the street and the workers up against the wall bowed; it was a different world, there was no communication between them. And then I would think that a great milestone was what we have already talked about, 1936 -- the general strike.

Q: What about the failures? Do you think there are some major failures?

A: I am reconciled with the present situation, but I myself think that the weakness was the incapacity of the trade union movement to maintain its unity. At the end of the First World War, the socialist trade unions had 750,000 members. The Christian Democrats had just about 150,000. On the eve of the last World War, the socialist unions had 600,000, they had lost and the Christians 300,000, they went up. At present the Christians have 1,200,000 - 1,300,000; I doubt the socialists have more than a million. In the subjective terms of the socialist trade unionists, that is evidence of failure. In objective terms one can say that all together you now have five times more members than before. Well, I don't think that. You know the workers don't always see clearly the progress which they have made. As I hinted before, one of the most difficult jobs in ending the strikes in 1936 was to persuade the workers that they had obtained a great victory. The labor movement has brought about a large number of improvements for the workers. It has failed though to convey to them a feeling of happiness. That I consider as our greatest failure.

Q: How do you feel about the division of the Socialist Party into Flemish and French-speaking parties?

A: I think it was a tragedy, but it just happened. You know, nationalism in my country, Flemish nationalism in particular, is like a worm working from inside. There are very small groups of Flemish nationalists that take a stand on different problems and which have a romantic hold on the minds of the young leaders of the Catholic Party and once they have adopted those positions, they stick to them when they become statesmen. And they in turn influence the Liberal and the Socialist Parties who could, in these matters, do no less than the Catholics. So from the moment when the Flemish Catholics decided to form a party of their own, the socialists and the liberals followed suit and broke away from their old party and set up a typical Flemish Socialist Party and a Flemish Liberal Party. It is through the parties that the Flemish peoples were influenced in a way which I consider very unfortunate.

Q: In 1944, you made the decision that you would not return to Belgium and that instead you would work in international organizations. What did you do from 1944 until your return to Belgium?

A: Well, the activities of an official in the International Labor Organization are manifold. I always had a militant conception of my role. To me, there was no fundamental difference between my role as trade union leader before the war and as an official of the International Labor Office, except difference of scenery. I always came out openly and actively in favor of what I considered was in equity due to the workers. I decided once to take open stands against the views of the shipowners, which made me not very popular in that group and not very popular with some governments. But I think I may say that I have contributed to some fundamental changes towards progress in social matters in different parts of the world, especially in the Far East and in South America.

Q: Do you think that socialism has accomplished its main goals in creating the welfare state?

A: Oh no, I don't think that socialism has accomplished its main goals. As I see socialism, it is an unending process of change towards bringing out into the open and into public life what is best in man. I really think socialism touches on ethical values.

Men carry within themselves the worst and the best. Take for instance a movement like Hitler, and now the Khomeini movement. They speculate on what is worst in the crowd: hatred toward foreigners, hatred towards certain groups of the population. I think socialism is essentially based on trying to build a society in which the best things that men carry in them, justice and a thirst for freedom, will prevail. And that is an attempt which has to be done all over again by each generation in the light of its own goals, which will change from one generation to another. Of course, as time passes by, society becomes more complicated, it is perhaps more difficult to see those goals as clearly as Vandervelde and Jaurès and Bebel could see them, and Marx. In their time, society (at least for the first three) was clearly based on oppression and exploitation. I don't say it has come to an end, but it has become less clear. The whole game of our economic institutions is much more complicated than a hundred years ago. But nevertheless, I think our generation has a task, and begins to see it, not necessarily in our country, but in our world. There is still a tremendous job to be done in order to restore a minimum of justice and well-being, when one knows what is going on in India and in South America. I said before that in a certain way I think I made the wrong choice in 1944 by not going back to Belgium. But I console myself with the fact that I have been able to see elsewhere in the world injustice, oppression, discrimination and exploitation against which I have fought, I think, as good a battle as an international official could have done. But this is not seen as a political goal of great immediacy by the European labor movement. Some of them see it. Among the labor leaders, I think the man who sees it clearly is Brandt.

The primary direction that socialism has to take is concern with development of the third world, that's a goal which has not been sufficiently treated. We have not yet learned to become world citizens.

Glossary of Names, Organizations and Terms in the Rens Interview

--<u>Edward Anseele</u> (1856-1938). The socialist boss of Ghent; a founder of the cooperative movement.

--<u>Michael Alexandrovich Bakunin</u> (1814-1876). Russian revolutionary anarchist, his dispute with Marx helped destroy the First International.

--<u>August Bebel</u> (1840-1913). Leader of the German Social Democratic Party.

--<u>Isabelle Blume</u> (1892-1975). Blume, a leader of the socialist women, came into conflict with the party over the Cold War and joined the Communists in the late 1940s.

--<u>Max Buset</u> (1896-1959). President of the Socialist Party from 1945-1959.

--<u>Conseil d'état</u>. The highest administrative jurisdiction of the State, consulted by the government on the legality of legislative proposals.

--<u>cinquième bureau</u>. The intelligence service of the French army.

--<u>Commission Syndicale</u> (Trade Union Commission). The original name for the federation of socialist trade unions indicating they operated under the auspices of the party.

--<u>compromis des belges</u>. An agreement in 1932 by which the administration of Flanders and Wallonia would be conducted exclusively in the dominant language.

--<u>Sir Stafford Cripps</u> (1889-1952). English Christian socialist, Chancellor of the Exchequer 1947-1951.

--<u>Louis de Brouckère</u> (1870-1951). One of the leading ideologists of the Belgian socialist movement and a close collaborator of Vandervelde. President of the Socialist International 1935-1939.

--<u>Achille Delattre</u> (1879-1964). A leader of the miners union, Delattre served as Minister of Social Affairs from 1935-1939 and was elected Vice-President of the party in 1939.

--Jules Destrée (1883-1936). The leading socialist man of letters of his time in Belgium, Destrée was also a spokesman for the Walloon movement.

--Edo Fimmen (1881-1942). A Dutch trade union leader, Fimmen played an important international role as secretary of the International Transport Workers Union.

--Bad Godesberg program. In 1959, the SPD adopted a new non-Marxist program at the Bad Godesberg conference.

--Camille Huysmans (1871-1968). A major Belgian socialist politician and Flemish leader, Huysmans served as mayor of Antwerp, Secretary of the Socialist International, President of the Belgian Chamber of Representatives, and Prime Minister 1946-1947.

--Paul Hymans (1865-1941). Liberal leader, Foreign Minister 1918-1920 and 1927-1931.

--Internationale Sozialistiche Kampfbund (ISK). An organization of German socialists which continued the fight against nazism after Hitler's coming to power, especially abroad. The leader of the group was Willi Eichler (1896-1971) who had been secretary of the philosopher Leonard Nelson (1882-1927) from 1924-1925. Eichler was inspired by Nelson's ideas about the relationship of socialism and ethics. After the war, Eichler was a member of the SPD's executive. For further information about the ISK, cf. Werner Roder, Die deutschen sozialistischen Exilgruppen in Gross Britannien 1940-1945, (Hanover, 1968).

--Paul-Emile Janson (1872-1944). Liberal leader, Prime Minister 1937-1938.

--Henri Jaspar (1870-1939). Catholic party leader, Prime Minister 1926-1931.

--Michael Kropotkin (1842-1921). Russian anarchist leader and author.

--Paul Krueger (1825-1904). President of the Transvaal Republic, Krueger was a prominent leader during the Boer War.

--George Lansbury (1859-1940). Christian socialist and pacifist, Lansbury was leader of the English Labour Party from 1931-1935.

--**Louis Major** (1902 -). Trade union leader, secretary-general of the socialist trade unions after 1952.

--**Karl Mannheim** (1893-1947). Sociologist; founder of the sociology of knowledge.

--**Pierre-Joseph Proudhon** (1809-1865). Influential French anarchist, Proudhon advocated the notions of mutualism and federalism.

--**Elisée Reclus** (1830-1905). A noted geographer, Reclus was an important anarchist thinker; he participated in the Commune of 1871.

--**André Renard** (1911-1962). A radical trade union leader, Renard was the leader of the general strike of 1960-1961. He then founded the Mouvement Populaire Wallon.

--**Henri Rolin** (1891-1973). A lawyer and socialist Senator, Rolin clashed with Spaak on two occasions. First, he was a strong opponent of establishing consular relations with Franco in 1938. Second, he fought the creation of the European Defense Community in the early 1950s.

--**Carlo Rosselli** (1899-1937). An active anti-fascist and intellectual, Rosselli was the main founder of Giustizia e Libertà, and formed an Italian detachment to fight on the Republican side in the Spanish Civil War. He was assassinated by members of the Cagoule, a terroristic French fascist organization.

--**SAP** (Sozialistiche Arbeiters Partei). A splinter party of the left of the SPD which wanted to form a united front including the communists against Hitler.

--**Victor Serge** (1890-1947). A Belgian anarchist who went to Russia to serve in the Communist International, Serge was imprisoned by Stalin and saved from probable death only by the protests of left-wing intellectuals in Western Europe. Serge lived for a time in Brussels in the late 1930s.

--**Paul Tillich** (1886-1965). A leading Protestant theologian and philosopher.

--**Emile Vandervelde** (1866-1938). The most important political leader and ideologist of the Belgian socialist movement in the first third of the 20th century, Vandervelde also served in many cabinets. He was Foreign Minister in the Poullet-Vandervelde ministry of 1925-1926. Vandervelde was a reformist and a Marxist.

--**Herman Vos** (1889-1952). Vos was an intellectual and leader of the Vlaamsche Front, an organization founded in 1919 which stressed the primacy of the language issue in Flanders. He later joined the Socialist Party, and served as a Senator and then as Minister after World War II.

--**Joseph Wauters** (1876-1929). Socialist leader and minister.

--**Paul Van Zeeland** (1893-1973). A well-known banker and Christian Democrat, Van Zeeland served as Prime Minister from 1935-1937.

3
Riccardo Lombardi
and Italian Socialism

> In my eyes, the Socialist party had only one
> man, Riccardo Lombardi, who could state the
> problems of modern Italy properly.[1]
>
> Ugo La Malfa

Riccardo Lombardi is one of the most respected
elder statesmen of the Italian left and indeed in
Italy today. He has made major contributions to the
intellectual life of his party by emphasizing
socialism's responsibility to provide a genuine
socio-economic alternative. Lombardi's primary
concern has been to elaborate a blueprint for a
worker-managed, democratic socialism. He conceives
of political alliances as means of bringing about the
step-by-step realization of a socialist society.

It has been said that Lombardi is more a
theoretician than a practical politician. Indeed,
Lombardi and his allies, despite considerable
influence, have never controlled the Socialist
Party. Yet was he less practical than Nenni?
Nenni's support of the Popular Front with the
communists after World War II and then for a
governmental alliance with christian democracy in the
1960s led to schisms within the PSI and the loss of
its autonomy and electorate. Craxi's political
activities did not significantly increase the
socialist vote in 1983. In the first post-war
elections in 1946, the PCI and PSI received
approximately the same number of votes. Today, the
communists receive almost three times as many votes
as the socialists and Italy is the only country in
Western Europe whose Communist Party is stronger than
its Socialist Party.

To understand the chronic weakness of Italian
socialism and the significance of Lombardi's role, it
is necessary to take a look at the history of the
Italian socialist movement. The Italian Socialist
Party was founded in 1892. The northern industrial
area provided fertile ground for socialism. In
addition, after 1870, many intellectuals who were
disenchanted with the results of unification found in

---

[1]   Quoted in Furio Columbo (editor), In Italy,
Post-War Political Life (New York, 1981), p. 145

socialism a logical continuation of the Mazzini-Garibaldi tradition of the <u>risorgimento</u>. The landless agricultural laborers of the Po Valley were attracted to the movement as well.

The curse of the movement from its inception to today was factionalism. Revolutionary and reformist socialists, themselves divided, fought each other, while a large part of the labor movement, suspicious of all politics, was anarcho-syndicalism. Bakunin had not spent many years proselytizing in Italy in vain. The reformists dominated the party from 1900-1912, partly because liberal leader and perennial Prime Minister Giovanni Giolitti cooperated with the socialists, trading social legislation for their critical support. Relations between Italian socialist and the liberals were similar to those between French socialists (at least the Jaurès wing) and the radicals. All shared a commitment to laicity.

The Libyan War of 1912, however, produced unexpectedly strong opposition among the socialists and the left wing of the party took power. One of its most boisterous members, Benito Mussolini, became editor of the party newspaper, <u>Avanti</u>! Widespread strikes and radical demonstrations took place. In the general introduction, we have already examined the impact of World War I and the rise of fascism.

Organized opposition was relatively weak within Italy and from abroad during the Mussolini era; most significant were the communists and a new movement, Giustizia e Libertà, created by Carlo Rosselli, which attempted a synthesis of socialism and liberalism. The socialists, finally reunified in 1930, preferred rapproachement with the Communists to close relations with Giustizia e Libertà. In 1934 a Pact of Unity of Action was signed between the socialists and communists, which was destined to continue in one form or other until 1956, with the exception of the period of the Nazi-Soviet Pact of 1939-1941. Socialist leader Pietro Nenni believed that the socialist-communist split had been the major cause for fascism's success; such a division was to be avoided at all costs. In practice, because of the organizational weakness and disunity of the socialists the party was never an equal partner in the alliance and the PCI became the dominant party of the left.

Mussolini fell in 1943, the Allies landed in the South and the Germans occupied the North. There, partisan activity developed on a large scale, dominated by the communists and the Action Party, the offspring of Giustizia e Libertà. The socialists as a party played a lesser role in the Resistance. Socialists and actionists took a strong stand against the continuation of the Italian monarchy which had

allied itself to fascism for two decades; the
communists, displaying their political suppleness,
agreed to drop the monarchy issue as long as the war
continued. Even then, Togliatti was thinking of a
potential historical compromise with the right.

During the fascist period, Riccardo Lombardi had
become an active opponent of fascism, first as a
member of the left wing of the Popolari Party and
then as a member of Giustizia e Libertà and the
Action Party. As a member of the Committee of
National Liberation in Milan (CLNAI) he was
intimately involved in the insurrection against the
Germans and was named Prefect of Milan at the
liberation.

After the liberation, the unpopular Bonomi
government was replaced by a ministry under Parri,
the leader of the Action Party, which lasted from 20
June 1945 until November 24. Politics was already
eroding the Resistance mystique and the Action Party
was really a general staff without electoral
following. Parri was replaced by De Gasperi and a
basically tripartite coaliton of communists,
socialist, and christian democrats. The elections of
2 June 1946 gave the three parties 18.9, 20.7, and
35.2 percent of the vote respectively; the actionists
received only 1.5 percent.

The results, however, were somewhat deceptive.
Many people who voted for the left in an anti-fascist
mood later voted for center parties. In particular,
the strength of the socialists proved ephermeral.
There was indeed a large potential socialist
constituency; never again, however, would the
socialists be able to garner the support of this 20
percent of the population. The socialist lacked the
organizational strength to compete with PCI and DC.
Equally important was renewed factionalism, a result
of Nenni's determination to maintain Unity of Action
with the communists despite the onset of the Cold
War. This resulted in the schism of 1947, when
Saragat and the social democrats established their
own party. The situation now paralleled 1922, with
social democrats, maximalists, and communists all
organized separately. During this entire period,
Riccardo Lombardi led the autonomista current in the
party against Nenni's frontismo.

Krushchev's revelations about Stalinism and the
suppression of the Hungarian Revolution in 1956
prompted Nenni to break the communist alliance and
contemplate working with the DC. The DC likewise
showed a new willingness to consider an opening to
the left, in particular once Vatican policy shifted
under John XXIII. The result was a socialist entry
into the government in 1963. Nenni held to his
rapprochement with the DC as tenaciously as he had

supported frontismo with the PCI; Lombardi wanted the party to keep its distance from the DC. Lombardi developed a theory of the socialist alternative and revolutionary reformism to make the PSI an instrument of long-term radical transformation of Italian society while maintaining its distance from the two larger political formations. The "opening to the left" was soon followed by reunification of the PSI and the social democrats in 1966, but this in turn led to the departure of the PSI's left wing. Reunification collapsed in 1967, leaving the socialist party with a score of 9.6 per cent in the elections of 1972. The socialists continued to play an important role in government formation, yet their organizational and electoral weakness prevented them from exerting much influence on policy. The PCI dominated the left; its eurocommunism attracted new adherents.

Lombardi supported a government of communists and socialists to bring about reforms along the lines of his socialist alternative. But this policy, never popular in the PSI, was not accepted by the PCI either. The "historic compromise" advocated by Berlinguer and the PCI in 1975 called for an understanding with the DC, not the PSI.

In 1976 Bettino Craxi replaced Francesco de Martino as Socialist Party secretary. Craxi hoped to encourage the growth of an autonomous PSI along the lines of other European socialist parties, like that of France. In 1978 Craxi began a polemic against the marxism-leninism of the PCI, which seemed also a criticism of marxism. His goal was to contest the supremacy of the communists on the left and to attempt to regain socialist strength in order to increase the party's influence in the government. To do so, he was willing to make political alliances in a highly pragmatic fashion. His primarily political perspective differs from Lombardi's emphasis on structural reform. Following Nenni's death on 31 December 1979, Lombardi was elected President of the PSI. After only three weeks he resigned as a result of conflict with Craxi.

Interview with Riccardo Lombardi

RICCARDO LOMBARDI:

   I am the son of an army officer. My father died
when I was three months old. I was educated by my
mother, a very religious Catholic, who educated me in
religion with much tenacity. I am an industrial
engineer; I studied at the Polytechnic Institue of
Milan and practiced the profession of engineer for
many years, at the same time as being politically
active from the age of 18 on. Because of my
religious upbringing, until 1921 I belonged to the
new Popolari Party. I was active in its left wing,
the so-called miglioliste wing, named after a deputy,
Guido Miglioli. I left the Popolari party because I
thought that it didn't take an active enough role in
the struggle against the fascists, who in those years
had begun their terrorist activities. During my time
at the Polytechnic Institute and after finishing my
studies, I always took part in the anti-fascist
struggle without joining any political group, but
maintained relations with almost all the anti-fascist
movements. The main focus of my activity was the
underground press.
   In one of the public demonstrations against the
fascists in 1930, I was arrested, not by the police
but by the fascists. I was badly beaten. I lost one
and a half lungs, which very much limited my activity
all my life. According to the doctors, I should have
died at 40; I am now 80. I just made it, caught as I
was between two fires, the fascists and the official
police. The fascists accused the official police of
weakness for not having succeeded in arresting me.
The official police, that of Mussolini, the OVRA,
tried to downplay the matter and it's due to that
conflict that I survived. The vice-director of the
OVRA, Petrillo, told me frankly: "You are very lucky
because we tried everything to liquidate you, but
those imbecile fascists" (these are his words,
textually) "botched up the job." After that I
continued my activity and, after 1939, was engaged
even more intensively in the struggle. Then in 1943,
Badoglio's coup d'état took place.

   Q: At that time, what were the means of action
employed by you and your associates?

135

A: Well, I was always determined not to leave
around any document as evidence of my clandestine
action. In the police archives, a note was found --
it has been attributed to Mussolini -- which says
that one must beware of Lombardi, because he is very
cunning. And I must admit that I was. I exercised a
profession, that of engineer, and consequently no one
could say anything. I had a job, and at a given
moment, I went to work for a German firm that
manufactured turbines and chemical products; thus I
had a double cover. Despite that, I don't know how I
succeeded in getting by. Aside from two arrests, I
was left alone despite being very active. In those
years, I maintained relations not only with the
socialists but with the communists who disposed of an
underground apparatus in Italy. I was very close to
the Communist Party during the years 1926-1931,
without ever belonging to it. I worked so much with
them that I became their homme de confiance to
reestablish the links between the communist center in
Paris and the Italian communists when the leaders
they had sent to Paris fell. My relations with the
communists were interrupted in 1930, after the change
in the party line. The persons in whom I had the
most confidence were expelled. The Communist Party
assumed a very sectarian position. Things couldn't
continue as before; I maintained good personal but
not political relations with them. So I joined the
new movement, Giustizia e Liberta, in which I had
also been involved even before its official
constitution. In 1926, when the exceptional
legislation was implemented banning political parties
and movements, I had collaborated with Ernesto Rossi
and Riccardo Bauer to organize the underground
emigration of political figures under persecution.

Q: During the 1930s, did you have much contact
with the Italian anti-fascists in France?

A: During the fascist period, when I went
abroad, I did it in a secret fashion. Thus, I had
very limited contacts. I had contacts, for example,
with the Italians like Turati, Modigliani, etc., with
communists in France and Switzerland, with Tasca
before his expulsion. In 1942 I was one of the
founders of the Action Party. The Action Party
resulted from the fusion of two groups. One included
many socialists from Giustizia e Liberta, the other
was more bourgeois-democratic and was based on
intellectuals, former democrats, republicans, etc. I
was involved in the first newspaper of the Action
Party, Italia Libra. Later I was director of the
underground magazine of the party, Quaderni de
Giustizia e Libertà. Thus, in July 1943, at the time

of Badoglio's coup d'état, I was the representative of the Action Party at the meeting of the anti-fascist parties. Naturally, this event had been prepared for numerous years; in 1943 we had a meeting in which I participated along with <u>Gronchi</u>, who represented the Christian Democratic Party. This party was not yet officially constituted, but the process was under way. There was a communist representative, <u>Professor Marchesi</u>, two socialist representatives, <u>Basso</u> and <u>Veratti</u>, and a liberal, I think it was <u>Casati</u>. After that first meeting which took place at a publishing house in Milan, Principato, there were many others to organize a common struggle at a time when it was thought that a crisis in the regime was near. And that was very opportune because when the <u>coup d'état</u> occurred, we were prepared. That very day, we held a first meeting in the course of which we issued an appeal to the nation to organize the struggle against fascism and denounced Badoglio's <u>coup d'état</u> as a camouflage prepared by the right to create a fascism without Mussolini. And it was very important to have obtained this platform and to unite behind it the parties favorable to making certain concession to the monarchy, including the communists, who were very determined to maintain collaboration with the monarchists, so as not to prejudice the future.

In 1943, at the armistice, I was one of the representatives of the Action Party in the Committee of Liberation of Northern Italy. You know that a Committee of National Liberation was formed in Rome, but naturally, foreseeing the division of Italy, we held a meeting in Florence to define our respective tasks. We foresaw that the allied armies would arrive at the Po line. As to that part of Italy occupied by the Allies, there was no problem; the Allies would take care of it, even if they were slow in arriving at the front. But in the North, we apportioned the tasks: press, production of underground documents, arms, etc., in such fashion that we were almost as well prepared as the communists. It was not an act of Providence if the Action Party was, after the communists, the best prepared for the underground struggle.

Q: Why were the Italian socialists not as successful in organizing the resistance as the communists?

A: In general, the socialists suffered a systematic extermination when fascism triumphed. The socialists were in the majority on the left, the communists in the minority and naturally almost all the mayors of major cities, almost all the leaders of the trade-union organizations were socialist and better known. Then the emigration of socialists amputated the party of middle-level leaders and of major leaders like Turati, Treves, etc. and that was very damaging to the socialists, who never succeeded in constituting an underground network in Italy equal to that formed by the communists. They tried with Morandi, who was brought back to Italy but who almost immediately was captured and imprisoned and liberated only after the coup d'état of Badoglio. Many have criticized the Socialist Party for passivity, but that's not true. The reason was the extermination, not always physical, of the socialist leadership.

So at the moment of the armistice, 9 September, 1943, all the anti-fascist parties met, and proclaimed our message that the armed struggle was to begin. Nothing was ready from the logistical point of view, but much was prepared politically. We had already chosen the men who were to become active in that task. As for the Action Party, we had an important person, Sr. Parri who almost naturally became the recognized leader of the armed struggle. But we had a lot to do because many cultivated what was called attentismo; many said that we should collaborate with the fascists against the Germans, or with the Germans against the fascists so as to divide them. Their pretext was: "How can we engage in armed struggle without unifying the fascists?" And I still remember a conversation with Parri the first day after the armistice in which we were discussing the question of armed struggle. I informed him of the opinions which were circulating. Parri said to me: "Listen, in that case, let's settle the matter. We are discussing whether or not to engage in armed struggle. Let's begin the armed struggle and the question will be resolved. Let's start something." "But we don't have any military organization." "There is no need to wait for a perfect military organization, let's begin with coups de main." So we began with one of the first coups de main which I pulled off with a bunch of comrades. We disarmed two German patrols during the night, taking advantage of the fog which in the month of November in Milan was providential. During the entire autumn and winter of 1943 we had a thick fog. One night I myself got completely lost.

Naturally, life during this period was full of dangers. But I must admit that I am very lucky. In Milan, the secretary of the Fascist Party, Sr. Resega, was executed by a group of partisans. In reprisal, five partisans were executed, including one of the leaders of the Action Party. The day of the funeral of this secretary of the Fascist Party, my wife and I were in an underground printing plant where *Italia Libra* was published. We left at about seven, our clothing stuffed with newspapers which had to be brought to the distribution point and we passed by the Piazza del Duomo, the principal square of Milan. We didn't know that the funeral procession of Resega, accompanied by the fascists, was to pass by the Piazza del Duomo. When the procession reached the Piazza, someone fired shots at the crowd from the roof of a building. The fascists fled, leaving the body, but afterwards returned to the Piazza at the very moment I was passing through with my wife. The Piazza was sealed off by the militia, the army, and the carabiniers. We were caught in the bottleneck. I never wanted to tell this to the publishers who asked me to write the story of my life, because it is unbelievable. But the fact is that the morning of the very day of the funeral, the newspaper of Farinacci, *Regima Fascista*, came out with the following on the front page: "Here are those guilty for the assassination of Resega: Giorgio Amendola and Riccardo Lombardi." You see, the police had seized the document signed by all of us the day of the armistice in which we said that the fascists had to be exterminated. Thus my name was on page one of the paper. If I had been arrested, I would have been shot on the spot. So my wife and I tried to escape. At the corner of the Via Torino, what does my wife do? She arranges the papers on her chest in such a way that she seems pregnant and when we arrive in front of the carabiniers, she makes believe she is fainting, saying, "I am pregnant." So the carabiners said "Pass through!" When you ask how I survived I had a series of strokes of luck.

I ought to tell you, not my story but the story of my wife, Eva Viatto, who was a former communist, had been in prison, etc. In many equally dangerous circumstances, she saved my life with her incredible presence of mind, her extraordinary initiative. I could write a novel based on her story.

Well, we get to the end of the war. Perhaps you know that there was a meeting with Mussolini; I participated as a representative, not of the Committee of Liberation, but of the Insurrectional Committee. The Committee of Liberation had accepted the proposal of Cardinal Schuster, the Bishop of Milan. He had proposed a meeting between the Committee of Liberation and Mussolini, because the Cardinal suffered from some illusions. He believed that we could let the fascists leave without fighting. It was the 25th of April. The Committee of Liberation had agreed to the meeting, but with very precise instructions. All compromise was to be avoided. We were to tell Mussolini that we accepted the terms of the Allies; Mussolini had to give himself up without conditions. But we had constituted an Insurrectional Committee to insure that the end would not be peaceful. We attached an extreme importance to the fact that Milan would behave in a way different from Rome. The Allies were to arrive with acclamations, of course, but we wanted to liberate the city by fighting with the fascists. To this end, we created the Insurrectional Committee in which the christian democrats and liberals did not participate. Only the left parties participated, socialists, communists, and Action Party. It was an informal committee. But when the Committee of Liberation accepted the meeting with Mussolini, this committee delegated me to be present to guarantee good results. I participated in this meeting in which Mussolini, at a certain moment, understood that there was nothing more to be gained and asked for half an hour to consider his decision. In reality, he went to the prefecture where he was living and took flight. Then, after waiting almost an hour, we decided that the game was up and gave orders for an insurrection in Milan. I was named that very night Prefect of Milan and took possession of the prefecture. My comrade Antonio Greppi of the Socialist Party was named Mayor. All the organs of power were put in place without delay because we had already divided up the tasks and responsibilities. But what is most important is that we had prepared for the provisioning of Milan. During the last months of the resistance and German occupation, we had constituted groups of technicians in association with the other parties. They had assessed the possibilities of furnishing rice, wheat, and even industrial products (rubber, gas, fuel, etc.). Our plan was the following: the very day the fascists were evicted from Milan, bread was to be distributed to the population. No one was to find conditions in the city abnormal, at least from the point of food-supply. That was a very good thing. I remember that during the night, before going to occupy the prefecture, I went to the Ice Palace where the supplies of fuel were hidden and said to the two gendarmes: "Shoot anyone who tries to get hold of these precious things for which you are responsible." Everything went well for me. Little by little, the situation returned to normal.

Fortunately, provisioning took place with a great deal of rigor. The Milanese suffered from hunger, but for the first time, rationing was honest. That takes strong action. When two government ministers arrived from Rome, I knew that they had gone to a black market restaurant to eat outside the norms. That very evening, I sequestered the restaurant. There were shortages because there was a tendency to put aside supplies for the local population and it was almost impossible to thwart that. For example, the Prefect of Novara telephoned me saying that he would give me rice if I gave him bicycle tires. But looking back at this period, in general, and in all modesty, I think we did the best that could be done.

In December, the fall of the Parri government led to a crisis. Parri was determined that I belong to the new government, something which I dreaded very much. I was sick the day he came to Milan and he saw my wife. I tried to escape. I said: "I accept, but if I join the government, the Prefect of Milan will have to be changed." And the governmental crisis had occurred above all over that question: the liberals and christian democrats no longer wanted political prefects. So I went to the newly appointed Prime Minister, <u>De Gasperi</u>: he had much esteem for me, possibly because as an engineer, I was good at figures, whereas he trembled before them, and said: "The Prefect of Milan must not be a civil servant." For the civil servant prefects were necessarily fascists. "But, that's impossible," replied De Gasperi. We nevertheless succeeded in having the Prefect of Milan who was to replace me chosen following the advice of the Committee of Liberation. Thus I participated in the government as Minister of Transport. Parri wanted me to participate above all to have some influence on planning the forthcoming Constituent Assembly, because the government's principal task was to write a draft of the new constitution. He wanted someone he trusted to deal with political questions. I remained in the government until the election of the Constituent Assembly and after that I did not want to accept any political position in the government.

Q: Did you expect that the Action Party would maintain its political importance after the war?

A: No, the Action Party began its crisis before the Constituent Assembly. In January 1946 it held a congress. The socialist and liberal wings of the party confronted each other and a schism resulted. Parri left along with many others, especially those from the democratic-republican wing. What remained was the Giustizia e Libertà group. We took part in the elections. What interested us most was the referendum on the abolition of the monarchy. We didn't think we would elect a single deputy. On the contrary, we had seven. In Milan, for example, I didn't present a list although it was a city where I had a certain popularity. I didn't present a list because Parri was running. We preferred to sacrifice one or two seats rather than to run against Parri.

Those were the practices of the Action Party, a little elitist, a little aristocratic. But we held to them. For example, at the moment of the liberation of Milan, there was a swarm of people who thronged to the headquarters of the political parties wanting to join. We in the Action Party refused to allow automatic registration. Men over 25 had to prove that they had not been fascists. Obviously we didn't gain a lot of members. We didn't envisage a mass party but a party of intellectuals, naturally a minority.

I joined the Socialist Party in 1947, because we didn't think that the Action Party could survive, above all for a political reason, not simply because of its numerical weakness. The question was the following: could the coalition of the Allies survive after the war? After the Fulton speech, we were convinced that the Action Party had to be disbanded. The last congress of the Action Party took place in Rome at the Valle Theatre in July 1947. We invited all the parties to participate, not simply to send their greetings, but to participate in the discussion with full equality with the members: there was Saragat, Lelio Basso, Silone, Secchia who discussed the future of the Action Party. This problem interested all democrats. After the discussion, we joined the Socialist Party, making at the same time a very clear democratic and anti-totalitarian declaration. We demanded no posts, no positions in the party leadership. We didn't want to have any privileges.

Q: In 1947 when you entered the Socialist Party, what was your ideological position?

A: As I had the occasion to tell you, I was of Catholic origin. Afterwards I had a background which curiously was both democratic and Marxist. I studied a lot. I believe I belong to that small category of people on the left who studied Marx. If one discusses the superiority of Marx, the question of the pre-marxists, what Marx calls the utopian socialists must be raised. For a long time, the Catholics, the Christians, attempted to substitute Proudhon for Marx. But Proudhon was merely a pre-capitalist socialist. The analysis of capitalism was done by Marx. The capitalist society of the time of Proudhon was an artisanal and not an industrial capitalist society. Even at the time of Marx, industrial society had begun to develop in England and nowhere else. I was very seduced by Marx without becoming a dogmatic Marxist. I was very seduced by his analysis; I still am. When someone asks me: "Are you Marxist?" I reply, "I don't feel the need to be." I answer in the same way Che Guevara replied to the same question. When someone asked Che Guevara if he was Marxist, he answered that he didnt's feel the need, because today one is Marxist in the same way one is Galilean or Newtonian. Galileo and Newton are necessary landmarks despite the fact that one can no longer calculate according to their models but must do so according to those of Bohr, Einstein, etc. Likewise, Marx is a necessary landmark although his rules can no longer be applied to a society which has profoundly changed.

In Italy, study of Marxism began with Morandi and especially with Basso. It must be said that one of the real weaknesses of the Socialist Party has been and still is its lack of ideological formation. It is necessary to know one's ancestors, one's history. If we are socialists, it is because we are anti-capitalist. What does it mean today to say anti-capitalist? One does not learn the meaning of that even when one understands the texts of those who elaborated the critique of capitalism. In Italy, although Marxist studies were cultivated for some time even before fascism, the real knowledge of Marx was very sketchy. The greatest numbers of socialist and communist leaders before the schism had read only the last works of Engels which were simplifications of marxist theory, like Anti-Duhring. As might be expected, it was a Marxism more positivist than dialectic. Moreover many of Marx's fundamental works were not known in Italy until 1955; the Grundrisse appeared in 1954; the philosophical manuscripts of 1844 were published in 1932 and known in Italy in 1955. One can assert that there is nothing in common between the Marx of Capital and the Marx of the 1844 manuscripts. In my opinion, that is not true. But the polemic, the discussion of these questions could not take place until the intellectual world had at its disposition the works in question. I fear that criticism of Marx will be transformed everywhere into an anti-Marxist polemic. Sometimes I choose to open Marx as a study in perfectionment. There is such a power of analysis, even in his errors.

Q: After the Second World War, Nenni and Morandi followed the policy of frontisma with the Communist Party. What was your attitude towards....

A: I was opposed to that political line, even at the end of the electoral campaign leading to the defeat of 1948. I was a signatory of the motion which led to the Congress of Genoa, a congress which gave us autonomists a victory against the coalition of Nenni, Basso, and Morandi who not only refused to accept our position but refused to participate in running the party. And so we were obliged to take the direction. In fact, we were the minority because we represented only 33%. And we governed with the rest of the party in opposition because no one wanted to assume the task. But we were forced to. It was a situation of weakness. We lased a year, until 1949. We succeeded in dissolving the Popular Front, dissolving the alliance and preparing the way for an autonomist policy. The policy Nenni began in 1953 -- Nenni never admitted it -- wouldn't have been possible if this preliminary experiment had not taken place.

Q: What happened in the Italian Socialist Party was very different from what happened to socialist parties in other countries of Western Europe. Italy is the only country where a socialist party at the end of the 1940s made an alliance with the communists. How do you explain that?

A: There are many explanations. The most important is the anti-fascist struggle. In the battle against fascism, the communists and socialists were often separated, at certain times, for example, by the theory of social-fascism. In Italy this theory was never popular. Still, even in the worst moments when the official position of the international communist parties was that of branding the socialists as social-fascists, Italian communists and socialists always collaborated at the base in clandestine activity. There was above all that solidarity in the resistance. Today, despite the animosity of our politics between, for example, christian democrats and liberals, there is still an essential bond which imposes respect and sets limits to our political battle. The reference to the resistance isn't completely rhetorical in Italy, as long as my generation survives. After that, I don't know. That is one of the causes for the socialist-communist collaboration. After that, there is the fact that the communists, because of their activism in Italy during fascism and because of the absence of the socialists, succeeded in taking over socialist-reformist constituencies.

After the war, the Socialist Party thought it would be able to maintain a reformist clientele, for example, in the industrial centers, in the agricultural areas, in the cooperatives. In fact, the communists seized all that and the Socialist Party found itself largely deprived of social bases. I remember clearly that in 1950 when I was living in Milan, there was a big strike of peasants in the province of Pavia, which is near Milan and which is a historical region of social conflict. Things were different from today. Almost no one had a telephone in his house. Some of us left by cars, some by bicycles, some by train for the strike. I remember the mayor of that little city, now communist, but formerly socialist, who explained to me that they were communists because, he said, "at the end of fascism we looked for a contact, we didn't find any and the communists said that there wasn't any difference between communism and socialism." That's perhaps a cavalier way to pose the problem but there is much truth in it. Moreover, the communists took care not to enunciate a different kind of ideological propaganda, at least on the level of practical action. A second reason for this alliance of socialists and communists is the following: there was a terrible persecution of workers, an insane persecution after 1948. For example, the American Ambassador, Mrs. Claire Booth-Luce proclaimed officially that whether or not the American army or American organizations ordered supplies from FIAT depended on whether the CGT (left-wing trade union) lost its majority there. This proclamation resulted in the reinforcement of the unity of communists and socialists.

I was a member of the commission established by the Italian Parliament in 1956 to study working conditions in different industries and I was able to take the pulse of this situation. The community of persecution creates many bonds. The bonds formed during the resistance and renewed by common persecution at the hands of management supported by the police and the magistrates are very strong. Imagine, if someone wanted to take part in a competitive examination to be an army officer, the carabiniers had a note card with the mentions "communist" or "socialist" and could prevent his entry if there were communists or socialists in his family. The fascists were admitted on equal terms with everyone else towards the end. In 1956, the Minister of War was a social democrat, Sr. Tramolini, an old friend of mine. I went to see him and said: "Listen, end those practices." After that I had the occasion to see one of those cards thanks to one of my friends in the carabiniers. There was still the mention "communist" or "socialist" but with the subdivision: "of socialist origin," or "social democratic origin." This mentality of persecution helped to tighten the links between socialists and communists.

Q: Did the personality of Nenni play an important role?

A: Yes, certainly, it played an important role. He didn't prevent a schism when the party decided to collaborate in the government. It was the first center-left experiment and we suffered a very grave secession because militants left the party and that was a great loss. And I always reproached Nenni for having done nothing to stop it. He was so convinced that this minority would have always blocked his policy of collaboration with christian democracy that he preferred to let it drop out. Nenni was so persuaded, he told me many, many times, that "the comrades on the left were ready to seceed from the party." It wasn't true, because the schism of 1963 was experienced by many comrades with anguish. It wouldn't have taken much effort to stop it. De Martino and I were engaged in negotiations to keep them in the party. They posed some conditions, for example: "If Lombardi did not hold a position in the government" -- I had no intention of participating in the government -- "if he assumed the direction of Avanti! so that the party maintained a separate identity from the government...." Maybe these were ruses, but there were nevertheless some people who were sincere. But, while these negotiations were being conducted, by De Martino and me and others, Nenni denounced the left to the control committee for indiscipline. Nenni bears a very heavy responsibility. But it must be said that once he began to envision a political project, he had to carry it out. That was part of his greatness. It was the same way for the political coup of the center-left. If we had been able to stop the schism of 1963, the fate of the center-left would have been different. After the nationalization of electricity, the christian democrats didn't want to pursue new reforms. At that time, we could have repaired the schism by provisionally withdrawing from the government because many dissidents were not against all collaboration with christian democracy; they accepted a provisional, limited, conditional collaboration.

Indeed, when I began to write articles in the newspaper Avanti! against the governmental alliance between the christian democrats and the socialists, an alliance which seemed to have become eternal, many comrades who had left the PSI were ready to return in case of an interruption, even temporary, of the collaboration. Things hapened like that. Even if one succeeds in defining responsibilities it gives little solace.

Q: To return for an instant to 1947, you entered the Socialist Party just at the time when Saragat and the social democrats left. Could that rupture too have been stopped or was it inevitable?

A: No, the rupture, in any case, was desired by both Saragat and Basso. The latter proclaimed officially that his intention was to eliminate the Saragat reformists from the party. The reason was that he wanted to create an ideological party. That was the obsession of Basso, which was in contradiction to his operational pragmatism, a pragmatism totally different from the fundamentalist rigor of his ideology. Nenni didn't expect a break. It's curious that a man like Nenni who had such intuition was convinced to the last minute that Saragat would remain in the party. I remember, several days before the congress which marked the schism -- I was still in the Action Party -- I paid a visit to the Ministry of Foreign Affairs, still in the Chigi Palace. Nenni said: "Don't believe that there will be a schism." The Saragat reformists and the Iniziativa Socialists were both eliminated from the party. This latter faction wanted to outflank the communists on the left. It reproached them for being moderate. The schism of the Palazza Barberini was made by these two factions.

Q: There were two constants in your thought, the ideas of the "socialist alternative," and "revolutionary reformism." Could you explain the meaning of these terms?

A: The two themes are tied together. What does revolutionary reformism signify? After the experiments of Marxism, so called Marxism since the October Revolution etc. to install socialist societies, I am persuaded that the path to follow in the advanced countries, in the countries which have accomplished their industrial revolutions, is the path of reformism. But I invented the distinction between these two words. It is not simply a question of a purely verbal distinction. The politics of reformism is one thing, reform (la politique réformatrice) is another. Reformism in the historical sense of the term following Bernstein, etc. signifies the acceptance of the capitalist system. It may involve reforms within the system in order to eliminate its evils, its major injustices, but leaves intact the framework. The socialist and social democratic parties which have followed that reformist direction have introduced great reforms, have improved the situation of the working class and the lower classes, have reformed society, rendering it less injust, more equitable, etc. The political line of leaving to the capitalists the major responsibility for production and limiting the action of reform to distribution has been followed especially in Sweden where the most interesting experiment has been made. Capitalists have been allowed to pursue their profits. They have been permitted to take initiatives with the least possible intervention on the part of society, while at the same time, the State has intervened energetically on questions of distribution. At a given moment, this situation ran up against what has been baptised today the fiscal crisis. The profits which were to be redistributed disappeared and taxation began to absorb almost the totality of revenue. La politique réformatrice signifies on the contrary an intervention of society and of the State, which is not limited only to redistribution of profit, but involves also the area of production, including a non-statist planification utilizing forms of self-management, democratic forms which prevent the soviet degeneration. Nevertheless the State takes charge of the program, no longer leaving it to the pleasure of the entrepreneurs. That is my point of view, which is not only mine and which contributed to that principle of "revolutionary reformism." There are many socialists in Italy and elsewhere who arrived at the same conclusions. What is necessary in my opinion is a peaceful series of reforms which are not limited to redistribution, but extend to planification, utilization of resources, to the choice of what is to be produced, how to produce it and for whom. That does not prevent (on the contrary!) a policy of energy and territory, or a policy with regard to the Third World. This then is the task of a socialist government which, by means of a chain of reforms, succeeds little by little in transforming the capitalist system into a self-managed socialist system.

By what means can we arrive at that transformation? Homogeneous majorities need to be constituted. That refers above all to the Italian situation, because our electoral system makes very difficult a clear-cut opposition between a conservative and a progressive party. We are almost forced to form coalition governments. There is another solution, that of creating a homogeneous government of the left. There are many voters who are not regimented in parties, who are active even in conservative parties but who have their hearts on the left. Consequently, it is necessary to promote a left-wing political line by eliminating as far as possible the differences which exist among the parties of the left (differences which often come from historical disagreements) in order to establish a platform of the left specifically addressing this program of revolutionary reformism. That is the liaison which exists between revolutionary reformism and the socialist alternative.

Naturally, this task could not be proposed at a time when the Italian Communist Party, which is an important element of the left, was tightly linked to the Soviet Union and acted like a black sheep of the revolutionary forces. But that is no longer the case. It must be recognized that much progress has been made. Without making concessions, we should encourage the tendencies to reform within the Communist Party and not isolate them. The Communist Party's pretension that it is the providential historical representative of the working class and left-wing politics should be challenged. I must recognize that some successes have been registered, in France, Italy, and elsewhere in this regard and that the process of profound modification of communist mentality is a sine qua non for the change of communist policies. Maybe what is necessary is to give a push. In politics as in life, I think there is no last step, the last step doesn't exist. We must always push forward, always unsatisfied. I am never sated.

Q: So, since 1963 you have lost hope in the possibility of working with the advanced elements in the christian democrat Party, isn't that so? After the nationalization of electricity you decided that a center-left government was no longer capable of putting into effect the program on which it had been based.

A: Yes, I was very much involved in the politics of the center-left. I supported the alliance with Christian Democracy, in order to draw the Socialist Party out of the abyss in which it had been plunged by its errors, by its unequal alliance with a Communist Party which dominated it. Thus, in my judgment, the policy of alliance with the christian democrats was a step forward, provisional but important, for our political orientation. That was the reason for my alliance with Nenni when, together we sired the center-left orientation. But for me that alliance with christian democracy was supposed to be provisional, limiting to promoting certain priority reforms, to begin a process of multiplication which would have given currency to that series of reforms which is the essential trait of revolutionary reformism. For Nenni, a great man without doubt, but more skilled in political maneuvering than at substantive issues, this alliance was in reality a permanent alliance, whose goals were seen exclusively in terms of governmental policies.

The latter is important, but does not in my opinion
suffice for a socialist party. So, I supported the
first formation of a center-left government in
alliance with the christian democrats. I supported
it, but I refused to participate personally. Why?
Because I thought, and rightly, that this provisional
alliance was limited in time, could only accomplish
certain reforms and then would end. By its nature,
its voter base, traditions, history, and ideology,
christian democracy is a party with which one can
have agreements and provisional compromises in order
to accomplish certain initial reforms. But the
limits of a collaboration with christian democracy
are very quickly exceeded. And that's exactly what
happened, because after the first reforms on taxation
and the nationalization of electric energy and school
reform, we came to blows on the second part of the
program. At this stage, we encountered the explicit
stubborn opposition of christian democracy which
almost did not hesitate to threaten us with a coup
d'état. In July 1963, a few months after the
formation of the first government of the center-left,
certain milieux of christian democracy (invoking the
higher responsibilities of the President of the
Republic, Sr. Segni, a christian democrat) menaced us
with a coup d'état by the SIFAR (organization of
official military and political intelligence). This
program of a coup d'état was organized to threaten
the Socialist Party in case it insisted on the third
great projected reform, that of territory, housing
policy, urbanization, etc. something of enormous
importance to Italy. At that point, the SIFAR would
have organized the deportation of the leaders of the
left, a veritable coup d'état.

At that time, I directed the party organ, the
newspaper Avanti!: I had asked to be in charge of
the daily precisely to prevent the party's political
policies from totally and permanently coinciding with
those of the government. I wanted to preserve
liberty of action for the party; the Socialist Party
is one thing, a government of the center-left is
another. In July, when I refused to continue
supporting the government's policy, I was not aware
of this plan for a coup d'état. I knew that
christian democracy would try at all costs to prevent
the implementation of the program. There were
revelations in the press which provoked an enquiry
and confirmed that a coup d'état had been planned.
Indeed, there was a parliamentary commission which
concluded that there really had been plans for a coup
d'état. But the direct relationship of this coup
d'état to the program of reform was known only
tardily. Nenni said loyally in public that the
President of the Republic had threatened him with not

signing the laws that Parliament might have voted,
especially in the area of urbanization. He even
added that the President of the Republic, Sr. Segni
had said to him: "If that crazy Lombardi, and Sullo
(a christian democrat who was convinced of the
rightness of the policy of reforms) continued after
the madness of the first nationalization of
electrical energy, if they want to do another crazy
act with this law on urbanization, I won't sign it."
That had been said in confidence but Nenni made it
public. After that, it was clear that the
center-left orientation had no more future for the
socialists. From the point of view of governmental
stability, the policy of administering from one day
to the next is not necessarily bad. There are
compromises which I don't refuse. One must in any
case pursue things which have a chance of success in
a government, even if they are small improvements.
None the less, one must always have before one's eyes
the ends to be attained: small things are all right
if they are in the direction desired. That's what
provoked a perpetual dispute between my comrades in
the party and myself, which lasts to this day and
which is in the nature of things.

Q: So you refused to see in the participation of
the socialists in the government a sort of historic
compromise between socialism and christian
democracy. It was merely a provisional alliance for
certain specific goals which went in the direction of
socialism. And if the government refused to go in
that direction, there was no reason to remain in the
government.

A: Yes, but the word historic compromise is
inappropriate. I always said that I accepted
compromises but not historic compromises. The word
compromise is in the nature of politics, of political
action. The adjective historic is false. Even Nenni
revealed his real purpose when in 1963 he spoke of
historic agreements with christian democracy: that's
the word which the communists took up again later.
The question of "historic" is not a semantic issue,
you understand me, it is a question of substance, of
reality.

Q: Thus, you would make the same criticism of
the idea of a historic compromise on the part of the
communists?

A: Yes, the very day in 1975 that Sr.
Berlinguer, secretary-general of the Communist party,
interpreting incorrectly in my opinion what happened
in Chile, proclaimed that political line of the

historic compromise, the Central Committee of the Socialist Party was holding a meeting. I immediately got the floor to criticize the idea of a historic compromise. That policy, which the communists thought was something new, was a deceptive form of old-fashioned reformism. Working together with the christian democrats cannot go beyond certain limits. Christian democracy has an electorate which is not progressive even if it contains certain progressive strata. If it followed a policy of reform, christian democracy would risk losing the greater part of its support. That renders provisional, if not null, the engagements which must be made, engagements limited with regard to time, subject, the substance of the compromises to be actualized. We are suffering today the consequences of the historic compromise. For, during the years in which the communists obstinately proclaimed that they wanted concord, etc. real problems were thrust aside and nothing important resolved. And if we are in a situation which is not satisfactory from the economic point of view, it's also because of the weakness of those years of so-called understanding between communists and christian democracy.

Q: What do you think of the present leadership of the PSI in Italy? You now have that "young generation" of Sr. Craxi, etc.

A: There has doubtless been an important change of generation. That's a good thing, because one should not be dominated by old people, but it is also necessary to prevent the emergence of false young people, of a false youth, because there are young people who are really older than old people. For example, Craxi is a young man unquestionably endowed with qualities: character, tenacity, etc. Nevertheless, he has the same faults as Nenni with a difference of culture, history, etc. That is to say, he almost always thinks exclusively of governmental questions, so-called political questions. His political perspective is not in the tradition of the Socialist Party and that's a tradition which must be respected. He began an anti-Marxist offensive. No one in the Socialist Party can liberate himself from the Marxist idea. The first thing to do, in the Socialist Party, is to understand capitalism. Capitalism is not eternal. In all our party congresses, I always began my statements thus: "Let's first see where capitalism is today, what are its tasks, what transformations it is undergoing, what are its new attitudes, etc. Let us understand the enemy the better to combat it." One must understand the state of society to determine the position of a party which wants to transform things. Without that, we would always be engaged in opportunism....

Q: Why did you resign as President of the PSI in 1979?

A: I resigned after 20 days of dissension with the secretary of the party. If the president and the Secretary of a party are not in agreement, it can't work.

Q: It seems to be that the present policy of the Socialist Party is much closer to the social democracy of other countries of the 1950s. I wonder whether this orientation won't ultimately damage the PSI since any offensive against the PCI gives the impression that it is the socialists who are dividing the workers?

A: Yes, and that has an unfortunate consequence because it discourages the current in the Communist Party which works for a real change. It accentuates the differences between communists and socialists. There are many theoretical and practical differences between them. I don't say that communists and socialists are the same thing. That is not only because of historical reasons. But to encourage the divisions, when to my point of view, operational unity is necessary in Italy, is to prevent the left from having the force it deserves. For some, the situation is discouraging. For me, the encouraging fact is that in Italy, all the parties are in the process of analyzing or transforming themselves. The situation is not hopeless because the resources, the initiatives, the fantasies, the will to work, are much greater in Italy than is thought. People abroad naturally tend to see above all terrorism, certain forms of disaffection, etc. in Italy. There is another side to the Italian situation which is encouraging.

Q: At this time, what in your opinion should be the position of the Socialist Party?

A: The priority is, and I have suggested it many times, to propose to the Communist Party a meeting designed to clarify the existing conflicts between the two parties, to establish a realizable program of reforms in Italy, even accepting the unpopularity that would come from taking that on. Only after that can we face elections, even bring them about. I certainly understand the reluctance of my party to provoke a governmental crisis, which could lead to the dissolution of the legislature before the scheduled elections. That would make four times. But if we arrived at elections of a new kind, if for the first time in ten years, the entire left, communist and socialist, presented itself united with a common program to offer to the electorate, these elections would not resemble the former elections. The left, in my opinion, would not win on the first try, but it would have presented a real choice for the first time.

Five years ago I suggested to the communists a common program. And they constantly refused, because they were engaged in the historic compromise. A common program with the Socialist Party would have signified a refusal of the historic compromise. Now, in an article on unity, published on the occasion of my 80th birthday, Giorgio Napolitano for the first time wrote that he thought that the communists were perhaps very wrong to constantly refuse my propositions for a common program. Today, the difficulties come from the new Socialist Party; the opportunity should have been seized before. For five years I waged a campaign, which was not, as some pretend, a pro-communist campaign. It encountered the indifference, the hostility of my own party, without encountering a more receptive audience from the communists either. And in my opinion, that caused considerable delay in the formulation of a left-wing political orientation. It is difficult to regain time.

Q: Indeed, what you are suggesting is close to the French socialist line of the last ten years.

A: Yes, Mitterrand followed my line. When the communists directed a fierce campaign against him, he said: "I want to be unitary for both parties. Because the communists are not in favor of unity, I am in favor of it on their behalf!" The French electoral system gives Mitterrand an advantage. The President of the Republic has great powers and is elected for seven years; the electoral system does not make coalition governments necessary and makes possible governments which are clearly on the right or on the left. It is much easier there to create homogeneous governments. For that reason I support Craxi's proposals to modify the Italian electoral system to simplify it. I am in favor of proportional representation but not to the point of making coalition governments necessary. In Italy there is an almost complete balance between right and left, because the fascists cannot be counted in any majority. If the fascists could be utilized the right would have an advantage but there is agreement to eliminate them from the democratic competition. Ten votes would be enough to change the balance.

Q: Would a presidential system be possible?

A: Yes, during the Constituent Assembly, the Action Party to which I belonged was the only party favorable to a presidential regime. But there were perhaps some reasons why this kind of system was held in disfavor. The Constituent Assembly came immediately after fascism and an excessively strong executive was feared. But I didn't have any fears on this account because to make a new Mussolini, we would have had to have a victorious general. We didn't have a single one who could present himself as a man of destiny. Not only didn't we have one, but we didn't have a De Gaulle. No General Lefebvre. Absolutely nothing. Only defeated generals.

Q: If I understand correctly, for a long time you have felt that worker self-management (auto-gestion) will play an important role in a socialist society, because you don't feel socialism means simply state control of the means of production. Can you explain how you envision self-management in a post-industrial society?

A: I must admit that the concept of self-management is still a little nebulous, because nowhere have there been possibilities of experimentation up till now. But I wish to emphasize that there is a movement of thought, up to the present only theoretical, above all, in France. This movement, which we have followed very closely in Italy, is trying to produce a practical proposal. However, I can define the concept of self-management in a negative way, by what it is not. First of all, it is not to be limited to factories. This is important. Of course, we can begin with co-gestion (shared-management) as it is practiced in Germany, for example. The essential thing is to begin to experiment in this area. In Italy, we have not made many studies to define a program of participation of workers, technicians, etc. in the management of enterprises. One of the preliminary conditions is to know all the facts about the enterprise. That is a major difficulty. Another is that it is necessary to have personnel with the requisite aptitudes, the necessary background. That said, I think there is no sense in self-management limited to enterprises. In my opinion, the fundamental reason for self-management should be this: the State does not organize by itself the essential services of society. The State provides the means, the power to local or managing or municipal or regional groups to organize certain services. It provides the means to decentralize and to localize the services in such a fashion that they can become independent. That is, as a theoretician, <u>Gilles Martinet</u> said: to restore to civil society the powers usurped by the State. The State does too many things, even in the area of social reforms, and statist management has shown itself to be weak and destructive. Self-management might cause errors, but no worse than those committed by the State in trying to administer everything by itself, by centralizing power. It is not a question of substituting the logic of public property for the logic of private property. For that, in my opinion, would have little sense. The very right to property must be challenged. I am not saying that property is theft! I want to say something else, that the enterprise is henceforth no longer founded on one right but on many rights. There is the State's right of taxation, or rather, its rights of taxation, there is the power of the stockholders and that of the board of directors which is different from that of the stockholders, there is also the power of the trade union which imposes its point of view, negotiates and arrives at a coordination, sometimes voluntary, with the owners. Thus, following this logic, it is necessary to end up by legalizing all these different forms of power which are being exercized. Henceforth, what is certain is that there is no single power in the enterprise. Juridically, yes, there is the power of the board of directors, but in fact this power is shared. There are slices of power which are exercized. Therefore, it is necessary to find out how to organize a communitarian society in which the different powers, the different responsibilities would even be institutionalized by law. But that implies experimentation.

I am not in favor of doing things on the spur of the moment. One must begin with limited forms of participation to educate the workers so that they can assume their responsibilities, learn and use their knowledge in the enterprise where they work. This experimentation would be tied to the process of decentralization of the State which I just mentioned.

I am against establishing a program of self-management from one day to the next. One must proceed progressively but always following the logical process which is to subtract powers from the State in order to give them, to the extent that it is possible, to society, in the areas of the organization of production and the distribution of income. I think that henceforth one can create management autonomy in the nationalized enterprises, an idea discussed everywhere but which is not practiced in Italy.

One can henceforth have a category of small and medium-sized enterprises which could be self-managed sooner. One can even have cooperative enterprises of a significant size; we are beginning to have some. So there could be three sectors, a private sector with forms of State intervention, a nationalized sector with forms of control and the progressive acquisition of means of intervention and co-management, and the sector of medium-sized enterprises and cooperative sector. A framework can be formed which, once put in place, can give an idea of the relations between market and planification. One can frame a proposal which takes into account the international ties from which naturally we cannot be liberated. We live in an international society with many constraints; we can see up to what point the plan is compatible with a certain freedom of the market. Too great a freedom of the market would prevent socialism; too little would provoke dictatorship. We must find the correct relation between market and plan. This is the problem faced by all socialists throughout the world: the relationship between plan, program, and market. The problem is complicated by the existence of multinational corporations which escape from state regulation and would tend to escape regulation under a system of self-management. This is frankly one of the most anguishing problems for socialist politics but has not been given a solution either by socialists or capitalists. The problem of multinationals exists even for the capitalist system, which has a lot of interest in regulating them but which doesn't know how to do it. The failure of all the efforts by the Common Market to regulate them proves in a convincing fashion the difficulty of the problem. We are in an international economy dominated by powers which escape our grasp.

Often there are more problems than solutions. We are in a society which transforms itself so rapidly that I am not surprised by the new difficulties we encounter every day. One must always come to terms with new situations.

Q: I have to tell you something, not to flatter you. You don't seem to be 80 years old, you seem much more like 40, because you are so involved in everything which is happening.

A: What helps me to live -- I am in bad health -- is an enormous curiosity. I have not lost interest in events and that helps me bear my age. I was saying to you before that there are false youths, perhaps there are also false older people. The important thing is not to arrive at old age senile. What frightens me is just that, to end up feeble-minded. That would be very disagreeable. The question is, when one becomes like that one doesn't realize it.

Q: I think you are very far away.

A: What you say is encouraging.

Glossary of Names, Organizations and Terms in the Lombardi Interview

--Giorgio Amendola (1907-1980). Active anti-fascist and communist since 1929.

--Attentismo. An attitude of fence-straddling by which a large part of the population avoided taking sides during the occupation.

--"Badoglio's coup d'état." In late July of 1943 the Fascist Grand Council ousted Mussolini. He was replaced by Marshal Badoglio, the Chief of Staff of the Army. Mussolini was imprisoned; he was later rescued and brought to Northern Italy, where, under German protection he created the so-called Republic of Salò.

--Lelio Basso (1909-1978). Member of the maximalist wing of the Socialist Party. An active anti-fascist, he was arrested on several occasions. In 1945 he became vice-secretary of the party and in 1947 secretary-general. He left in 1963 in opposition to the center-left coalition government.

--Riccardo Bauer (1896-1982). An anti-fascist journalist, Bauer helped anti-fascists to emigrate. He was arrested in 1927-1928. A founder of Giustizia e Libertà, he headed the Action Party's military junta from 1943 to the Liberation.

--"Behave in a way different from Rome." Rome was liberated by the Allies without a popular insurrection.

--Count Alessandro Casati (1881-1955). An early supporter of fascism, he resigned as Minister of Public Instruction in 1925. He helped establish the Central Committee of National Liberation in Rome in June 1943. Minister of War (1944-1945); later Senator.

--"Change in the party line in 1930." Following the Comintern, the PCI denounced other movements on the left as "social-fascists." This policy was opposed by Tasca, who was expelled.

--Coup de main. Surprise attack.

--Francesco de Martino (1907-   ). Anti-fascist and member of the Action Party, De Martino became a leading member of the Socialist Party after the War.

He was secretary-general from 1962-1968 and is an opponent of Craxi.

--<u>Roberto Farinacci</u> (1829-1945). A leader of fascist bands, Farinacci was considered to be on the radical totalitarian wing of the movement. Secretary-general of the Fascist Party 1925-1926, he later supported an alliance with Hitler. From 1938 on he edited <u>Regima Fascista</u>. Farinacci remained loyal to Mussolini during the Salò period.

--<u>Alicide de Gasperi</u> (1881-1954). A leader of the Popolari Party before its dissolution, de Gasperi spent the fascist period in the Vatican. A supporter of the Republic, he was leader of the Christian Democrats and Prime Minister 1944-1953.

--<u>Antonio Greppi</u> (1894-1982). Socialist militant active in anti-fascism, Greppi was a member of the partisans and a member of the Committee of Liberation of Northern Italy. Mayor of Milan at the Liberation, he served as deputy 1958-1968.

--<u>Giovanni Gronchi</u> (1887-1978). A founder of the Poplari Party. He helped De Gasperi found the Christian Democratic Party and was a member of its left wing. Gronchi was elected President of Italy in 1955.

--<u>Concetto Marchesi</u> (1878-1957). A member of the Communist Party since 1921. In 1943 he met with liberals to attempt to organize an anti-fascist coup d'état with the monarchists. Member of the Central Committee of the PCI after the war.

--<u>Gilles Martinet</u> (1916-   ). French theorist of <u>auto-gestion</u>, a leader of the PSU and later a member of the new Socialist Party. He was named Ambassador to Italy by Mitterand.

--<u>Guildo Migliole</u> (1879-1954). Lawyer and Catholic trade union activist; leader of the left wing of the Popolari Party, Migliole strongly supported division of large estates into peasant small holdings. A proponent of cooperation with the Marxist left against fascism, he was expelled from the Poplari Party in 1925. He was an active opponent of fascism during his exile.

--<u>Guiseppe Modigliani</u> (1872-1947). Socialist leader and anti-fascist, Modigliani participated in the reconstruction of the socialist movement in exile.

--**Rudolfo Morandi** (1902-1955). An active anti-fascist, Morandi joined Giustizia e Libertà and then the Socialist Party, to whose ideological development he contributed. He advocated close collaboration with the communists. He was President of the Committee of Liberation of Northern Italy in 1945, and secretary of the Socialist Party 1945-1946.

--**Giorgio Napolitano** (1925-   ). Major contemporary communist leader.

--**Pietro Nenni** (1891-1980). Editor of Avanti! in 1921, Nenni became the major socialist leader during the 1930s and remained so during the rest of his lifetime.

--**OVRA**. Meaningless acronym for the Special Inspectorate of Public Security, a branch of the state police supposed to act against clandestine opposition to the fascist regime. It was often in conflict with the MSVN (Milizia Volontaria per la Sicurezza Nazionale), the police of the fascist party.

--**Ferrucio Parri** (1890-1982). A leading anti-fascist, Parri represented the Action Party in the Committee of National Liberation of Northern Italy. He was Prime Minister from June to November 1945. Parri headed the right wing of the Action Party; he joined the Republican Party after the Action Party split. He was elected Senator in 1948.

--**Popolari Party**. A party of christian democratic tendencies founded just after World War I.

--**Ernesto Rossi** (1897-1967). Democratic radical activist in the anti-fascist underground; one of the founders of Giustizia e Liberta in 1929. Imprisoned 1930-1943; after the war, a leading advocate of European federalism.

--**Giuseppe Saragat** (1898-   ). Leader of the social democratic tendency in post-war Italian socialism and founder of the Social Democratic Party in 1947. President of Italy 1964-1971.

--**Pietro Secchia** (1903-1973). A communist militant active in the underground, Secchia was imprisoned from 1931-1941. He was a leader of the party in the North during the partisan period. At the liberation, Secchia was a member of the Constituent Assembly and then Senator.

--<u>Ignazio Silone</u> (1900-1978). Leading Italian novelist and active anti-fascist. Originally a communist, he later joined the Socialist Party.

--<u>Angelo Tasca</u> (1892-1960). Leader of the right wing in the Italian Communist Party, Tasca opposed the "social-fascist" line of the International. Expelled in 1929, he moved to France and worked with the French socialist party. He was a journalist during the Vichy regime. His <u>History of Italian Fascism</u> remains the classic work on the subject.

--<u>Claudio Treves</u> (1869-1933). A reformist socialist closely tied to Turati, Treves escaped to Paris in 1926 where he was active in the anti-fascist movement.

--<u>Fillippo Turati</u> (1857-1932). One of the founders of the Italian Socialist Party and leader of its reformist wing, Turati supported collaboration with the bourgeois parties. He was expelled from the Socialist Party in 1922 for advocating a governmental coalition to stop fascism. He escaped from Italy in 1926 with the aid of Parri and Carlo Rosselli and was a leader of the anti-fascist opposition in exile.

--<u>Roberto Veratti</u> (d. 1943). Northern secretary of the underground Socialist Party, Veratti died when the SS captured the party's clandestine headquarters on November 25, 1943.

4
Socialism in Scandinavia

   Socialism in Scandinavia has followed a path different from that of most of Europe. The reasons lie in the distinctive nature of Scandinavian society.
   Scandinavia did not experience feudalism; certain areas, like Norway had hardly any indigenous nobility. Even peasants had some access to political participation very early on, for example, the Fourth Estate of the old Swedish Parliament. Compared with the rest of Europe, Scandinavian societies were relatively homogenous.
   A decisive factor was that Sweden, Denmark, and Norway all industrialized very rapidly in the late 19th and early 20th century. The struggle for political equality and democracy coincided with the struggle for social justice. Social democracy became a major carrier of both. In addition, social democrats were sufficiently pragmatic to modify their originally Marxist programs to appeal to groups in the population besides industrial workers. All the Scandinavian socialists showed a penchant for mass organizations and developed enormous trade union federations which made social democracy far more than a purely political phenomenon. The socialists were fortunate in not having to cope with a clerical issue as was found in Catholic countries; indeed, they soon assimilated certain demands that had been supported by evangelical protestantism, like temperance.
   In the late 19th and early 20th centuries, socialists worked with radical liberals for universal suffrage; in the 1930s in Sweden and Norway they found support from agrarian parties in their efforts to alleviate the economic crisis. Whereas Scandinavian socialists were generally successful in maintaining party unity, they faced a "bourgeois" opposition divided into at least three parties. Social democracy became the largest political party in each country by World War I.
   The 1920s saw minority socialist governments of brief duration in Sweden, Norway and Denmark. In all three cases, the social democrats had little opportunity to act decisively and had no clear program for immediate action. The Great Depression forced a rethinking of party strategy, and the social democrats, in coalition with other parties, were able to successfully apply counter-cyclical economic policies to fight the depression and also implement

significant reforms in social welfare. Their success in doing so made them the dominant party and the normal party of government in Sweden and Norway. In Denmark, the social democrats are the largest party, but have never attained an absolute majority.

Starting in the 1930s, the Swedish Social Democrats undertook health, education and pension reforms and redistributive tax policies, which laid the basis of the welfare state. At the same time, they emphasized maintenance of full employment and economic efficiency. Nevertheless, the social democrats did not see the welfare state as the ultimate goal of their movement.

Nils Karleby and Ernst Wigforss contributed to the development of a distinctive Swedish social democratic theory. Karleby (1892-1926) attempted to show that contrary to Kautsky's belief, capitalism and socialism are not absolutely distinct systems and that socialist development could proceed within capitalist society. Karleby insisted that property really was a bundle of different rights which could be modified and reformulated. Karleby also argued the virtues of a market economy, but demonstrated that by changes in distribution, such a market economy could be made to serve the interests of socialism.

Ernst Wigforss (1881-1977) was a member of the executive of Social Democratic Party from 1928-1952 and the Minister of Finance from 1925-1926 and from 1932-1949. He deserves much of the credit for Sweden's success in dealing with the economic crisis and laying the groundwork for the welfare state. Timothy Tilton summarizes the importance of Wigforss as the leading ideologist of Swedish social democracy:

> Wigforss' Social Democratic strategy, then, is a policy of permanent reform...Each series of reforms sets the stage for new ones and weakens the capitalist's privileges....He pleaded for Social Democracy as an alternative to liberal welfare statism and to state socialism. He noted that the liberal welfare state extended a safety net to protect its citizens from dire poverty, and strove to maintain full employment, but otherwise left the inequalities of bourgeois capitalist society intact. Large fortunes still serve as the basis for class distinctions and the administration of enterprise remained oligarchic. This liberal welfare state, Wigforss argued, could and should give way to a classless society, a Social Democracy characterized by general equality of

condition, social planning of investment and economic development, and industrial democracy. This vision of Social Democracy regards socialization only as a possible means not as an absolute necessity for socialism and shows no inclination to abolish wage labor, but its emphasis upon equality, democracy, and public control of society's economic resources reflects socialist values.[1]

In the 1930s Swedish social democracy entered into the phase Walter Korpi calls the "historic compromise" with capital:

Since the mid-1930s, the policies of the Social Democratic government came to be dominated by what we have called the historical compromise between labour and capital made possible, as well as necessitated, by the fact that political power had become separated from economic power. As we have seen, the historical compromise resulted in a shift from a 'zero-sum' conflict situation to a 'positive-sum' strategy of class conflict. It was based on a formula of cooperation between the labour movement and the representatives of capital to increase economic growth. Decision-making in the sphere of production was largely left to capital. The labour movement undertook responsibility for affecting distribution of the increasing product by political means, through the government, according to criteria of social justice. This strategy was also seen as speeding up the maturation of capitalism and thereby as facilitating the movement towards socialism. The historical compromise was an achievement for the Swedish labour movement, made possible by the increased political support for the Social Democratic Party. This compromise therefore provided the base for policies which were to have important positive consequences for the wage earners. Of crucial importance were the economic and labour market policies which made it possible to decrease unemployment in the 1930s and to maintain a very high level of employment in the inflation-unemployment dilemmas facing governments in the west in the postwar period and up to the 1970s.[2]

This historic compromise meant that social democracy became responsible for promoting economic growth, without which welfare capitalism could not function. But unrestricted economic growth produced negative side effects, like the destruction of the environment, and tended to make social democracy appear as merely an appendage of the system. In the late 1960s, social democrats in Sweden renewed demands for social equality, including reform of the school system and attention to lower paid workers. The deteriorating economic situation of the 1970s prompted an even more radical idea, the so-called wage earners fund.

Social democrats were concerned about the tendency towards stagflation; wage increases increased inflation and at the same time investment was declining. These two phenomena called into question the "historic compromise." In 1976 a commission of the trade unions under Rudolf Meidner proposed the creation of "wage earner funds." These funds would be constituted from monies put aside in lieu of wage increases, thereby discouraging inflation; they would provide capital for investment and at the same time would enable the workers to ultimately acquire control over businesses. The concept was left in rather vague form preceding the election of 1976, and may have contributed to the socialist defeat. The party congress of October 1981 accepted the idea in principle. Despite strong opposition, the Palme government elected in 1983 has tried to implement a modified version of the program. This represents an end to the "historic compromise," and demonstrates that Swedish Social Democracy is following an original and innovative path.

The willingness to experiment demonstrates the rightness of Korpi's argument that Swedish social democrats remain true reformist socialists and are not simply social reformers. This vision of a society based on social equality and the desire to transfer the means of production from private to public ownership has not been lost; the Swedish Social Democrats have traveled slowly but irrevocably along this road. Thus, they are at once the most reformist and the most truly radical of European socialist parties.

The Norwegian Labor Party has a different history. Norway was more rural, industrialization occurred not in urban but in isolated rural areas. Norway has always been more of a frontier society than Sweden with a more individualist social ethic. Rapid industrialization and the creation of a working-class from former farmers or fishermen produced a strong syndicalist strain; Martin

Tranmael, for example, the leading figure in the movement, had migrated to America and joined the IWW before returning to Norway to become a socialist leader. Consequently, the Norwegian Labor Party joined the newly-formed Third International. Tranmael and his friends looked on Russia as a successful effort at revolutionary syndicalism. When they discovered the realities of the Comintern, they withdrew in 1923; by 1927 the split that had developed between the majority of the Labor Party and the schismatic social democratic wing was healed. Nevertheless, Norwegian labor has tended to alternate between the two poles of radicalism and reformism; as the former party chairman, Reiulf Steen, put it:

> On the left, you will find people who define themselves as socialists, on the right you will find people who don't think that is too important, people who, if they define themselves, would call themselves social democrats. But that's superficial. When it comes to political realities, you will find the left wing is more a driving force on issues like development of industrial democracy. Take a current issue -- oil policy. The left will try to get as much state control as possible. The right wing will have a more pragmatic view, and say that private interests should also be allowed to take part in exploitation of oil resources. The left wing is also closer to the trade unions than the right, at least the traditional trade unions, the factory workers, the building workers. I belong to the factory workers union and that union is supposed to be on the left. When it comes to foreign policy, the right will strongly defend NATO positions and links to the US. The left will be more critical. They accept NATO membership as a necessity, not as a virtue, and they will be more skeptical towards the US system and integration with US power....It's much more a question of mood than opinions.[3]

The persons interviewed in this section represent significant figures in Scandinavia socialism. Tage Erlander, who began his career as a member of the city council of Lund in 1930, became Prime Minister of Sweden from 1946-1969, holding office longer than any other democratically elected head of government. Under his administration, Sweden consolidated its position as a welfare state and engaged in major reforms of pensions and schooling. Sigrid Ekendahl

represents a feminist dimension in the socialist
movement. Her experience reveals the difficulties
encountered by women within socialism. She was
elected ombudsman of the Hotel and Restaurant Workers
Union in 1937, headed LO's Women's Council from
1948-1964, and served in Parliament from 1941-1948
and 1957-1968. Trygve Bratteli, Minister of Finance
1951-55 and 1956-60, Minister of Transport 1960-1964,
party chairman in 1965, was Prime Minister of Norway
from 1971 to 1975.

FOOTNOTES

1   Tilton, Timothy, "A Swedish Road to Socialism: Ernst Wigforss and the Ideological Foundations of Swedish Social Democracy," American Political Science Review, 76, (June 1979)) p. 518. I am also indebted to Professor Tilton for showing me an unpublished article on Karleby, on which my comments are based.

2   Walter Korpi, The Working Class in Welfare Capitalism, London, 1978, pp. 320-1.

3   Interview with Reiulf Steen, Oslo, 10 December 1981.

Interview with Tage Erlander

TAGE ERLANDER:

My father was a teacher in my home province, Värmland, and he was a liberal. He had very little sympathy for the trade unions because he thought they were destroying the free market which, as for many other liberals, was important to him. But in other things he was very radical. He worked for universal suffrage. The struggle for the vote was very important for radical people in the beginning of the century. He was also interested in social reforms. He was deeply religious. Although a teacher's salary was low at the beginning of the century, he found the means for me to go to the gymnasium at Karlstadt, in the south of Sweden. It was the richest province, and still is, but the agricultural workers were extremely poor. We have always talked about Värmland as a poor province, but such poverty as I saw in the rich Skåne was unbelievable.

It was a starting point for me, this poverty among the rural workers. During 1923 I remember seeing rural workers being carried away from their house during a strike. That gave me the feeling that Sweden couldn't continue the way it was. Who could make it better? Of course, it was the trade unions and the Labor Party. At that time, I had the pleasure to read a translation in Swedish of Karl Kautsky's <u>Marx' Economic Theory</u>. It came at just the right moment, it gave the explanation why there were such terrible conditions for the workers. Therefore, I became a socialist, working with the trade unions in Skåne and thereafter with the party.

Q: Did you read Marx directly or did you learn about his ideas only indirectly?

A: I read very little of Marx directly, and I should think it was a good thing (laughs), because I was also occupied by practical political work very very early among the students of the University of Lund, and thereafter, as a member of the local authorities in Lund. I bought <u>Das Kapital</u> and I have that copy here, but I can't say that I read it really carefully.

171

Q: Were you influenced by the ideas of particular people in the Swedish Party?

A: Yes, of course. The 1920s was a period when the former generation of leaders was growing very old. Branting passed away in 1925; his collaborator, the Minister of Finance, Thorsson died the same year. I went to both of their funerals. Two young leaders of the party were Ernst Wigforss and August Möller. They visited the radical students at Lund very often, and both of them made a very strong impression. Wigforss had just been engaged in the Ford Peace Movement, a great attempt by Ford against war. In Sweden, it was led by Wigforss. He was trying to create democratic socialism; he was not particularly in favor of state socialism but advocated syndicalism. August Möller is the creator of socialist Sweden, he believed in state socialism; he thought the only way to create a good society was to let the State take over economic life. But it was very interesting for us young people to meet two very young leaders of the Social Democratic Party who had opposite opinions on these important questions. It created tension, it made a much more interesting picture of political life to have them there. Later came Karleby; his analysis of Marxism from the pragmatic Swedish point of view was very important. His book came out in 1926 and made a very great impression on young people. He was seriously ill and died that year. He was the theoretician of the pragmatic socialism that the party has pursued.

Q: When you talk about pragmatism in Swedish socialism, are you talking about a pragmatism which is itself founded on a very definite ideological point of view, or the pragmatism one finds in America, of just doing things and seeing what happens?

A: No, we look upon pragmatism as a theory of problem-solving; by its basic nature, it keeps to the guidelines of reforms which suit the future of a more just society. And Karleby developed this very brillantly. Wigforss continued his analysis. Wigforss was also a great practical politician and Minister of Finance for many years.

Q: As Prime Minister, did you always have a particular idea of the ultimate goals for Swedish society?

A: No, on this point I am a Marxist! Development always confronts us with new problems. It is clear that we strive for equality, full employment, etc. but we do not have some direct plan. Another aspect of our pragmatism is that we try to see where every step we take will lead. Many of our solutions are very long-range, for example, the pension system. It was both a reform to safeguard future security and to provide a ground for future welfare in this country.

Q: Would it be correct to say that the wage earner funds proposal, which could lead to actual worker control of enterprises, is an inherent part of social democratic thought?

A: Yes, but the question is more complex. One has to go back and look at the history of the party at the beginning of the 1920s. There were strong forces, among them led by August Möller, which thought that one could make very great advances. But at the Party Congress of 1932, the first I attended, there was a great discussion about the problems of socialization and planning of resources. Wigforss succeeded in convincing the Party Congress that previous plans of socialization were not the road for the party to follow, that the so-called reformist line was preferable. But there was a majority of only eight votes on this point.

After that, the party has worked according to a line of partial reforms. Then after the Second World War came a more stable leadership in the country. We had an enormous cultural and social reform program in front of us, family policies, housing policies, food policies, etc. We let private enterprise work undisturbed by the State. Korpi describes this in his book as the "great historical compromise." It meant that private enterprise could work for itself but we took its fruits and distributed them. But we were fully aware that there was always a need for state control in a free enterprise system: it wasn't as free as one might have thought. When we reached the 1960s, more and more we discovered that there were things almost as dangerous as unemployment. There was the destruction of the environment both inside and outside. Many people were completely broken down by this. The environmental destruction was the proof that one could not let private enterprise work as freely as the historic compromise supposed. Therefore the 1971 LO Congress became a turning point; that's when we started to discuss how the workers' influence could be great enough to prevent the destruction of man in private enterprises. That's when the Meidner funds plan came out. But it is important to observe that the international crisis thrusts before us the question of getting production to work. Thus we come back to the ideas of the 50s and 60s, the question of giving the private enterprise system the capital necessary.

The economic crisis that has spread all over Europe has destroyed very many thoughts we had had in the early 70s. But we hope that the world will be reasonable again, that we can return to them. If we create full employment the ideas of giving workers increased influence over their enterprise will come back again. They have not completely disappeared; they are still there. But the emphasis has come to be much more on the necessity of getting production rolling again.

Q: In any case, this marks the breakdown of the historical compromise. To increase investment the State will have to increase its role in economic life, in the productive area, not the area of distribution.

A: Exactly. You're perfectly right.

Q: To what extent did you and others in the Social Democratic Party perceive a threat to Sweden in the 1930s not only from the depression but from fascism?

A: Our closeness to Germany worried us very much. The Swedish Social Democrats always thought that the Western democracies would have to defend themselves. They were rather worried by both the Norwegian and British Labour parties' willingness to drastically reduce defense capabilities. Had they succeeded, Europe would have been almost defenseless when Hitler came. Safeguarding democracy involved a relatively strong defense. It was, of course, not sufficient against the Big Powers.

Q: How was it possible to reconcile neutrality with the defense of democracy?

A: That is, of course, a moral problem. We thought that peace was important, not only for Sweden, but for neighboring countries. The contributions we could make against Hitler were rather insignificant compared to the gains that all states could have from our neutrality.

Q: Did you have much contact with resistance movements in other countries?

A: Of course we had. Sweden was a breathing space for German socialists and communists. There were a number of leaders of the Germany labor movement here, including Bruno Kreisky, Willy Brandt,

Herbert Wehner, and also a large number of ordinary party members. Also we tried to help the Norwegians and the Danes. We received several thousand refugees. At the end of the war, in 1944, we delivered quite a large number of weapons to the resistance movements. We trained almost 10,000 Norwegian soldiers here in Sweden. That may not have been all that neutral! In the beginning, when the Germans had occupied almost all countries in Europe (they were also at first allied with the Russians) the Swedish government's freedom of action was not particularly great. After the defeat at Stalingrad, the German war machine was so much weakened that even we, with our limited war resources, could be a problem. From August 1943, we had a rather independent policy. But the first years were not very amusing.

Q: Did the war have an impact on the development of social democracy?

A: The experience of the war years taught us that there were almost unlimited resources in Swedish society. Before the war we discussed reforms that cost 10 or 20 million kroners and thought that was a lot. When the war came, Swedish defense outlays rose from 14 million to two billion. We looked upon social reforms in a more realistic way after the war because we knew we had productive resources. At the end of the war, I was chairman of something called the Building Regulation Board, which was to plan the whole investment policy and structure of the Swedish building industry, to create a productive apparatus that could carry all these expenses. There we learned that the productive resources were much greater than we had thought. But we also learned that it was much more difficult to stimulate investment resources centrally; after the war we were more willing to allow private industry to take a larger role than we had thought in the beginning. We were scared of our own incapacities.

Q: In 1946 you became Prime Minister and remained so until 1969, the longest term in a democracy....

A: The Swedes are a patient people.

Q: When you became Prime Minister, did you have a series of priorities? How far had you planned in advance?

A: I'd rather like to answer that I didn't have any plan but that would be wrong. The most important thing was to create conditions for full employment; second, was greater people's education which would correspond to the demands of the new society. I put the emphasis on full employment and the new school. Under the new school, I also include the emphasis on technical research development. Nowadays, I think people understand that the precondition for increased welfare is a high education of people. If you make the comparison of the reading abilities among the populations in Europe, already in 1875 Sweden was above all other countries. In the 20s, 99% were able to read in Sweden, next came Germany with 97%, France and Italy were much lower. An English author has recently pointed out that this helps explain the ease with which the Germans defeated the French.

Q: That goes too far, I think.

A: Only 80% of the French soldiers could read.

Q: The problem was mostly with their generals, and they could read, but not think!

A: We are fortunate in Sweden to have a literate people for about 150 years. I'm quite sure that our emphasis on technical and medical science has played a great role in our development.

Q: In foreign policy after 1945, Sweden maintained her position of neutrality under a social democratic government. Why did you make that choice?

A: We never accepted the belief that the Russians were interested in conquering Europe. The Russians had enormous internal problems. We can see how the Finns have been able to keep their independence. Therefore, we did not agree with the British Labour Party that it was necessary to form an alliance. We made an attempt to form a Scandinavian defense alliance, with Denmark and Norway. I still think this would have been a positive development.

Q: The call for a nuclear free zone was a continuation of that idea?

A: For once, the two superpowers were quite agreed to prevent the foundation of a neutral Scandinavia. I asked Krushchev, "Why is it when you and the US so rarely agree, you do it to prevent something wise?"

Q: I wonder if there isn't a logical coherence between your domestic and foreign policy. In each case, Sweden takes it own course -- independence of the two blocs in foreign policy, and a social and economic policy between American capitalism and the Soviet model.

A: Thank you! That's exactly the way we look on it.

Interview with Sigrid Ekendahl

SIGRID EKENDAHL:

I was born in a big family with eight children. My father had a small farm. I had only six years of schooling, nothing else; I went afterwards to study circles. I had to go out and get my first job at 13 or 14 to earn some money and help the family. I first worked in an old people's home. Then I went to Stockholm and began to work at small cafés and konditorei; it was a heavy job. I wondered, can nobody do anything for us? I met an old woman; I was only 20 and she was 60, and she said: "Go to the trade union; they can help us to get better facilities here." I did. I was very interested in going to meetings; they were at 10 p.m. because the cafés and konditorei just closed, you see. Very soon I came to sit on the board of the union. We had 2,500 members ten years later. They chose me to be their representative; ombudsman, as we say here in Sweden. So I had to give up my job as a waitress and just work in the union. And I went around to the cafés and asked the girls to join the unions. And then in 1947, I came to LO as an organizer or an ombudsman.

Q: Were you influenced by any thinkers or books, or was your education essentially practical?

A: Working at a café or restaurant, we had such long working hours, 60 hours a week, and some days, 12 hours, that there wasn't much time to read. But we tried to go to the labor education service and take part in the study circles, but it was also difficult for us in the hotel and restaurant business, because one day, I was free from 5 o'clock, and another day, I worked to 10 or 10:30 p.m.

Q: I'd like to ask you questions specifically about your experience as a woman in the labor and the socialist movement. First of all, were you accepted by the male trade unionists, and by the male socialists? Did they make you feel out of place when you began your career?

A: The union I belonged to all my life was only women. 2,500 women and 29 men, and we had a man as a paid officer. We had to elect a second officer in 1937. This man and the 29 men worked to have another man. Many of the women, and of course, myself, said: "No, we have to have a principled discussion about what kind of person we shall have, a man or a woman." And we had a two hour discussion and then decided by a big majority to have a woman. And then the men said: "Do you have any woman?" We hadn't. One of the girls, one of my best friends, who was also a waitress said: "Sigrid, you have to take this job." And I said: "No, I can't, I can't. I have only six years school and I can't write and...." And she said: "You have been talking about women during the whole discussion here. What kind of woman are you? I had to say: "Yes, I'll take it." Then the men in the national union, the Hotel and Restaurant National Union, said: "Wait and see. We don't think it will work, but let her try." I had the women beside me every time. They said: "We're going to help you. If something happens, call us, we will come and help." And later when they asked the party to have a trade union woman on their list for the Parliament, the party in Stockholm decided: "Yes, we'll try. What experience does she have? We know that she is a social democrat and we know she is working hard for the trade union, but what about politics?" You laugh, and I laugh too, today, but it was like that. I was placed twelfth on the list, and nobody thought we would take 12 seats, but we did. And then I had to again show that I knew about politics and I had to work with questions like the labor market, women, day nurseries, and everything that women should have to make it easier to work and have a family. Then I can say that I was accepted. But the man in this union I had told you about said: "You can't have this job and also hold the seat in Parliament." And I replied: "We have to ask the board about this." And the board was only women. The chairman, who was a cook in a big restaurant said: "We're going to let Sigrid try. If she doesn't manage to do both, we'll take up the question again, but not now." And he had to sit down. Parliament met Tuesday, Wednesday and Thursday. And then the members of Parliament just went to the community and I went to my job. The women said: "We'll help you. Tell us what to do, we can go to these cafés and konditorei and talk to the workers, then you just can come in and negotiate for them."

Q: So there was a very strong sense of solidarity on the part of the women who supported you?

A: Yes, there really was. And it's a good feeling to know that. When I came to LO in 1947, I had to try to see that women's wages were raised a little. Before 1960, women were not paid the same as men. But in 1960 we reached an agreement for equal pay.

Q: In all this struggle, were there men in the union and the party who supported the efforts of women?

A: Yes, they did, finally they did. They didn't from the beginning, and they didn't care about day nurseries, and things like that. But nowadays they do.

Q: Was there any discussion within the party or the trade unions on the theoretical problems of the women's question? Was that discussed at party congresses or at party meetings?

A: Not in the party congress, but in LO Congress of 1946; we had written some resolutions and asked the Congress to decide that we women should have the means to work to get women more active in the unions and in the LO. And of course, the men said: "Why? Women have all the facilities and all the possibilities." But the Congress decided that we should have a committee working out the proposal. I was the chairman of this committee. And one of the men in LO was secretary. He was a very good and just young man. His feeling was that women were just as good as men if they got the same education, the same opportunities, and he did a very good proposal. And the board of LO decided that we should have such a committee within LO and that the LO should appoint a woman secretary. They chose me. I had to travel around the country and ask the women and men to let the women take part in the organizations. Nowadays, it's easy; it wasn't then. But it was a very interesting job, very interesting.

Q: One of the great efforts on the part of Swedish Social Democracy was to establish an effective system of pensions and facilities for retirement. At the same time, there's been a certain amount of criticism in the last decade that Sweden has become bureaucratic, and older people are segregated from the rest of the community. Do you think that's a valid criticism?

A: Oh, yes. Of course, when you leave your job, you leave your social contacts, and you have to try to get other contacts, and I think it's more difficult for men than for women, because women always have something to do in the home and in my generation men aren't so used to that. But I am now working very hard in the old people's organization. We have a big organization, almost 400,000 members. I am just chairman of one local organization here -- 400 pensioners, and I also belong to the district's board where we have 37,000 members. We try to get in contact with the pensioners who just sit in their home and don't do anything.

Q: So, in a certain way, you continue the same kind of role.

A: Yes, I really do. I feel it's just as important as it was with the young people.

Q: What kind of changes is that organization working for?

A: We are going to try to get the community and the government to give money to rebuild old houses, so people can still live in their own homes. Many of the houses in the city don't have a lift and old people can't stay if you don't rebuild them. So we have to always, every day, push on this. Remember that we have been working very hard for our whole life and we don't want to stand with our hat in hand and say: "Can we have this or that?" We ought to have it. Young people ask for swimming pools and we ask for better communications, hospitals, and home service, and for people to come in and help. I can't wash windows and do the heavier work myself. And we have to make them realize that it is almost as important for older people to raise their voice as for young people.

Interview with Trygve Brattelí

TRYGVE BRATTELI:

My parents settled in 1908 in the town of Oslofiords, about 20 kilometers from Oslo. My father was a shoemaker and had finished his training in the beginning of this century. He was a real handicraftsman; he made new shoes, but he also had a very small farm. This was the time of big families. My father was the eldest of 12 children. My mother was the eldest of six. They had 11 children; I was the fourth. Conditions were very bad. It was a life of hard work, very little else.

During the First World War, the handicraft shoemakers were destroyed by the new factories, and that created very difficult economic conditions for my family. My father, like many handicraftsmen in such a situation, was rather hostile to the shoe factories and refused to take a job there. In the last years of his life, he was a muncipal worker, under very bad conditions.

My father and I joined the Labor Party at the same time. I was 17 years old; he was 30 years older. Like many handicraftsmen at the time, he first became conservative, but some years later, after having been a municipal worker and coming into contact with the trade unions, he joined the Labor Party. 1927 was a great period of political upheaval in this country. The election led to the first short-lived Labor Party government. Just before Christmas we went to a meeting and became members.

I asked for immigration papers to the United States in 1928, but didn't get them. In the beginning of the 1930s I received a message from the American consulate that I could ask again, but by this time I was politically active and I refused to emigrate.

Q: How did you become involved in politics?

A: This was a difficult time for the country. There were tens of thousands of jobless young people. I joined the Labor Party and shortly after the youth organization and became very active in studying social and economic problems. In 1932 I got my first professional job in politics. I was sent to the far north to a small industrial town. Since

183

then, my job has been political activity except for
the years of war and concentration camp.

Q: What were the major ideological influences
you experienced?

A: The dominant issues were economic, that was
our main line. The bulk of us were in opposition to
Soviet communism. The election of 1933 revolved
around full employment and growth. I always studied
quite a lot, not in institutions, but in organized
groups in the youth organization and socialist
party. First I was a leader of the socialist youth
organization, then of the party. After the war, I
was elected secretary-general of the party
administration. I was chairman of the first defense
commission after the war. My education has always
been in organizational and practical political work.
After several years, I can say that I knew more about
economics than youngsters who had spent several years
in universities. I specialized for a long time in
economic questions. I was Minister of Finance two
times, in all, for seven years, and prepared eight
state budgets, more than anyone else.

Q: In the 1930s, how concerned was the Labor
Party about the threat of fascism from within Norway
and from without?

A: The Labor movement all over the Nordic
countries was on its guard against fascist movements;
aside from the United Kingdom, they were the best
prepared to stand up against fascist-nazi expansion.
Fascism never got any firm base in this part of
Europe. Looking back, I can say that there was a
very great consolidation of democracy in the Nordic
area.

Q: In general terms, what was the significance
of the occupation and resistance for Norway and for
the Labor Party?

A: Not very much. If I take the main lines of
domestic policy in this country, I think it was an
almost unbroken general line from the beginning of
the 1930s until this day, a new economic policy with
Keynes as its big prophet. There was certainly a lot
of discussion with my younger friends in German
concentration camps. We used to discuss what we
would do after the war -- that was a more cheerful
subject! Our intention was very clearly to go on
further with the policies of the 1930s: full
employment, better education, greater social
justice. The Labor Party was very strong after the

war. The real break was the 1930s. There were changes in other fields, in foreign and defense policy.

In our discussions about the future, we didn't believe it possible to safeguard this country through the defense policies of the 1930s. To avoid the outbreak of war a sufficient number of states must keep together. Norwegian neutrality disappeared in the feelings of people when Norway was actually attacked. Even when that happened, it was difficult for many people in this country to believe it was possible. At least since 1905 when we broke the old connection with Sweden, the Norwegian people believed that as long as we didn't provoke anyone, no one would attack us. It was a real shock. That's why there was sufficient support for foreign and defense policy which ended up in membership in NATO.

Q: What is extraordinary about Norway is the rapidity and extent of change in this century.

A: When I was about 20 years old, most people believe that really profound change in economic conditions wasn't possible. The big break was to discover that it <u>was</u> possible by appropriate means to control economic conditions. We're in the midst of that discussion again today. To me, it's rather horrifying to listen to these arguments from the 1920s.

In my childhood, especially in the countryside, but almost all over Norway, it was looked upon as a natural thing that all families have six-11 children. Then in the 1930s, this changed entirely, not by propaganda. This was the foundation for economic and social policies in Norway for a long time after. These big groups of children helped create the unemployment of the 1930s. When this generation married, they protested against having such large families. It just happened, without any help from authorities, religious or political, in the course of a decade.

Q: What has made the Norwegian Labor Party more radical than, say, the Swedish Social Democrats?

A: Norway experienced very fast industrialization. Young families left their homes and protested their conditions in the new factories.

Q: The situation seems like a speeded-up version of what happened in England in the early 19th century, with one exception. The socialist and trade union movement was already here. It was able to channel the very radical sentiments of dispossessed artisans and peasants, whereas in England, such protest often turned into Luddism and the working class needed over half a century to evolve an effective doctrine and organizational structure.

A: One example is Martin Tranmael. For several decades, he was looked upon as our most influential leader. He was born in the countryside; he was never exactly at home in the town. He was very skeptical about many things which followed industrialization. He was typical of two generations, of the youngsters who had their roots in rural areas and small towns. He was very doubtful about the new political alliance which came with the Russian Revolution. He was the main opponent of the Comintern in Norway. He opposed all kinds of heavy centralization in the hands of a few people. He was a typical Norwegian. For this reason, you find very opposing tendencies here, more marked than in Denmark and Sweden.

Q: You were Prime Minister at the time of the Common Market referendum and resigned after its defeat. Why was the issue so divisive?

A: I had tried to study the main lines of European development back to the German-French wars. I was convinced and still am convinced that the stabilization of Europe was only possible with developed and formalized contacts between the various nations. The situation was nearly ripe for Norway to go into the Common Market. After the war, I supported the idea of new forms of economic, political and military contacts between nations to lay the foundations for more stable conditions and a safer future for this part of the world but here you found our whole history repeated for hundreds of years. All traditions had spokesmen in the discussion which followed. In my party, in the party organization, we had solid support the whole time, but there was all kinds of criticism. Then it was decided to hold a referendum. The government unanimously took the stand that if the referendum did not back the government's proposal to prepare for membership in the Common Market, then, in accordance with parliamentary rules, the government had to resign. It was a long-term perspective. Today, Norway's economic relations with the Common Market countries are much greater than at the time it was decided not to go into the Common Market. I doubt very much that economic integration would have gone much further had we been full members. The most important consequence of not being a member is that we don't have a political voice.

Q: To conclude, what do you think have been the major accomplishments brought about by the Labor Party and what are the main problems for the rest of this century?

A: I've had a rather long life, over 70 years. I remember what I saw with my own eyes, in small towns and in the countryside. It was a real class society. Norway is <u>entirely</u> different from what it was when I was 20 years old in 1930. There were no real social connections between the owners of farms of a certain size and small farmers. For example, one of my friends, a leader of the Norwegian trade union movement, found his father when he himself was over 50 years old through the Salvation Army. The father had had a job on a farm. The owner had a daughter of the same age and they had contact with each other and wanted to marry. The parents of the woman refused and the result was that the man just disappeared. Even on a comparatively small farm, it was <u>impossible</u> to accept that a real proletarian without social and political position could marry the daughter of a Norwegian farmer. It was a real class society. But it is very different today. I see much more inheritance from the old class society when I visit Soviet Russia than in this country.

Q: And the main priorities for the rest of the century?

A: To give a very general answer, just go on continuing in the same direction.

5
Bruno Kreisky
and Austrian Socialism

Austrian Social Democracy dates from the Hainfeld Congress of 1889. It was founded by Viktor Adler, who remained its leading figure until 1918. It was a mass party, which sought not only electoral support but also a large and active membership, a membership which, since World War I, has fluctuated around 10% of the population of Austria. The socialists created a veritable state within a state. This tendency reflected and contributed to the division of Austrian society into three rival compartments during the First Republic, compartments referred to as lager or armed camps.

The movement was based on three pillars; the party, the trade unions and the cooperatives. After World War II, the trade union movement, desirous of including all political persuasions, became officially neutral. Although the socialist faction has the clear majority within the unions, relations between parties and unions are restricted now, especially with regards to financial contributions from unions to the party. The unions are no longer the "siamese twin" of the party. Nevertheless, there persists a system of interlocking directorates. The same development took place within the cooperative movement. Although the many organizations associated with the party are somewhat less important now than in the past, they remain significant: the sports association, for example, has about 700,000 members, the Friends of Nature 126,000.

Prior to 1934, intellectuals, many of them Jewish, played significant roles within the party leadership. There was an informal rule that Jewish membership on the party executive would be kept below one half. The relationship between men like Viktor Adler or Otto Bauer and the party was almost patriarchal. Adler, Bauer, Max Adler and Karl Renner were all provocative thinkers, who synthesized Marxist thought with other currents like neo-Kantianism or the empiro-criticism of Mach. The term "Austro-Marxism," invented by the enemies of the socialists, soon became a mark of this stimulating movement. The Austrian party, unlike the German, was not dominated by uninspiring party hacks and bureaucrats after World War I. Concern with ideology declined, however, after the Second War ; one reason was perhaps the destruction of the Vienna Jewish community, another the "end of ideology."

Austrian socialism has placed a premium on party unity. The party has never undergone a major schism. Leadership has known how to move with the tide to avoid a rupture; communism never got far.

Austrian socialism in the Empire was predominantly the party of German Austrians. The nationalities formed their own parties. If the imperial authorities were originally antagonistic to the socialists, they soon assumed a benevolent neutrality; the socialists wanted to establish autonomy for the nationalities within the Empire; they were among the few centripetal forces in Austria-Hungary. Universal male suffrage was established in 1906; by World War I the socialists had the largest parliamentary group in Austria.

When war broke out, the party leadership supported the Empire against its nemesis, Russian autocracy. But as time went on, opposition to the war increased. In 1916, Friedrich Adler, son of Viktor Adler, assassinated Count Sturgkh, the Prime Minister. Adler became a hero to many militants; his act, as much a protest against his father's policies as against those of the State, may have helped avert a significant post-war schism in the party. The party moved towards an increasingly resolute opposition to the war.

With the collapse of the Empire, many socialists hoped for union with Germany. Naturally, the Allies were not thus inclined, and the rump Austrian state was forced to continue. The socialists participated as the leading party in the provisional government of 1918-1920. In this period, the party showed much greater wisdom than its German counterpart. It saw the enemy on the right, not on the left. Rather than emphasizing the struggle against bolshevism and joining forces with the right, the party moved to the left, at least rhetorically, thereby limiting communist influence. At the same time, the socialists tried to create a loyal republican army and police.

The tragedy of Austrian socialism was that the party fell short of a parliamentary majority. Because of its leftist leanings, it was reluctant to continue the collaboration with the Christian Social Party after 1920. Thereafter, the right dominated the federal government, the socialists, Vienna. Vienna was turned into a model of the new society. Rents were controlled, vast public housing complexes were built, providing sanitary amenities never before known by the working class in Vienna. An impressive system of education, health and welfare programs were established, largely paid for by high taxes on the

wealthy. This division of power between christian
socials and socialists might have worked had not the
former developed an increasing aversion not only to
socialism but to democracy. Under Ignace Seipel, the
christian socials cooperated with the fascist
Heimwehr. Especially after 1927, polarization
increased, and the socialists were placed on the
defensive. Seipel's successor, Engelbert Dollfuss,
hoped to resist the pressures of the nazis for
anschluss by creating his own brand of
clerical-fascism with the support of Mussolini. He
eliminated political freedoms step by step, finally
provoking an unsuccessful socialist uprising in 1934,
which took place against the wishes of the party
leadership. But at least Austrian socialists, unlike
German, fought back. They continued to do so. An
underground organization, the Revolutionary
Socialists, was formed. Highly critical of the old
leadership, the Revolutionary Socialists demanded a
more radical, even Leninist line; nevertheless, the
ties were never broken with Bauer and the rest of the
party leadership who had established headquarters in
Czechoslovakia. In 1938, it seemed as if Schuschnigg
was willing to legalize the socialists to create a
united front against Hitler; the anschluss ended that
hope. Resistance proved more difficult under nazi
rule than under the bumbling clerical-fascist
dictatorship.

The Socialist Party was reconstructed after the
war. The Russians supported the creation of a
provisional government under Karl Renner, which was
accepted with reluctance by England and America.
Nevertheless, Renner and the socialists once again
proved successful in resisting communism, even with
the Soviet army occupying half of Austria. The
communists received only five percent of the vote in
the first elections; "popular democracy" got nowhere.

One result of the experience of nazi rule was
that the socialists and christian socials were
resolved to avoid repetition of the internicine
conflicts of the First Republic, a decision rendered
all the more important because of the continued
presence of Soviet occupation forces until 1956.
Austria was run by a series of coalition governments
which until 1966. Jobs in the public sector were
proportionately divided among party loyalists on the
basis of election results. After 1966, regular
alternation in government has taken place, but
important issues are still carefully discussed by
party leaders before they are presented to
Parliament. Both parties have moved to the center,
ideological fervor has diminished; the old
laic-clerical conflict has slowly faded. Unlike the
SPD, however, the SPO has not renounced Marx.

   Much of the credit for the success of the SPO in
the last 20 years goes to Bruno Kreisky. A leader of
the Young Socialists in the 1930s, Kreisky joined the
Revolutionary Socialists and was arrested. His
speech in the trial of 30 Revolutionary Socialists
and communists in March 1936 was described as the
high point of the first day of the trial. Kreisky
prophetically called on the government to restore
political freedom as the only way of making a defense
of Austrian independence possible. Kreisky went into
exile in Sweden and where he remained until 1950,
learning much about the practice of Swedish Social
Democracy. He returned as State Secretary for
Foreign Affairs and took part in negotiating the
Austrian State Treaty with the USSR. In 1957-58 he
headed a commission to prepare a new party
programme. In 1959 he became Foreign Minister, in
1967 party leader and in 1970 Prime Minister.
Kreisky's charisma and his appeal to social groups
which had not previously voted socialist help explain
the party's success in obtaining an absolute
parliamentary majority for the first time in its
history.
   During the 1983 electoral campaign, Kreisky
threatened that he would step down as Prime Minister
if his party lost its absolute majority. The
socialists, although doing well in the election, did
not retain their absolute majority and formed an
alliance with the small Freedom Party. Kreisky
resigned as Chancellor, a decision which may also
have been prompted by his ill health; for several
years, Kreisky has had to receive kidney dialysis.
Nevertheless, he remains active in the Socialist
International, where his radical positions on the
Palestinian and other issues make him a controversial
figure.

Interview with Bruno Kreisky

BRUNO KREISKY

Q: Would you please briefly describe your family background and its impact on your development?

A: As to my ancestors, they were industrialists, inasmuch as one can speak about industry at that time, as well as lawyers and politicians. A great-uncle of mine, Joseph Neuwirth, was active for decades in the Austrian parliament in the second half of the 19th century. He belonged to the liberals and his main interests pertained to economic issues, a novelty at that period.

Thus they all contributed their best whether as judges, prosecutors, or attorneys. And apart from problems of disease which befell one or the other there were essentially no problems in this family up to World War I.

Many people, however, at that time lived in conditions of misery and legal deprivation unimaginable to our contemporaries. With sensitive persons growing up in a bourgeois environment this misery naturally very often led to an attitude of protest. With some this attitude was even exaggerated and motivated them to become active communists. But many who thought about these things more seriously, turned to social democracy and helped to overcome them.

In this context I should not like to fail mentioning that there were obstacles put in the way of young intellectuals wishing to establish themselves in the social democratic movement. Many were shown a cold shoulder and it was almost considered virtuous to repeatedly repulse them in order to observe how they would react. Some were driven away for good. It was said at that time that nothing was lost in those who let themselves be rejected. I must say that even I might have succumbed to such rejection had there not been friends in the labor movement retaining me with great insistance. If, however, an intellectual had once found acceptance it was almost touching to see how pleased people were to have him in the labor movement. There was then a relationship of mutual friendship and faithfulness which belongs to the greatest experiences one can have.

Q: What were the major ideological influences you experienced when you first became active in the socialist movement? Were you influenced much by Marx directly, or more through Austro-Marxist writers? Were you influenced greatly by any of the old party leadership?

A: In my youth I read the important works of Karl Marx, such as "Lohn, Preis, Profit", "Lohnarbeit und Kapital" and of course the Communist Manifesto. I had always avoided reading Das Kapital itself.

While imprisoned for political reasons I found ample time to carefully study Das Kapital. To this day these volumes which I then underlined and annotated are in my possession. Besides I also read in prison a large part of the exchange of letters between Marx and Engels.

In addition to socialist literature I was, of course, also strongly influenced by people who at that time played an important role in social democracy. In particular I was impressed by Otto Bauer, Karl Renner and Max Adler and I should like to stress that I have never since met a person of greater intellectual capacity than Otto Bauer. But there were situations when I felt that in his political actions Otto Bauer was not always right and sometimes failed to act decisively.

I was the youth representative for the fourth Viennese district which belonged to Otto Bauer's constituency. Thus I had the opportunity to often closely observe Otto Bauer. Occasionally, I imagine, he took an interest in me and, for example brought me along to meetings of the Arbeiterzeitung, the official newspaper of the Socialist Party. At the same time I served as an agent and party representative in Lower Austria, in the midst of Karl Renner's constituency. All the party politicians in Lower Austria were friends and partisans of Renner's policy which I therefore also became familiar with. The fact that I have personally been acquainted with both leading figures much more closely than many others, helped to lead me to a certain fundamental balance. Everything I am I owe to these two men. Certainly, Viktor Adler was the great teacher but he was already more remote. Bauer and Renner were the two poles between which I moved along with some others.

Q: Could you describe your activities within the Revolutionary Socialists? What did you hope to accomplish? To what extent did you share the RS's radical critique of the old party? What was the significance of the RS on the subsequent development of Austrian socialism? How valid do you think were

Buttinger's ideas and why did he fail to play any role in the post-war era?

A: In 1933 I was elected chairman of the Committee on Education of Labor Youth by 600 delegates in Salzburg. Due to the dissolution of all socialist institutions in February 1934 I was, of course, precluded from continuing my function. But I continued to feel responsible to those who had elected me and therefore to work for the party as far as this was possible in conditions of illegality. I admitted as much during the trial against socialists in 1936 in which I was one of the accused.

The work of the Revolutionary Socialists can only be understood in the context of the circumstances then prevailing. There was no democracy, only a dictatorship against which we struggled. Thus, during the trial I confirmed that we were in favor of the revolution in the meaning given to it by Ferdinand Lassalle: "Revolution signifies radical change and thus a revolution always occured when -- with or without the use of force, the means do not matter in this regard -- a new principle replaces the existing state of affairs".

But let me turn to the role of Joseph Buttinger which you expressed interest in. At the turn of 1934-35 the first big wave of arrests took place against the leadership of the Revolutionary Socialists. Buttinger then assumed the leadership of the illegal party and provided all his energy for its political activity.

Later on Buttinger accomplished a great deal in humanitarian matters. Together with his wife he helped many persecuted people escape, thus saving them from extinction which almost certainly awaited them.

After the war Buttinger decided to stay in the United States. For the first time a union of the old social democracy and the illegal Revolutionary Socialists was achieved. The name "Socialist Party" in itself was already a compromise. To this designation was a bracket added reading "Social Democrats and Revolutionary Socialists".

Joseph Buttinger later on described the events in a very personal manner in his book Am Beispiel Osterreichs, parts of which caused a lot of criticism on the part of some of his former party associates. If one takes due account of the subjective nature of his account one must however recognize that it constitutes a significant contribution to our history. Buttinger nevertheless never severed his ties with Austria as I know from his numerous visits and the letters I exchanged with him until most

recently and from the fact that he put his valuable
library at the disposal of an Austrian university.

Q: You spent almost a decade in Scandinavia
during and after the war. Could you describe your
political activities during this period? How much
did the conceptions of Swedish Social Democracy
affect your vision of socialism?

A: During my exile in Sweden I worked as an
employee in the secretariat of the consumers
association in Stockholm. Besides, I was
correspondent of various foreign newspapers and
magazines and also wrote for Swedish daily and weekly
publications. In the summer of 1939 I travelled to
the Congress of the Socialist Youth International in
Lille, France. There a confrontation occured between
us and the representatives of French and British
socialist youth organizations which accused us of
being in favor of the war since it was French and
British soldiers who were supposed to fight for our
liberation in the trenches.* We tried to explain
that fascism means war and that they would be faced
with this danger sooner than they thought. At that
time someone shouted at me: "we don't want to die
for Danzig". A few weeks later the World War
started. I have recently recalled this episode a
couple of times as I believe that everything must be
done to foster the peace movement, that the big
parties too must work towards this end. But we
should also be aware that peace cannot be preserved
through demonstrations and love of peace alone, that
we need a genuine policy of peace.

Shortly after my return from France I met Willy
Brandt for the first time and this was the beginning
of a life-long friendship. In my political work I
was mainly involved in those issues which were of
particular concern to the emigrants: for one,
political asylum for members of the German military
forces who had escaped to Sweden. In addition and at
a very early stage we drafted a declaration
announcing the support by Austrian socialists in
Sweden for the re-establishment of an independent
Austria and the convocation of an Austrian national
congress in London with participants from all
countries.

As to the other part of your question it is
certainly correct that the concepts of Swedish Social
Democracy have had a great influence on me. When

---

*I had to answer them that their freedom too was at
stake.

Austria and Germany succumbed to dictatorship a new political philosophy emerged in the social democratic parties of the Scandinavian countries which finally brought these parties to power and strengthened them. They carried out an economic policy which helped to overcome the economic crisis which had only just begun to subside. In carrying out this policy they abided by the teaching of an economist of the liberal school, John Maynard Keynes. He was one of the most important economists precisely because he refused to simply accept the fatalistic view according to which the laws of the market will finally overcome the crisis. In contrast he believed and taught that the state had the means at its disposal to counteract the crisis. It is interesting to note that at an international conference one of our young economists recently referred to our economic policy as a form of "Austro-Keynesianism". To this I responded that "Austro-Keynesianism: is to Keynes as Austro-Marxism is to Marx." In all likelihood both would have shaken their heads at what happened in their names. But, in spite of all, these terms carry a certain significance.

Q: There is much talk about the differences between pre-war and post-war Austrian socialism. You have sometimes seemed to suggest that the differences have been exaggerated. How would you describe the main continuities and discontinuities of Austrian socialism?

A: As a socialist one must again and again address the most cruel phenomenon of this economic order, namely unemployment. For it constitutes a great social cruelty if 35 million people wishing to work have no possibility to do so. And if someone is removed from the productive process, from work, this naturally also bears serious psychological consequences.

I am one of those who bear witness to the effects the crisis had on the labor movement and above all the Austrian labor movement. The number of unemployed had reached gigantic dimensions. One could only estimate it since tens and even hundreds of thousands had ceased to be eligible for unemployment benefits. It was undoubtedly more than half a million in a total population of 6 million.

There were then two completely contradictory views held in the labor movement, and it occured that conferences had to be repeated in order to continue discussions. Some comrades believed that we were faced with the last crisis of capitalism and merely had to wait for the moment when this would become evident. Then there would be revolutionary change.

They were opposed, surprisingly, mainly by Otto Bauer who mustered the entire resources of his intellect to prove that this was a serious crisis, the most serious of capitalism, but not the last.

Behind this debate also lay an ideological dispute about the tasks of social democracy. Some thought that the social democracy was a party which at times would be reformist and at others revolutionary. This goes to say that in the periods between revolutions, as they are brought about by wars and crises the party should maintain and strengthen the fighting ability of the working class, preparing it for the big confrontations. Its revolutionary spirit should be preserved. But as we must also fulfill functions in the communities and provinces we must opt for a reformist policy in practice. At the time in question this became known as the theory of the "pause between the revolutions".

In opposition to this the partisans of unconditional reformism espoused the view that the capitalist system could be altered through social reform such as to make revolutions superfluous.

Max Adler called the first theory "revolutionary social democracy". Others believed in social democratic reformism and both failed.

For it became evident that the great crisis was not the last, whatever led to its being overcome. And at its end there was no revolution but a development towards extremes -- not only fascism, but also communism. For the country which next to Austria was most hit by the crisis, Germany, then had a communist party of millions, a phenomenon certainly caused by the crisis.

Thus, as a matter of fact, a process of political disorientation occured during the great crisis. The working class disintegrated into those who had work and those who didn't.

And those who dreamed about a revolutionary development were proven just as wrong as those who believed in reformism. For it very soon became evident that these reforms, as good as they might have been, could not be financed. Thus, both these trends in social democracy foundered on the problems of the crisis. Only when social democracy drew the lessons from this development could it decide on utilizing the possibilities of economic policy of the state in mastering the crisis. The fact that this struggle against the crisis can be carried out with success is proven by the excellent situation in which Austria finds herself today compared with other industrialized countries.

Q: Along the same lines, some authors suggest that the SPO has "abandoned" Marxism without finding an acceptable substitute. How valid is that generalization?

A: For me the way Marx and Engel's explained the world and history remains convincing. Their way of thinking has helped me a lot. For even if today you cannot study physics relying on a textbook from the beginning of the century, Newton remains one of the really great, even though there was an Einstein after him. The same applies of course to Marx.

I live and work for a developed democracy. In my view its law is the evolutionary process and I am therefore very pleased that the notion of reform today receives a more contemporary and appropriate interpretation. There is the well-known distinction between reforms which maintain the system and those which change it, whereas I should like to stress, this distinction is very often to be understood in a dialectical meaning, i.e., the quantity of reforms may alter the quality of a society. No question about that. But I continue to believe without hesitation or limitation that wherever there is a dictatorship, a total dictatorship, the people has a right to revolt against it. And wherever this occurs I shall support such movements as much as I can. Quite frankly, for those parts of the world ruled by brutal tyranny I advocate the principle that the oppressed, unable to find justice, have the moral right to revolt and thus obtain their rights. This may come as a shock from a social democrat and an old politician. For me it is a moral obligation.

In this context I am always asked about my views on the idea of class struggle and a classless society. The class struggle is a historical phenomen and takes place continuously. Today it is often called a distribution struggle, the struggle of distribution in the society. This is a term of modern economics coined in order to avoid the word "class struggle". The class struggle is a historical fact and it will be carried on in different forms at certain times. It is being sublimated, so to speak. A classless society, however, is a notion which cannot be realized. We have seen this in the communist states where new classes replaced former ones. Sometimes we are dealing with economic characteristics of class, sometimes with bureaucratic ones, a third time they are of a military nature. In my opinion in socialism it is most important to continuously question this formation of classes and to exercise some control over it. And this is only feasible in conditions of democracy, every other form of government having failed in this respect. The communist dictatorship has turned the dictatorship of the proletariat into one over it, something which Max

Adler already predicted. It is only democracy which
time and again challenges class domination. The
degree of mobility is, however, important for the
quality of a society. It is essential that gifted
people have a chance to advance in the areas of their
competence. Everything which impedes such mobility
is detrimental.

The democratization of society in all areas
constitutes another important element. To achieve
this end different means must be applied for each
area. In the economy, it cannot simply be
accomplished in mathematical terms. One cannot
juxtapose 500 workers to one manager, for example,
but one must attribute a certain functional position
to the emplyees, carefully balanced with that of the
employer who must be able to discharge his functions
while blue and white collar workers are granted the
right to participate in decision-making. The process
of democratizing the economy must, however, not lead
to destroying profit. Economic laws have to be
recognized also by those who are not enrepreneurs.

Q: Austria before the war was a bitterly divided
society; since 1945 it appears a model of stability.
What are the main reasons for this change, and to
what extent has the SPO helped produce this evolution?

A: In the 1930s all efforts to escape Hitler's
fascism by favoring common interests over dividing
ones failed due to the intransigence of the bourgeois
politicians. Instead of cooperating with the social
democrats they dissolved the Parliament and
developments led to the bloody civil war of February
1934 and the destruction of the organizations of the
labor movement. Following these events there was
such incredible pent-up hatred against the regime
that some people naively remarked that they would be
content with anyone just as long as he would end this
rule. But I am firmly convinced that we would have
been able to save Austria from nazism if a political
agreement like the one after 1945 could have been
reached. I should like to repeat what I said in
1936, namely that the Catholic farmers, at that time
much more numerous than today, together and united
with the social democratic workers, hence 70-75% of
the population, could have formed a political force
which could not have been defeated by nazism. Maybe
through military force but things had not come to
that yet. We were not defeated on the military
plane, we were already exhausted politically and one
of the reasons for that was the fact that the right
had already conceded Austria to Mussolini.

After 1945 we not only succeeded to remove the
rubble fairly quickly but men who had been on

different sides of the barricades very quicly found common ground. To me this is the greatest accomplishment of post-war Austrian history. It goes to show that Austrians have proved the famous expression by Hegel wrong, according to which we learn from history that people learn nothing from it.

The Austrians learned their lesson from history and the same happened more recently in Spain. If a people has really become acquainted with civil war it does not want it to happen any more.

Since 1945 we also benefit from regular contacts between the socially and economically relevant forces of the country. These contacts take place in the framework of our system of social partnership which is admired by many people abroad. Strong trade unions are a precondition for the functioning of this system and they are fully aware of how much they can reasonably demand from the other side. Thus both sides consider carefully whether or not to leave the negotiating table in critical situations. In almost all cases negotiations continue as everyone knows that he will have to return to the negotiating table anyway. As each side knows the strength of the other, futile threatening gestures are dispensed with.

To define social partnership I once used a term coined by psycho-analysis, namely a "sublimated class-struggle". Its object is the distribution of what has been achieved by common efforts. Wages, salaries and profits play a role as much as prices, in this context.

Q: Austria has always played an important role within the Socialist International and you have certainly continued this tradition. What goals can the International pursue for the next decade?

A: The close connection between the Socialist Party of Austria and the Socialist International which was called "Socialist Workers International" between the two World Wars is proven by the fact that Friedrich Adler, the son of the founder of SPO Dr. Viktor Adler, was Secretary General of the Sozialistische Arbeiterinternationale from 1923-1940 when he resigned and the International collapsed. Later on Julius Braunthal was Secretary General of the SI from 1949-1956 and Hans Janitschek from 1969-1976.

Bruno Pittermann, at that time Vice-Chancellor of Austria, was elected President of the Socialist International in 1964 which function he retained till 1976. At the SI congress in Geneva in 1976 SPO-party chairman Federal Chancellor Dr. Bruno Kreisky was elected as one of the Vice Presidents of the Socialist International, a function he still holds.

The main aims of the Socialist International in the current decade are: disarmament (SI has appointed a special Advisory Council on disarmament questions). Closely connected with disarmament a further goal constitutes the improvement of North-South relations (e.g., report of the so-called Brandt-commission which was also adopted by SI), finally human rights as the basis of the above-mentioned efforts.

Areas of special SI-activity in the current decade are: the Middle East (fact-finding missions led by Bruno Kreisky), Latin America where SI offers strong support to liberation movements and resistance fronts, in some cases led by SI-member parties, and Southern Africa (in particular support to Front Line States SI mission of the Front Line States led by Olof Palme, 1977). Overall themes of activity are, of course, détente based on the recognition of the fact that in the nuclear age on the international scale the dialogue with the political opponent is the only possible way of action.

6
Michael Foot
and the British Labour Party

Michael Foot was elected Leader of the Labour Party in November 1979. He resigned in June 1983, following the party's overwhelming electoral defeat. His years of leadership proved a frustrating experience. Foot had difficulties asserting control over the intensely divided party. Foot was committed to left-wing causes like unilateral nuclear disarmament; he also supported withdrawal from the Common Market. His election as leader helped provoke the secession of the social democrats. Yet Foot's "soft" leftism differed from the "hard" left of leaders like Tony Benn who did not share Foot's respect for parliamentary institutions and concern for party unity. Foot depended on the right of labour for support against this new left. The electoral defeat of 1983 indicated that the public either did not like what the left-wing party platform said (an opinion shared by many labour MPs) or did not have faith that a Labour Party which could not rule itself was capable of leading the country.

The crisis of the Labour Party mirrored a deeper crisis in English society. The economic decline of England led to a radical critique in both the Conservative and Labour parties of the centrist orientation that had generally prevailed in both parties since the 1950s. Margaret Thatcher pushed the Tories to the right; her political skill and the Falklands Island war enabled her both to overwhelm moderate opponents within her party and win an unprecedented electoral victory at a time of massive unemployment. In the Labour Party, however, no group or individual was able to provide direction. The period of crisis brought to the fore historic differences between party factions, as well as pointing out incongruities in party structure. A brief historical survey will help explain how labour arrived at this point.

Although the Industrial Revolution occurred first in England, the rise of a labor party occurred in England later than in most other European nations. And unlike the working class parties of the continent, the English party was not established as an explicitly Marxist or even socialist party.

There had been no lack of radicalism among the English working classes during the Industrial Revolution. Robert Owen pioneered both a national trade union movement and a system of cooperatives. The chartists fought for male suffrage in order to give the workers political power. But these efforts failed because of the inexperience of the working class and the sheer might of its opponents. So long as the workers movement seemed radical, the full power of the Establishment was mobilized against it. With the advent of Victorian prosperity and the apparent failure of revolutionary politics, the workers turned towards reformist solutions and moderate trade unions. The growing "reasonableness" of the workers prompted the Liberal and Conservative parties to extend the suffrage in 1867 and 1884. In the last part of the 19th century, most workers supported the Liberal Party, although small numbers joined Keir Hardie's Independent Labour Party found in 1893 or Henry Hyndman's Marxist Social Democratic Federation.

Frustrated by the small gains made through collaboration with the liberals, the Trade Union Congress united with the Independent Labour Party, the Fabian Society, and the Social Democratic Federation to establish a Labour Representation Committee to back candidates for Parliament (the dogmatic Social Democratic Federation soon withdrew). In 1900 two MPs were elected; in 1906, 29. From the beginning, the Labour Party was more a coalition than a cohesive party. The dominant force was the TUC, which, as a result of the party's structure of indirect representation based on collective membership of affiliated organizations, controlled an overwhelming majority of the votes at party congresses. It is significant that the party established a political structure first and only later defined its ideology. In that process, a number of influences proved significant. Intellectuals like Sidney and Beatrice Webb and George Bernard Shaw of the Fabian Society supported a gradualist, reformist line. Many labour leaders were actively involved in non-conformist churches, and were deeply marked by christian socialist ideals. On the other hand, the influence of Marxism was extremely limited.

The majority of the party supported involvement in World War I and from 1915 labour members sat in the cabinet, though a minority of the party, under Ramsay MacDonald opposed the war. In 1924 labour won 142 seats and became the leading opposition party. For a brief period in 1924, MacDonald, who had returned as party leader, formed a minority government. Since it was dependent on liberal support, the government made no notable reforms. It did demonstrate that labour was capable of governing within the parliamentary system.

In 1929 labour returned to power, again without a majority. This proved a trying period. MacDonald and Snowden, his Chancellor of the Exchequer, stubbornly applied deflationary measures as remedies for the Great Depression, encountering mounting opposition from within the party. Faced with labour unwillingness to countenance his policies, MacDonald decided to form a National Government with the conservatives and liberals, carrying with him virturally none of his own party. After this blow, Labour remained in the opposition for the rest of the '30s. The trade unions reasserted their predominance and Ernest Bevin emerged as éminence grise. In 1935, the pacifist Lansbury was replaced as party leader by Clement Attlee, and the party's new foreign policy line stressed collective security. Even at this point, however, Labour had difficulty in arriving at a clearcut position on fascist expansionism.

During World War II, labour again participated in the wartime cabinet; this time, however, its role was greater. Many party leaders developed experience in government which proved useful afterwards. Attlee served as Deputy Prime Minister. In 1945, to some astonishment, labour won the elections. The Attlee government nationalized several key industries, implemented many of the welfare proposals of the Beveridge report and established the National Health Service. Centralized planning, however, was not attempted and labour rejected membership in the European Coal and Steel community. The domestic policies of the government were not radical enough for the party's left, who were no more pleased by its unqualified support for American Cold War policy. The leader of the left was Aneurin Bevan, a charismatic orator and the political mentor of Michael Foot. The Bevanites expressed themselves through the Tribune, which Foot edited from 1948-1952. When the government decided in 1951 to charge fees for eyeglasses and false teeth to offset deficits incurred because of the Korean War, Bevan resigned his cabinet seat. After Attlee's retirement as party leader, the moderate Hugh Gaitskill defeated Bevan as party leader. The conflict between the two men and their factions continued through the decade; Gaitskill, however, could count on the support of the big trade unions. One particularly acerbic and futile debate occurred in 1959 when Gaitskill advocated removing Clause Four of the party program which pledged the party to the common ownership of the means of production. On the critical issue of unilateral nuclear disarmament however, Bevan made common cause with Gaitskill, to the consternation of Bevanites like Michael Foot. In 1960, the Scarborough congress of the Labour Party narrowly approved English renunciation of nuclear weapons. Gaitskill and the Parliamentary Party opposed the measure. This raised the question of the relative authority of party congress and parliamentary group, a question which reemerged in the 1970s. The next year, Gaitskill was able to obtain a reversal of that decision by the congress. Bevan died in 1960, followed by Gaitskill only three years later. The new party leader, Harold Wilson, was considered to be of the left but soon disappointed his former comrades. The Wilson years produced frustration in all factions of the party.

The Wilson governments of 1964 to 1970 demonstrated Wilson's remarkable skills as a pure politician, but were less successful in substantive issues. Wilson faithfully backed U.S. policy on Vietnam, found no effective way of disciplining breakaway Rhodesia, was plagued by constant economic and monetary problems, and showed little inclination to develop effective economic planning. The government's efforts at trade union reform, based on the White Paper In Place of Strife, unleashed such opposition from the unions that they were withdrawn. The trade unions' opposition to any limitations on their prerogatives brought them closer to the left of the party, a phenomenon accentuated by the declining state of the economy and labor market. Despite the defeat of 1970, Wilson remained at the helm of the party and became Prime Minister when labour was returned in 1974.

Up until 1974, Michael Foot stood on the periphery of the Labour Party. He had been a leading Bevanite spokesman, more Bevanite than Bevan in the case of nuclear disarmament. After Bevan's death in 1960, Foot represented his old constituency of Ebbw Vale. By the 1970s, Foot decided to play a more central role in the party. In 1974, he was named Secretary of State for Employment and in 1976, when James Callaghan became Prime Minister he was appointed Leader of the House of Commons.

When the Labour Party was defeated in 1979, resentment boiled over against Callaghan and his policies. The elections of 1979 marked the beginning of a new epoch in English politics. Margaret Thatcher became Prime Minister and breaking with moderate Toryism pursued a harsh monetarist economic policy. Callaghan's prestige was damaged by the electoral defeat of 1979, and he had difficulty resisting the demands of the Bennites. The latter demanded changes in the structure of the party which would have weakened the power of the Parliamentary Party, including mandatory re-selection of MPs by constituency parties (where the left had gained power), election of the party leader by an electoral college including unions and constituency parties as well as the Parliamentary Party. Benn also wanted to force the Parliamentary Party to follow the electoral manifesto devised at the Party Conference. These demands were accompanied by a political program which included withdrawal from NATO and unilateral nuclear disarmament, withdrawal from the Common Market, and renationalization without compensation of industries denationalized by the Tories. On September 30, 1980 the Blackpool Conference of the Labour Party passed resolutions for mandatory re-selection and the electoral college, but did not agree on the precise formula of the latter. They also voted for unilateral disarmament, but against departure from NATO. On 15 October Callaghan resigned as leader, perhaps to force election of a new leader before the electoral college system could be implemented. On 10 November Michael Foot was elected Leader, defeating Dennis Healey on the second ballot.

Michael Foot arrived at the helm of the Labour Party at a critical moment, facing problems both on his right and left. Shortly after his election the "Gang of Four," Jenkins, Owens, Williams and Rodgers left labour to form a Social Democratic Party, which subsequently entered into an electoral alliance with the liberals. The SDP did not take with it many labour MPs; nevertheless, it posed a potential threat to Labour, winning several key by-elections. The SDP schism weakened the right-wing of labour. At the same time Foot was involved in a series of skirmishes with Benn and his followers, who did not provide Foot with any more support than they had given Callaghan.

It is ironic that Michael Foot encountered difficulties from the left of his party. Foot has been on the left of the party for four decades. On national and international issues, Foot was not at odds with the Bennites. He favored British withdrawl from the Common Market and unilateral nuclear disarmament; he opposed any forms of legislation restricting trade unions. On the other hand, he was a believer in the prerogatives of members of Parliament, and instinctively opposed proposals which would put the Parliamentary Party under the thumb of constituency parties. Foot wanted to keep labour together, whereas the Bennites preferred to purge the right if need be to create ideological purity. Moreover Benn refused to respect party discipline. As labour lost more and more by-elections, there were continued calls for Foot's resignation. At the same time, Foot retained considerable trade union support. It seemed unwise to change leaders at the very last minute. Foot stayed, but his already weak authority was further damaged. The Falkland Islands conflict and the wave of jingoism it engendered gave Thatcher the perfect moment to call elections.

The elections of 1983 brought labour's score down to 23.3 per cent of the vote, its lowest in the post-war. Most of the losses were due to social democratic inroads, although ironically, the SDP received only six seats. The Alliance won few seats, but almost as many votes as labour. The schism of the party was a major factor in the defeat; conservative strength had actually declined by half a percent. Foot's experience as party leader had not been a happy one, but the problems went far beyond the personality or policy predilections of the party leader. The survival of labour itself remains in question.

Interview with Michael Foot

MICHAEL FOOT:

My father (Isaac Foot) was a strong liberal. In his very, very early days, he was a supporter of the old Social Democratic Federation of Henry Hyndman, but that was at the age of 18 or 19. He then became a strong West Liberal in the West Country in Plymouth and the whole surrounding area: he was a liberal M.P. in and out for many years and so I was brought up in a liberal family.

I'd had three years at Oxford; I think what I'd learned there had a considerable effect on influencing me towards joining the Labour Party and becoming a socialist. Several of my friends at Oxford were members of the Labour Club and the Socialist Society; then I was introduced for the first time to socialist politicians of the day, notably Stafford Cripps. I was very friendly with John Cripps, his son. But it wasn't till I left Oxford and went up for my first job in Liverpool, in a shipping firm, that I joined the Labour Party in the Walton constituency of Liverpool in 1934.

Q: Was someone with a university degree acceptable within that constituency?

A: Well, I wasn't adopted as a candidate. I just joined the Labour Party as an ordinary member. In the autumn of 1935, there was a general election declared by Baldwin, who was the conservative Prime Minister at the time. It was the election about sanctions against Italy. I wanted to become a labour candidate and so I went up to Transport House, which is the central organization of the Labour Party, and asked whether they had any constituencies that were still vacant, where they hadn't got parliamentary candidates for the election that was taking place in November 1935. They showed me a list; on the list was the constituency of Monmouth in Wales. The fact that it was in Wales made me first think. I was rather surprised that the list of constituencies where they didn't have available candidates should have included one in Wales, but they told me: well, first of all, that it was in the countryside, and second, that they had some disputes inside the party. Anyhow, I went down immediately; I was adopted that night because the election was going to take place in three weeks' time. I was defeated at the election. I wasn't surprised at that because it was a seat in which the conservatives, of course, have an overwhelming majority. But that was my political baptism in elections, at any rate. I fought that election at the age of 22, and I think that I've probably fought more elections than pretty well anybody else of the same age.

Q: At that time, in 1934-35, when you first joined the Labour Party and became active, what socialist thinkers had you read? What conditions influenced you?

A: Liverpool had a tremendous influence in my mind because I saw for the first time in my life what industrial England really looked like. And Liverpool, of course, was one of the cities hit by the slump most fiercely. There were very extensive slums. There was also a very high birth rate, it obviously influenced the situation, and the poverty in Liverpool was desperate. It was the midst of the slump. I don't know what the total percentage figure was then, but you could really see unemployment and its effect with your bare eyes, much more than you can in the England of today. So that obviously had an effect, but prior to that, and indeed in Liverpool, I started reading socialist writings on a much bigger scale than I'd ever done before. I'd talked a lot with socialists in Oxford, but I started reading in Liverpool. I read H.G. Wells, Bernard Shaw, Arnold Bennett, and Bertrand Russell. I don't know which one of them exactly I started reading first, but I read them all in a huge, great jumble, and I continued reading them for many years thereafter, and all of them had a very big effect on my ideas. Which of them had the greater effect, I don't know. In a sense, I was much more well disposed towards H.G. Wells and his approach to the whole question than I was to, say, Bernard Shaw. I read Bernard Shaw's Intelligent Woman's Guide to Socialism, as many of us did at that time; and, of couse, I think that it's a wonderful book, and I read several of his prefaces to his plays, but it didn't have quite the same exhilarating effect as H.G. Wells' books did have upon me, and I think that he did as much as almost anybody else to make me a socialist. But I also read Bertrand Russell's books, in particular, his book on Proposed Roads to Freedom and his books on the Soviet revolution and the political books that he wrote then and they had a very big effect on my mind.

Just after the election of 1935, which I've mentioned, I wanted to be a journalist. I came to London, I had a part-time job; first of all I got on the New Statesman. I was trying to be a reporter in London, generally on the freelance basis. But I used to work about a couple of days a week at the New Statesman, and there I was introduced to H.M. Brailsford, and I started reading him also, and reading every book of his that I could, as well as talking to him, or listening to him. I think that of all the socialist writers and journalist, he probably had a bigger effect upon me than pretty well anybody else. I've written about this in the book I've done, Debts of Honor, in which I've got a special essay about Brailsford. It was his description of socialism that appealed to me more than anybody else's.

Q: You've mentioned essentially English writers. What about French, German, Marx, etc.

A: Right, when I came to London, I started also to recognize that I had to read Marx. A lot of the socialists I'd met at Oxford talked and argued about Marx and of course, I argued with them. At Oxford, I'd usually adopted the kind of Bertrand Russell criticisms of Marx. I think the Bertrand Russell answer to Marxism remains generally valid. I suppose you call it a liberal answer in the proper sense of the word "liberal". But when I came to London, I started reading Marx, much more directly than I'd done before. And I read hugh amounts of Marx. I suppose in '36 and '37, I got through pretty well the whole of Das Kapital. I read most of that with Barbara Castle (she was called Barbara Best in those days). Bu we used to work for Tribune, which was started in 1937; and we did a column on industrial affairs or trade union matters which we were taught to do by William Meller, who was the editor of Tribune, and he also encouraged us to read Marx. I read Das Kapital, but I was always turning aside from Das Kapital to read the Eighteenth Brumaire of Louis Napoleon and much more attractive Marxist documents, which I think, of course, are absolutely magnificent, the Civil War in France, and Engels, Socialism, Utopian and Scientific and also the books on the English Revolution, the Industrial Revolution, and Engels' books on working class history. So I did have in the 1930s a good strong dose of Marxist reading; and I've certainly never wished to disown it, in any sense. I think anybody who doesn't read Marx in some form or other has hardly the right to talk on these political questions. I read quite recently, a couple of years ago, a very fine book on

Marx by S.S. Prawer, which reminded me of all the parts of Marx which had a very considerable influence on not only myself but on the whole range of English people who were educated partly by Marx. Marx himself was steeped in Shakespeare, and a whole range of the greatest figures in literature, so that Marx has a special appeal to English people on those grounds. I don't mean to suggest in any sense at all that it was just hard work reading Marx. I think it was a thrill, as well as instructive. Then also there were some of the people with whom I was becoming friendly at the time, Aneurin Bevan and others, who, of course, were also soaked in Marxism in one form or another; and Marx, undoubtedly described their world as they saw it, probably better than most other writers, although, the intelligent ones, like Aneurin Bevan, were not prepared to swallow it whole. There was also the Left Book Club, whose productions I used to read, and others used to read on a big scale. The quality of those books varied very greatly, in my opinion, but some of the best of them were very good indeed. And John Strachey's pre-war books and his popularization of Marx undoubtedly had a very big influence on many of us. And some of us who thought we understood Marx, maybe understood it because we read Strachey, who was explaining it to us a good deal more clearly. But what really captured my imagination much more than any other was Brailsford and I think that Brailsford's tradition and outlook and use of Marx was the way in which it should be done. Brailsford had a combination of a nonconformist conscience and an English radicalism and Marxist imagination rolled into one; and I believe that he interpreted Marxism for an English scene much better than anybody else.

Q: Let me ask you about your reaction to the practice of the 1930s. In particular, there seemed to be a problem for Bevan and many other people in the British Labour Party to reconcile a fundamental pacifism which derived party from the experience of World War I with the growing threat of expansive fascism. How did you deal with that?

A: Well, it's quite true what you say. There was a very strong anti-war, pacifist tradition in the left of the Labour Party. Not solely pacifist, but anti-imperialist, deriving from the opposition to the First World War, and it became, in the late '20s and the early '30s, the radical, left-wing outlook of the Labour Party. I don't say absolutely pacifist, although there was a strong pacifist element in it. But that continued until the early 1930s, until the rise of Hitlerism and fascism. That had already

happened to some degree in Italy, but the rise of
Hitler changed the mind of the left on these
questions. I don't say it changed it all suddenly; I
think the actual time when the change became
overwhelming was at the outbreak of the Spanish Civil
War. The pacifist opinion in the Party was
overwhelmed by fascism and the threat of fascism, and
in particular the appeal for support for the Spanish
Republic, which was undoubtedly the strongest
international cause for socialists in the whole of
the decade. And I believe that the record of the
Labour Party despite all the criticisms that can be
properly leveled at it -- the record of the Labour
Party was much better than that of any other section
of the community, in the sense that the Labour Party
did realize -- (the left of the Labour Party realized
it first -- but it helped to persuade the party as a
whole) -- that the Spanish Republic must be supported
-- and it could have been. In fact, if the Spanish
Republic had been properly supported, the whole of
the Second World War could have been avoided, and
fascism could have been defeated on Spanish soil.
That's what the Spanish understood, or the Spanish
socialists understood, and that's what many of their
supporters understood, and that's what could have
happened if it had not been for the betrayal of the
right, of the conservative government of the time,
and some elements of the Labour Party. Looking back
now, people talk as if it was a simple choice between
black and white, as if all the choices were easy in
those times, and much more difficult today for
socialists. But I don't believe that is the case. I
think that the choices in the 1930s were obviously
difficult ones, and they are exemplified in the
difficult choices that had to be made between
opposition to the Chamberlain regime and yet the
necessity to try and get some kind of opposition to
Hitler.

Q: Would you say that there was a particular
date at which point you turned from pacifism to the
preparation for the likelihood of war?

A: Well, I think people changed. Different
people on the left changed gradually; the exact time
when each of them changed would be difficult to set
down, but it undoubtedly was taking between, say 1934
and June 1936 -- the outbreak of the Spanish Civil
War. But by the time of the outbreak of the Spanish
Civil War or soon after, the pacifist element, or
mood inside the party, had become very much more
subordinate. Up till 1935, the argument had been one
in which the pacifist element was strongly
represented, of course, by George Lansbury, a very

fine person with a great appeal to the left of the
party for his own record over many years. He had
never been a member of the orthodox establishment of
the party, and indeed had only become leader of the
party by accident in 1931 because he was one of the
few left after the landslide disaster of 1931. But
he proved himself a pretty good one. Stafford Cripps
was also very friendly to him, and in a sense
Stafford Cripps was Lansbury's first lieutenant in
the party. They got on well together, partly because
of their common Christian allegiance and their common
religious associations, something I didn't share.
But you could see that it did have an effect upon
them. At the party conference in 1935, just prior to
the election of 1935, Lansbury was put out as
leader. It was not a happy way for the Labour Party
to go into that election, but the idea that all the
realism was on the side of Ernest Bevin, and all the
romanticism was on the side of Lansbury, wasn't the
case, because, as I've also explained in my book,
Ernest Bevin's attitude towards the Spanish Civil War
was not anything like as imaginative and realistic as
the left's attitude. And so those different elements
went to make the debates in the 1930s, but despite
the weaknesses or deficiencies of the Labour Party, I
think the arguments that were proceeding on the left
were a good deal more honorable kinds of arguments
than the ones that were proceeding in the
conservative establishment. Those were arguments of
the highly disreputable character because they were
arguments as to whether the fascism of Hitler was to
be condoned and accepted, and there were great
elements in British society, British Establishment
society, which were prepared to condone and accept
and indeed applaud fascism in one form or another.
Well, the whole of the Labour Party revolted against
any such proposition.

Q: To what extent did the experience of the war
affect your views on the role the Labour Party should
play? Could you trace your own personal career from
1939 until the beginning of the Attlee government?

A: The war had a very strong, deep, radical
effect on the British public mind and, indeed,
prepared it for the labour victory of 1945 and for
even more adventurous policies maybe than the Labour
Party actually applied. As Marx said, war is the
locomotive of history; well, the locomotive was
certainly at work in Britain between 1939 and '45.
First of all, there was a huge revulsion in the
public mind against those who had misled them against
the conservative leadership of the pre-1939 epoch,
not merely revulsion against their leadership about

fascism, but their leadership about mass unemployment and the rest but, undoubtedly, the effect on the public mind of having been led into that war by people who had apologized for Hitler, and Hitlerism in a sense. And then having to go through such moments of peril did sow a very deep anti-conservative, anti-Tory revulsion which Churchill, of course, had helped to enable them to escape. That didn't alter the fact that the Conservative Party as a whole justly took the great part of the odium for the fact that we got into the war in such a state, and the fact that Hitlerism and fascism had not been exposed before. So that was one major element in the whole change, and then, to fight the war, it was necessary to abandon most of the economic, laissez-faire doctrines that had been prevailing, and were still held by the conservatives. Keynesianism and such ideas had hardly had any influence at all in Britain before 1939. The figure of unemployment when we went into the war was still over a million, and laissez-faire doctrines still prevailed. Well, you couldn't run on that basis, although for some 9 or 10 months at the beginning of the war, they did try to do it. But once the country was in peril from 1940 onwards, every kind of radical idea for mobilizing the resources of the nation was accepted and many of them were adopted, and indeed, Britain mobilized for the war more effectively than probably any other country since; we mobilized more effectively than the Germans did themselves. I think that was kind of socialism in practice. Britain in the war period was nearer to socialist society than anything that I've seen. The common aims of the community were made dominant and I think they were translated into effective economic action in many fields. There was also a common purpose, accepted purpose. I think the war had to be fought, and that was also the overwhelming view of the Labour Party and socialists and therefore there was a kind of common socialist aim that was applied in the war. So all that had an effect in making ideas of socialism much more acceptable and tolerable. There were, too, the reports that were all brought out: the Beveridge Report and the rest. I think they had a very considerable effect on the public mind, but in many respects, I think that Beveridge was trailing along behind the public mood and the public spirit, rather than it happening the other way around.

As we move to 1945, I think that more and more there were people like Aneurin Bevan who were expressing the public mood; and I think he understood what was happening in the public mind much better than the orthodox Labour Party leadership, and he

expressed it when it came to the question of whether
the coalition was going to continue after 1945, after
the ending of the war in Europe. It was Aneurin
Bevan's view -- I didn't mean to say his personal
view but the view that he represented -- which was
decisive in breaking the association with the
coalition and preparing the way for the independent
labour victory of 1945. It was a transformation in
our politics which the Attlee leadership hadn't
appreciated. I don't believe that Attlee believed
that he was going to win the election in 1945, but I
think the same applies to Ernest Bevin. They thought
there was going to be a repetition of the 1918
political events, and that it was going to be another
Lloyd George, just as Lloyd George was the man who
won the war, acording to the conservative
propagandist of 1918; so that they thought that
Churchill, the war hero and the war winner,
supposedly was going to carry all before him in
1945. And it was certainly on that basis that the
conservative machine and most of the conservative
newspapers (and most of the newspapers were
conservative) decided that they were going to present
the case, but they had no understanding of the
tremendous education that had persisted throughout
the war. I think the whole of the Left Book Club
propaganda and everything associated with it went on
in the war and some of us contributed to the
pamphleteering that was done. And in some respects,
socialist education continued in the war on a scale
that people hadn't imagined. The reading of
socialist pamphlets in the war was enormous and the
people hanging around waiting to fight battles read a
lot of books; as it so happened, people didn't
exactly appreciate that that was the case. I
remember how Victor Gollancz, who was a brilliant
publisher, was very nervous about the first books
that we produced, Guilty Men and the others in 1940
and 1941. But they sold huge numbers, far bigger
than anything that he had calculated; then he went on
and produced a whole range of further books
throughout the war of a kind of propagandist,
socialist tone and temper and they had, I think, also
a big effect on the 1945 victory.

Q: Well, is that an implicit critique of the
Attlee administration? It didn't realize how much
was possible for the English public of 1945? Perhaps
you're suggesting that rather than being the
consecration of a labour victory, in many ways the
Attlee regime marked the inception of some of the
chronic problems of the Labour Party, as a result of
the frustration of the left of the party?

A: Well, I think that there was an Attlee-Bevin leadership. Attlee and Bevin were very close together, and Bevin was a much stronger figure than Attlee. Bevin was the effective leader of the party during the war, in the sense that he was the most effective labour minister in the government. I think he remained so, the most effective and dominant figure in the government after 1945. And I don't say that in derogation of him. He was quite prepared to hold the second post. He didn't want to be necessarily the leader as long as he held the power, and he was the most effective, powerful figure on the right. He didn't understand the party in Parliament as well as he understood the trade union movement, but he was a man of very great personal magnetism and power and determination. And together with Attlee and the official leadership of the party, they were able to steer things their way. The government undoubtedly did carry through great changes in our society, and even at the end of it, in 1950 and 1951, the labour vote in that period was very powerful still. Considering what the British people as a whole had been through right from 1940 to 1950-51, I think it's a great democratic achievement that they held the allegiance of such a big proportion of the people so long. After all, they went through horrific events, the dangers of near defeat and they also had to run a country where the food supplies were in a very risky state. They had to introduce in 1947 and 1948 even more rigorous systems of rationing. They had to do that partly in order to assist ourselves, but partly in order to avoid starvation in India and in Europe itself, and they also had to do that at a time when Britain's position in the world, comparative to other countries, was being greatly reduced, although we didn't know how much it was being reduced at that time. So I think that looking back on it, to carry through the whole of that change in the peaceful and intelligent way that it was done was a pretty big achievement, even though many of us on the left were critical and thought that more should have been done or could have been achieved; but I think that certainly after 1950 or so, there was every reason to be very proud of what had been achieved if we put it in its perspective. On the whole, that was the attitude of Aneurin Bevan himself, and those of us who were associated with him. Then came his resignation in 1951, but he didn't want to resign, he didn't want to have the break, and he certainly didn't want to have a situation in which a Labour Party was defeated at the election. I think he was genuinely surprised, in fact, when we were defeated in 1951. He believed

still that it could have been rescued, as indeed, it
could have been.

Q: Many European socialists seem to think that
the Attlee government missed two important
opportunities. One was not developing economic
policy based on the same kind of planning that Jean
Monnet and others introduced on the continent --
England introduced nationalization but not planning.
The other was not joining the European Coal and Steel
Community, the precursor of the Common Market.

A: On the first issue, on the investment one, of
course it's an absolutely major issue, and it's a
major issue for socialists, and always is. And in
the communist countries, what they've done is to
enforce the investment at the price of very heavy
economic burdens for their people, but maybe they've
only been able to do such heavy investment programs
because of their not having to answer to a democratic
electorate. Well, we had to try and carry through
such investment programs, even though we had to face
the electorate, and I don't believe that in the
period from '45 to '50 and '51 the criticism is a
very severe one in that I would have thought the
period when the lack of resolution was shown in
carrying through those changes on a sufficiently bold
scale was mostly in the 1950s. After all, in '45 to
'50, we were recovering from a war; and recovering
from a war in which Britain had had to divert her
resources to war more than pretty well almost any
other country, far more than the United States of
America, or Canada, or any other equivalent
countries. We'd had to spend much more on war than
any of the other countries, except maybe the Germans
themselves, although in some respects, our diversion
to war was even greater than the Germans -- which was
one of the reasons why we won the war. Not that I'm
saying that there weren't any mistakes made between
'45 and '50. Many of us thought that we were not
doing a sufficient amount of socialist planning and
many of those criticisms are included in some of the
pamphlets that we wrote at the time, in Keep Left
which came out in 1948, and another one called
Keeping Left which came out in 1949. Nonetheless, I
think that considering the burden left by the war and
the necessity to lift the country out of it, that
finally a pretty big investment program was
undertaken, and I think was carried through with some
success. And we also had to carry through very big
programs in the social field and the National Health
Service and the social security programs. Though, no
doubt, we could have done more in the planning field,
generally, if you compare the position with what

happened in France or Germany or other parts of Europe where undoubtedly later on much was done. I think you'll find the comparison is disadvantageous to us much more in the period of the 1950s and early 1960s when conservative governments were in power, and I think that the failure of Britain, or the beginnings of the comparative decline in Britain's productivity and Britain's productive effort was much more under the conservative government. And indeed, we were saying so.

Q: George Brown claims in his memoirs that in the Wilson government, he was trying to develop a serious economic plan, and that his efforts were undercut. Do you think there was an opportunity in the Wilson government that wasn't taken in that direction?

A: Yes. I think that in the period 1964 to 1966, it is difficult to complain or criticize them too much, because we only had a majority of three. It was very difficult to carry through a socialist plan with a majority of three. In 1966 when Harold Wilson by his political skill and arrangement and everything else (nobody should take that from him), did win a victory by nearly a hundred seats, the Labour Party was in the most powerful political situation we've known since 1945. It was, in my opinion, in those few months after 1966 that our greatest opportunity was lost because we didn't change gears when we saw the opportunity of having a five-year period ahead of us. I think it was squandered chiefly because of the determination of Harold Wilson and others, like Callaghan, to sustain the exchange rate and to extend the stable pound and not to have been prepared to face a devaluation. I think Harold Wilson greatly overrated the political disadvantages of the devaluation and thought that a labour government associated with devaluation would suffer great political, electoral damage. As it turned out, we had the devaluation, and all the other political disadvantages. So I think the criticism of the failure of the Labour Party to develop a more ambitious socialist program applies particularly to that period. Then there was also the fact that in that period the Wilson government embarked upon some of its highly disadvantageous quarrels with the trade union. The seamen's strike after 1966, difficulties concerning In Place of Strife, and the way in which the Wilson government of '66 to '70 allowed itself to become engulfed in a quarrel with the trade unions, which was a great and terrible error, was the major reason in my opinion which led to out setback in 1970 and to some setbacks later on. But let's go back to

the other question you mentioned before, about the
criticism from socialist parties in Europe about the
isolationism or the failure of the Labour Party in
the 1950s and early 1960s.

To return to the failure of the Labour Party to
have a policy for association with European
socialists, I think there's no doubt a great deal to
be said for that view. We had in the left of the
party in those days, in the book, Keeping Left,
criticism of the Attlee-Bevin government on these
subjects, although there was much division on the
left on the way we should proceed, when the precursor
of the Common Market, the Schuman plan for the iron
and steel industries was produced. In the Tribune
office, I remember at that time we had divergences as
to whether we should support it or not, and that
difference of opinion prevailed on the left,
generally. But, I think, there could have been, from
Ernest Bevin when he was Foreign Secretary and the
period after, a much more pro-European policy, if you
like. I don't mean to say in terms of the Common
Market, but a readiness to act with socialist parties
in Europe, and to see the way they wanted to move. I
think we made many errors in that field. I think we
made errors in the way in which we dealt with the
German party and the German position after 1945, that
is to say, the Labour government was much too
backward in acting with the German Social Democrats;
at that time the German Social Democrats had a
different policy from the one that they developed
later. In the same way, I think we were much too
hesitant in acting with Mendès-France when he was in
power. He formed the best French government of that
period and certainly, I think, we were lacking in
awareness thereto. But when it comes to the actual
propositions of the Common Market itself, I think
there were always, right from the beginning, good
socialist grounds for the hostility towards the
Common Market because it was founded on a free market
basis. It had a free market ideology associated with
it, and that was one of the reasons why the Labour
Party, and particularly the left of the Labour Party,
was always deeply suspicious of it. But in some
respects, that suspicion was translated into a
nationalistic attitude and I think that socialists in
Europe have a right to criticize us on that ground,
although we have the right to say to them that the
form of the market itself was bound to be hostile to
socialist developments. What we should have done was
to have been prepared to develop associations with
Europe and the socialist parties in Europe which cut
across the institutions of the Common Market itself;
and I believe the situation still prevails today. In
the Socialist International today, we have countries

that are in the Market and out of the Market. We
have countries, Socialist International countries,
that are in NATO, and outside of NATO. I don't say
that the Socialist International is a powerful,
coherent body, but I do believe that it shows how you
can have a socialist internationalist policy which is
not tied to the Common Market or tied to NATO. I
think the policies that the Socialist International
as a whole advocates on international affairs have a
good deal more to be said for them than those which
are developed through the Common Market institutions,
or through any of the other institutions. That can
be the way in which the Labour Party in Britain can
contribute to socialist developments in Europe as a
whole. I don't believe that antagonism to the Common
Market should be the sole strand of socialism; of
course not. It's only one element and, indeed, the
more we criticize -- or express the criticism by
coming out of the Common Market institutions -- all
the greater is the obligation of socialists in
Britain to build better relationships with socialist
parties in Europe and elsewhere, as I think we can,
through the Socialist International.

Q: You don't feel that if Britain were to leave
the Common Market, the result would be a
protectionist economic policy which would lead to
continued degeneration of the British economy?

A: No, I don't think so. Unfortunately, the
Common Market institutions have not been devised to
suit Britain; they were devised to suit the other
kinds of economies. I'm not blaming the countries
that devised them because they devised them to suit
themselves, but they don't suit us. That is to say,
what they've imposed on us is protectionism in the
field of food and agricultural products and free
trade in the field of industry. And the way it's
worked has been to injure the food supplies that we
want to get from different parts of the world and in
some respects, to undermine the old suppliers that we
used to have, and at the same time, to mean a free
trade in industrial goods, which has not been the way
in which we could have sustained any of our
industries. Some of the fiercest competition which
has hit our industries has come not only from Japan,
but from Europe itself. We also have to contribute
very largely in the budget arrangements, and the
budgetary arrangement was never one which suited us.
So what we should have done, I'm sure, when we
allegedly renegotiated our arrangements in 1975 under
the labour government, I think it would have been
much better if we'd made a breach then. But not a
breach that would cut us off from Europe. That's

ridiculous; we're part of Europe. There's a great deal of merit, I believe, in what De Gaulle proposed way back in 1957 or '58. He proposed a kind of associate status for Britain, and I think that that would have suited us economically better. And in some respects, I think it would have enabled our political influence to be better too, because it would not have involved us in quarrels about economic questions. And our membership in the Market means that we are perpetually quarreling with France on labor or economic questions, whereas if we were outside the Market, I believe that our common interests with France could become much stronger. Of course, I'm very much opposed to an arrangement which tempted any British government to play off Germany against France. I think that that's not an advantage to us; moreover, it has meant that France and Germany have very often had a common interest, apparently against us. Many of the smaller countries have shown that out of the Common Market they can still be good internationalists and can still also run economic policies that are a good deal more efficient than some of the ones inside. Austria, Norway, and Sweden are all three prime examples.

Q: To go back to the statement you made earlier about the policies during the Wilson administration towards the labor unions, there is the whole question raised by Barbara Castle's plan for industrial relations. The Labour Party is caught in the difficult position of being a party that represents to a large extent the labor unions, which at the same time, within government, is obliged to take positions against labor unions. There's no question that there is a fundamental problem of industrial relations in Britain that hasn't been solved. What do you think can be done in that direction?

A: Well, it hasn't been solved. But I don't think there's any doubt either that the Labour Party has an advantage in the end. I know that at the moment the trade unions are very unpopular, and there are some people who are prepared to exploit that unpopularity. The present conservative government is exploiting it to the maximum and maybe in the next few months will be attempting to do so even more deliberately. And this breakaway party, the Social Democrats, they are pretty anti-union in the way they express themselves. But I believe that's a very dangerous course, because if Britain's going to have the economic recovery that we've got to have, it can only be done in association with the trade unions. It can't be done in perpetual warfare with them. That does not mean to say that we have to accept,

that a labour government has to accept, whatever the
trade unions say, either. Of course, that's wrong.
And any labour government responsible to Parliament
represents a wider interest than the trade unions
themselves. But the trade unions represent such a
strong democratic element in Britain that to have a
government that is prepetually at war with them, in
particular, a labour government that's at war with
them, is nonsensical. So I think the labour
government's In Place of Strife approach to the
matter was a grave error, and I think most of those
who were associated, now would agree that it was.
Then the conservatives came along in 1971 and '72.
Their Industrial Relations Act was an even greater
error and, indeed, was shown to be utterly
unworkable, so much so that even the Conservatives,
up to this point have not yet been prepared to try
and revive anything of the sort. And when we
abolished the Industrial Relations Act of the
Conservatives in 1974-75, we had very considerable
support from a lot of the employers as well as from
the trade union movement as a whole.

Q: Well, my last question. Given the
unpopularity of the Thatcher government and its
obvious failures, this should be a good opportunity
for the left. Of course, there is the division
between the Labour Party and the social democrats,
and then the conflicts within the labour itself. As
leader of the Labour Party, how can you obviate the
social democratic split; how can you restore the
unity of the party, and what kind of program can you
use in an election to get the country behind the
Labour Party?

A: Well, that's a very large question to answer
in a short time. I think the general economic
program, the alternative economic strategy of the
party, as we describe it, is a good one, and I
believe that if we can present it properly, it can be
the way in which we can recapture support. I know
that it's regarded in some quarters as being an
old-fashioned, socialist doctrine. But there are
many old-fashioned socialist doctrines that haven't
actually been applied and so I don't believe that
that's going to be a disability. I believe if we had
concentrated as we should on presenting that economic
alternative, we would be in a better position than we
are. But we've been distracted by some other
events. The greater the intensity of the economic
crisis, the more I believe the debate, proper
democratic debate in the country, will turn on the
economic alternative, and I think we've got a much
better alternative than either the breakaway from the

Tory Party, or the breakaway from ourselves. And indeed, the appeal of the social democrats is a strong one, but it's a bogus one. It is an appeal to the coalition-mindedness of the public which is always there. There's always been in British history, an appeal to the kind of amorphous mood in the center by people who wish to see politicians engaged in solving all problems of the public without any troubles and hardships and controversies and without their pouring abuse on one another. This has got a great appeal, but once it comes up against the harsh realities of politics, I think it's inclined to be exposed. The National Government of 1931 was elected on exactly this kind of appeal, to all men of good will, supposedly. It was led by a breakaway from the Labour Party, and it was without a doubt the worst government in British history, but it was elected on exactly the same kind of appeal that the social democrats are seeking to make. I'm not underrating the importance of what's happening from our point of view, although I think that the prophecies that are made in the polls of their position are great exaggerations. What was the other part of the question?

Q: I asked what kind of strategy you could pursue as the leader of the Labour Party towards winning the new election, and then leading Britain out of the economic crisis.

A: Well, you know, it depends on what's going to happen in the world, too. We're not going to be able to cut ourselves off from the rest of the world, and we'd be ludicrous to pretend that we wanted to or should or could. Certainly as international socialists, which is what we are, I think it's nonsense to think that we could. Naturally, we are also extremely interested in what happens in France, and there is a socialist victory in France for the first time in history of that scale. There will be an attempt, I'm sure, by the Socialist Party there to apply their economic doctrines. We have differences with them on foreign policy and some other matters, but as regards economic policy we share many of the same ideas and the same applications and the same hopes. Of course, it will take some time for the full effect of their economic policies to be seen and I expect they will have their ups and downs. So I don't mean to say that we should just sit back and watch and see how they carry it into effect, but we will have discussions with them as they proceed, and if we can win here, whenever we can get the election, I believe we could play a very big part in getting common economic policies. One of the problems that we had as a labour government between '74 and '79 was the great difficulty of having any countries in the world that would prepare to pursue expansionist policies; when we first came in, in '74, we did try to pursue a more expansionist policy, and if we'd had a France then that was run by President Mitterand, or if we'd had a better chance with some other countries, we would have been eager to engage in expansionist programs ourselves. So, when we do secure the power, we're certainly not going to try to do it solely on a Little England basis -- such an idea would be nonsense. I know that this is difficult for people to appreciate in the light of our commitment about the Common Market, but I underline afresh that the very fact that we are likely to be coming out of the Common Market makes it all the more necessary that we should have common aims in more international economic policies. I believe that we will pursue a much better and more ambitious policy toward the Third World than that pursued by the present conservative government. You may say that that's a very small ambition, because they haven't done anything at all about it, except to cut the very miserly amounts that are devoted to overseas at the present. But I think, there too, there are great opportunities for us with the French government, which has got a much more hopeful attitude in these matters. But what would happen in the United States of America, that is maybe the biggest element of all.

If I can just say it in conclusion, even before we become the government of the country, I hope we may be able to influence in some degree the arms race. Undoubtedly, the greatest issue in the world is what is to happen to the nuclear arms race and whether we can turn it back. I believe there is a very powerful movement in Europe for altering the course of events there. I believe that one of the immediate necessities is to try to see that the negotiations opening in a few weeks between the United States and the Soviet Union on this subject are made to prosper. Socialist parties in Western Europe have a common desire and determination to try and make those negotiations succeed. And I think I've played a part already in getting the negotiations started, and can play a part in getting them to prosper.

Glossary of Names, Organizations and Terms in the Foot Interview

--Clement Attlee (1883-1967). Elected labour leader in 1935 to replace Lansbury, he served as deputy Prime Minister in the coalition government and Prime Minister 1945-1951. He resigned as party leader in 1955.

--Aneurin Bevan (1897-1960). The leading figure of the left of the Labour Party after World War II. As Minister of Housing and Health, Bevan sponsored legislation for council house construction and creation of the National Health Service. He resigned in 1951 over the cabinet's decision to charge patients for dentures and eyeglasses. In the next few years, the Bevanites became a definite faction within the Labour Party. Their divergence from the party line was manifested in opposition to German rearmament. In 1955, Hugh Gaitskill, the candidate of the right, defeated Bevan as party leader. Nevertheless, in the next years the former opponents managed to work together; Bevan was made shadow Foreign Minister. Bevan opposed unilateral nuclear disarmament by Britain, a position which led to a deep conflict with many of the Bevanites, including Michael Foot.

--Ernest Bevin (1881-1951). Leader of the Transport and General Workers Union, Bevin became a major power in the party when Clement Attlee was elected party leader in 1935. Minister of Labour in the war-time coalition government, he served as Foreign Secretary in the post-war Attlee cabinet. Bevin and Bevan represented the two poles of labour in the Attlee government.

--H.M. Brailsford (1873-1958). A distinguished journalist, Brailsford was a committeed socialist. From 1922-1926 he was the editor of the New Leader. Brailsford was concerned about the relationship of capitalism to war. He was a critic of both Stalinism and fascism. He wrote regularly for the New Statesman and Nation.

--Barbara Castle (1910-). A longtime MP, Mrs. Castle has served on the National Executive of the Labour Party since 1950 and was its chair in 1959. She held several ministries during the Wilson government, including Secretary of State for Energy and Production (1968-1970). She is presently a member of the European Parliament.

--Sir Stafford Cripps (1889-1952). A christian socialist, Cripps opposed rearmament and collective security during the 1930s; expelled from the Labour Party in 1939, he returned as Ambassador to Russia and then Leader of the Commons during the war. From 1947-1951 he was Chancellor of the Exchequer.

--Issac Foot (1880-1960). Liberal and Methodist, Foot served only eight years in Parliament. Parliamentary Secretary for Mines, he resigned in 1932 to protest the government's turn to protectionism, thereby ruining his political career for the sake of principle. Foot was also a noted orator and bibliophile; he amassed a collection of over 70,000 books.

--Lord George-Brown (1914-). A member of the right wing of the Labour Party, Brown was defeated for the party leadership by Wilson in 1963. He became Deputy Prime Minister and Minister for Economic Affairs in 1964. Brown's efforts at economic planning were unsuccessful, largely because of opposition from Callaghan at the Treasury; in 1966 Brown became Foreign Secretary, but he resigned shortly after in a disagreement with Wilson. This marked the end of Brown's role as a major party leader.

--David Lloyd George (1863-1945). Liberal leader and Prime Minister 1916-1919, he was returned to power in 1919 in the Khaki Election as leader of a coalition of liberals and conservatives. Churchill and the conservatives were thinking of this electoral success when they planned the post-World War II election.

--Industrial Relations Act (1971). This act, passed by the Heath government, created a National Industrial Relations Court to deal with various practices outlawed by the bill, like wild-cat and sympathy strikes. It also allowed the Secretary of Employment to order a conciliation period or a ballot before a strike could begin. It was repealed in 1974 by the labour government.

--In Place of Strife. A White Paper published in 1969 backed by Barbara Castle and Wilson which sought to have the Ministry of Labour empowered to require a one month cooling-off period before a strike could be called and a secret ballot of union members. Strong trade union opposition led to the withdrawal of the key provisions of the bill.

--George Lansbury (1859-1940). A christian socialist and pacifist, Lansbury took over the leadership of the Labour Party after the formation of MacDonald's

National Government. In 1935, he was strongly attacked by Ernest Bevin for continuing as leader despite his opposition to sanctions against Italy for its invasion of Ethiopia. Lansbury resigned and was replaced by Clement Attlee.

--Beveridge Report. A report prepared during the war by a committee under Sir William Beveridge on "Social Insurance and Allies Services"; it provided the basis for the post-war welfare state.

--Social Democratic Federation of Henry Hyndman. Hyndman (1842-1921) established the Federation in 1884 with a Marxist program; the movement never gained significant support, however. Hyndman expounded Marxist ideas in several books.

--John Strachey (1901-1963). A labor MP and friend of Oswald Mosley, Strachey left the party along with Mosley in 1931 and assisted in the formation of the New Party. When Mosley's fascist intentions became clear, Strachey broke with him and became identified with the Communist Party, although never becoming a member. During the 1930s, he wrote several influential books, including The Coming Struggle for Power. He severed his ties with the communists in 1939; after World War II he served in the Attlee government. Strachey's importance was above all intellectual.

--Tribune. The weekly newspaper of the left of the Labour Party, founded in 1937. In the 1950s, it was a citadel of Bevanism. Michael Foot was its editor on two occasions after World War II.